AF600303

MAPPING WITH WORDS

Anglo-Canadian Literary Cartographies, 1789–1916

Mapping with Words

Anglo-Canadian Literary Cartographies, 1789–1916

SARAH WYLIE KROTZ

UNIVERSITY OF TORONTO PRESS
Toronto Buffalo London

Toronto Buffalo London
utorontopress.com

ISBN 978-1-4426-5012-1

Library and Archives Canada Cataloguing in Publication

Krotz, Sarah Wylie, 1977–, author
Mapping with words : Anglo-Canadian literary cartographies, 1789–1916 / Sarah Wylie Krotz.

Includes bibliographical references and index.
ISBN 978-1-4426-5012-1 (cloth)

1. Canadian literature (English) – 19th century – History and criticism.
2. Canadian literature (English) – 20th century – History and criticism.
3. Cartography in literature. 4. Canada – In literature. I. Title.

PS8101.C39K76 2018 C810.9′32 C2018-902603-0

This book has been published with the help of a grant from the Federation for the Humanities and Social Sciences, through the Awards to Scholarly Publications Program, using funds provided by the Social Sciences and Humanities Research Council of Canada.

University of Toronto Press acknowledges the financial assistance to its publishing program of the Canada Council for the Arts and the Ontario Arts Council, an agency of the Government of Ontario.

Canada Council for the Arts Conseil des Arts du Canada

Funded by the Government of Canada Financé par le gouvernement du Canada

Contents

Preface

This book began to take shape in the library of Dalhousie University – not, as a literary scholar might expect, in the book stacks, but in the map room. I remember that place as dim and quiet, set apart like a small chapel off the transept of a cathedral. The vertical spaces of the dense floor-to-ceiling stacks opened up to a horizontal arrangement of low shelves with wide tops forming a broad, smooth surface where maps could be laid out and examined, pieced together in an ever-widening cartographic puzzle of the world. It was here that, with literary studies still far from my mind, I pored over maps of northwestern Ontario, searching for a route that would take me and eight other young women in canoes for six weeks through 650-odd kilometres of rivers, creeks, lakes, and portages that straddle the watershed between Lake Superior and Hudson Bay.

Long before I physically encountered this place, I was led there in my imagination by a number of connected 1:50,000-scale topographical maps surveyed by the Department of Energy, Mines, and Resources in the 1970s. They drew me into intricate landscapes tinted with pastel blues and greens, deceptive in their diagrammatic simplicity. From spare contour lines and schematic symbols grew rich mental images of the terrain's irregular shapes: the narrowing of river and stream, the openness of lakes, the soft edgings of marshland, the sudden steep rock face. Despite the dearth of roads and the distance from any city, the human features of the land were everywhere apparent. The names of lakes and rivers (Cellist, White Loon, North Spirit) were evocative, enlivened with personal association. Many toponyms spoke of the nations and histories that had converged on the land, with Anishinaabe, Cree, and Euro-colonial alternately resonating in the map's inscriptions: "Wapiskapika," "Agutua,"

"Windigo," "Weagamow," "Severn," "Flanagan," "McInnes." Not far to the east of our canoe route lay the portage that, I would later learn, had inspired Duncan Campbell Scott's poem "The Height of Land" almost a century before. Reserve lands, many of which he helped to delineate, were set cleanly apart from Crown lands with thin dotted lines, their mathematical exactness belying the dynamic and complex relations between these places and the people who have lived in them since time immemorial. The few roads were indicated by smoothly curving lines that tended to run north-south, between the Trans-Canada Highway, far below, and the shores of small lakes where they ended abruptly on some sandy bank, continuing only in winter across the ice.

There was, I soon discovered, something captivating – even addictive – about this process of cartographic exploration and translation. Like an armchair traveller, I revelled in the maps' compelling intimations of possibility. I imagined running rapids and portaging around waterfalls, setting up camp on rocky points and mossy forest floors. Cartography spoke in a vernacular of calming order and navigability. The pleasures of map reading, and of thus forging my own mental maps of these places, were at once practical and profoundly aesthetic, the route-log an emerging narrative of exploration, of making a world come into view.

Several months later, with our copies of these maps carefully rolled together in a long waterproof tube and three canoes and heavy packs of food and equipment loaded onto a trailer behind a bus, we found ourselves at the limits of the map before our journey had even properly begun. Far to the north of the community of Red Lake, the road, which had long given up on asphalt, dwindled until it disappeared altogether in the dense underbrush several miles south of the river where, the map had told us, we could put in. With nowhere else to go, we were forced to start our trip not on the mighty Berens River as we had planned, but on a slow meandering creek with no name that we knew (these were the last days before widely available satellite GPS, and our maps didn't cover this area). Disarmed and discombobulated, we paddled our way tentatively – and with a considerable amount of luck – back onto the map, and thus back into a world that, although none of us had been there before, was suddenly reassuringly readable. Our maps had betrayed us (and would do so again when we found that a promised creek had dried up, or a portage trail either grown over or never established), and yet we continued to put our faith in the cartographer's lines. Each day the landscapes that our maps brought into our daydreams were replaced by the elaborate, vivid world in which we travelled and lived – a world coloured by fluctuating weather and moods. If our maps had lied, they had also brought us here. Such is their tenuous and marvellous fiction.

As a scholar of early Canadian literature, I became interested in the affinities between the lines that writers create and the lines on maps. Words move through space in myriad ways. Whether marching or meandering across the page, they chart paths across their conjured geographies. Particularly when these geographies refer to physical spaces and places, their word-paths also traverse, and impress themselves upon, our mental maps of real, lived places and spaces. They inscribe and reconfigure signs of occupation and habitation, delineate topographies and territories, trace routes, establish roots, and distinguish places and peoples. From the page to the land itself, "the spacious word" (to borrow Ricardo Padrón's evocative descriptor) mimics the actions of the finger and the eye as they explore, define, and assign meaning to the surface of the earth. It is this meaning that this book explores.

Acknowledgments

They say that it takes a village to raise a child; it seems that it takes several of them to raise a book. I am profoundly grateful for the sustained support of institutions, colleagues, friends, and family that made the writing of this one not only possible, but also enjoyable.

Mapping with Words is the culmination of thinking that began in the English departments of McGill, the University of Toronto, and Western University. I am especially grateful to D.M.R. Bentley for his kind mentorship and encyclopedic knowledge; Diana Brydon, J. Edward Chamberlin, and Brian Trehearne for their inspiring guidance; and SSHRC for financial support in those early days. I completed this work at the University of Alberta, on Treaty 6 territory in Edmonton, amidst a nurturing community of colleagues and friends. Over these years Albert Braz, Lois Harder, Ian MacLaren, Keavy Martin, Liza Piper, Julie Rak, and Christine Stewart generously commented on parts of the manuscript; I thank them, along with Ben Authers, Robyn Fowler, Corrinne Harol, Eddy Kent, Terri Tomsky, and Teresa Zackodnik, for buoying my spirits at critical moments. The Department of English and Film Studies also provided graduate research assistants – I am particularly indebted to Deborah Ramkelawan for her cheerful and assiduous help preparing the manuscript for submission.

Among the many students who have energized my thinking, I wish to acknowledge those from my first graduate seminar, who ran with the idea of literary cartography, played with it, and critiqued it with such generosity and gusto; they confirmed what an enriching and collaborative experience a seminar can be. I have also benefitted from many conversations at conferences over the years; I thank Jordan Stanger-Ross and Johannes Riquet for organizing two of the most memorable ones, formative to my thinking about literature and spatial perception.

My editors at the University of Toronto Press guided me smoothly through the review and publication process. I thank Siobhan McMenemy for her enthusiasm and wise advice to slow down (even when there is so much pressure in academia to speed up); Mark Thompson for his grace, efficiency and good humour; and Frances Mundy and Carolyn Yates for their care with the copyedits and publication process. My greatest debt, though, is to the two anonymous readers who put such thought and time into the manuscript: their suggestions were invaluable, this book much better for their clarity and insight – thank you.

The support of friends, community, and family has sustained me through the many challenges of becoming a scholar. Jordan and Ilana Stanger-Ross (our intellectual "family") inspire me with their perfect balance of humour and rigour; my YM-YWCA Camp Stephens "family" taught me to read maps and took me into parts of Canada I would not otherwise have seen; and our Edmonton "family" – especially Jen and Chet, Lois and Curtis, Keavy and Richard, Christine and Graeme, David "not-another-book-about-Canadian-landscape" and Tikker, along with my warm community of North Glenora moms – keep life fun. Books need time, and this was given to me by the wonderful caregivers at Student's Union and Community Early Learning Centre at the University of Alberta, and then by generous neighbours and friends (especially Carolina Roemmich and Lysiane Campbell) who cared for my children after school so that I could work full days.

Throughout these years, my dad, Larry Krotz, has been my model for the writing life and a most generous reader. I also thank my mum, Gail Wylie, for bringing me into this world and sharing her love of literature; David Wright, who has read more *New Canadian Library* editions than I have; Michael Pettitt, Stephanie Woodside, Barb McCready, and Pauline McCrum (along with the vast networks of Adamses, Krotzes, Wylies, and Wrights) for their constant cheering support; and Brian Pettitt for his infectious passion for old maps, backcountry roads, and rare Canadiana. Many drafts were conceived or revised at the Morgan/Wright cottage on Lake of the Woods: I cannot thank this extended family enough for the deck in the pine trees overlooking the lake on which more than a few of these pages were written.

Needless to say, my deepest gratitude is for my immediate family, the three people who have spent the most time with this gestating book.

I cannot imagine going through any part of life without Eric Adams, my partner in all things. He knows this book inside and out, and it is much better for his unflagging intellectual curiosity, clear-eyed editorial advice, and appreciation for the subtleties of literary analysis. Fen and Timothy, you were born in the midst of this project and kept my heart light all the way through. At last it is done! It is dedicated to you three, for whom my gratitude is so profound there are no words.

MAPPING WITH WORDS

Anglo-Canadian Literary Cartographies, 1789–1916

Maps and Text-Maps

Cartographic Subjectivities

At the heart of *Roughing It in the Bush: Or, Life in Canada* (1852), Susanna Moodie's famous collection of sketches of life in nineteenth-century Upper Canada, is an encounter with a map. The author describes a visit from her "Indian friends," a group of Mississauga Anishinaabe on whose ancestral lands the Moodies had settled. Entering her dwelling in the sparsely settled township of Douro, her friends seize with great interest upon "a large map of Canada." "In a moment," she recounts,

> they recognised every bay and headland in Ontario, and almost screamed with delight when, following the course of the Trent with their fingers, they came to their own lake.
>
> How eagerly each pointed out the spot to his fellows; how intently their black heads were bent down, and their dark eyes fixed upon the map! What strange, uncouth exclamations of surprise burst from their lips as they rapidly repeated the Indian names for every lake and river on this wonderful piece of paper!
>
> The old chief, Peter Nogan, begged hard for the coveted treasure. He would give "Canoe, venison, duck, fish, for it; and more by-and-by."
>
> I felt sorry that I was unable to gratify his wishes; but the map had cost upwards of six dollars, and was daily consulted by my husband, in reference to the names and situations of localities in the neighbourhood.[1]

This is a rare description of an actual map in early Canadian literature and an oblique one at that, describing not the map itself but rather a particular encounter with it. Yet the vignette nonetheless registers the centrality of cartography, and cartographic ways of seeing, in settler culture. The appeal of the map as a miniature of the earth, a legible model that invites its readers to experience the wonder of locating themselves in, and affirming their familiarity with, the world, emerges with vivid clarity in this sketch. So, too, does the map's importance as a tool of colonization that inscribes the land for settlers even as it overwrites the presence and knowledge of Indigenous peoples.

As much as the conventions of the picturesque and the sublime, the pastoral and the gothic, cartography provided a lens through which settler writers saw the land and themselves within it. As this book explores the relationship between cartographic and literary practices in early Canada, it approaches the map not just as a figure or illustration, but as a perceptual model. Its questions take Moodie's vignette as an invitation to contemplate the cartographic figures and impulses that underpin not only other sketches in her collection, but also colonial writing more broadly – sometimes overtly, other times subtly. How did maps shape writers' expectations and perceptions of the spaces they described? To what degree can we understand settler writing as an extension of the colonial maps upon which emigrants depended? In what ways did this writing deepen and complicate the cartographic project of accommodating settlers in unfamiliar – and contested – terrain?

Maps, Moodie reminds us, connect us to the world. Their lines not only orient us geographically, but also are intimately bound up in notions of identity and of origins. This was true when medieval *mappae mundi* superimposed images of the physical world over Christ's body, with Jerusalem at his navel; it remains so today when in an uncanny secular echo of this archaic conflation of map, world, body, and origins, my son's birth certificate bears the imprint of an outline map of Ontario, the province in which he was born. Such designs confirm the rich metaphorical significance of maps. They express, and help to inscribe, what Tom Conley calls our "cartographic subjectivity": a subjectivity, he argues, that reflects a common "drive to locate and implant oneself in a named space; a drive to imagine necessary connections between the 'I,' the locale of its utterance, and the origins of its birth; ... a perceived need to burrow into and circulate about a body, a world, and a nation, of which all three components give credence and an illusion of heritage to the ego."[2] In the wake of the "spatial turn," humanities scholars across many disciplines have joined geographers in plumbing the depths of this subjectivity. Maps, they have found, "provide the very conditions of possibility for the worlds we inhabit and the subjects we become," some going so far as to claim that "no existence is possible on unmapped ground."[3]

Such assertions help to clarify the significance of cartography in the experience of settler colonialism, which was predicated on the reinscription of land and identities. While Moodie attributes a cartographic impulse to settlers and Indigenous people alike, the force of her vignette lies in the contrast it highlights between native and newcomer relationships to the map and, by implication, to the particular tract of earth that it depicts – a contrast of which the items of valuation ("canoe, venison, duck, fish" versus "six dollars") are richly suggestive. The shock and pleasure of recognition that Moodie's Mississauga neighbours experience as they pore so eagerly over the map arises from their ability to discern, in its contour lines, a terrain they know intimately. The map becomes a "coveted treasure" only for its novelty; they have no practical need for it. The Moodies, by contrast, would be lost without it. Made legible by its text of "names and localities," Ontario emerges as a product of the map that orients the emigrant family – especially Moodie's husband, who consults it "daily" – in foreign territory. That this vignette interrupts what is otherwise a sustained exploration of a genteel British emigrant's profound *dis*orientation in the Upper-Canadian backwoods makes its brief meditation on the power of cartography all the more poignant. Moodie's reluctance to part with it confirms that cartographers were, for newcomers at least, agents of certainty in geographical terrain that was anything but certain.

Settlers needed maps. As Moodie's sister and fellow emigrant Catharine Parr Traill complained in *The Backwoods of Canada* (1836), "a settler on first locating his lot knows no more of its boundaries and its natural features than he does of the northwest passage."[4] The unnamed map to which Moodie refers – likely James Chewett's *Map of the Province of Upper Canada* (figure 1), which the Canada Company regularly issued to new emigrants – not only extended the settlers' vision beyond their limited sightlines, but also affirmed their presence on the land. Its eloquent tracing of rivers and lakes, clear demarcation of districts and townships, and symbolic unification of the whole under the decorative crest that confidently asserted British governance compelled readers both to visualize the topography and to conceptualize it, and themselves within it, in particular ways. For British emigrants such as the Moodies (who would have heard the echoes of England in district names such as Newcastle, Northumberland, Durham, and Hastings), Chewett's map held the promise of belonging.

Offering the diagrammatic illusion of clarity, order, and containment, it reassured newcomers that their adopted home was knowable and navigable. Its blank spaces are no less significant than its surveyed ones: juxtaposed with the orderly grid of districts and townships, the unmapped regions that extend northward seem to await cartographic inscription – theirs is a blankness that beckons. Both in their eloquence and in their silences, such maps facilitated the multifaceted processes of orientation, accommodation, and appropriation through which settlers made themselves at home in foreign terrain.

Appearing in the sketch titled "The Wilderness, and Our Indian Friends," near the beginning of what was once the book's second volume, the Moodies' map of Canada subtly establishes their visual command of "the forbidding depths of [the] tangled wilderness"[5] around their homestead. At the same time, however, the narrative context in which Moodie embeds the map unsettles any sense of belonging that it might impart. As she makes clear, her adopted home was not *"terra nullius."* The string of "Indian names" that the map elicits from its Mississauga readers marks the land as a palimpsest, the map's comforting codes a colonial inscription against which lie another people's prior claims. The exclamations of her "Indian friends" disrupt the cartographic inscription even as they affirm its topographical accuracy: for a moment, the reader is invited to imagine beyond European cartography to another way of representing a terrain whose significance exceeds the map's colonial imperative.

In effect, as Florence Stratton observes, Moodie's vignette "actually features two maps, one of which conceals the other" one that is "alternative and prior but also present" in both the land itself and Moodie's description of it.[6] Gesturing to other possible maps that might be drawn of the same area, while also highlighting the chasm between settler disorientation and Indigenous knowledge, this sketch suggests the manner in which colonial maps could simultaneously connect and *dis*connect the "I" to and from "the locale of its utterance," not to mention "the origins of its birth" (which for Moodie, as readers of *Roughing It in the Bush* seldom forget, lay on the other side of thousands of miles of land and ocean). This exchange registers colonization and its cartographic inscription, then, as a profoundly ambivalent spatial experience – one anchored in Moodie's preference (shared with the majority of her contemporaries) for the term "emigrant" over "immigrant," which defined this spatiality in relation to the place of departure rather than arrival. The emigrant, she often reminds the reader, could conceive of herself as an "exile" severed from her homeland even as she displaced others, her cartographic subjectivity a confluence of mappings and counter-mappings of a place in transformation.

The themes that coalesce in Moodie's vignette – of the power of cartography as a perceptual framework for orientation and accommodation, of the encounter between Indigenous and emigrant knowledge of and claims to the land, and of the ambivalent spatial experience that emerges from the complex tensions between them – are the themes that run through this study. *Mapping with Words* foregrounds eight colonial texts from a period of unprecedented Anglo-colonial expansion that dramatically reshaped what is now Canada: Thomas Cary's *Abram's Plains* (1789), Adam Hood Burwell's *Talbot Road: A Poem* (1818), Moodie's *Roughing It in the Bush* (1852), Traill's *Canadian Wild Flowers* (1868) and *Studies of Plant Life in Canada; or, Gleanings from Forest, Lake and Plain* (1885), George Monro Grant's *Ocean to Ocean: Sandford Fleming's Expedition through Canada in 1872* (1873), Duncan Campbell Scott's "The Height of Land" (1916), and, in the concluding chapter, David Thompson's *Narrative of His Explorations in Western America, 1784–1812* (1916). Landmarks of an early Canadian literary cartography, these texts attest to a widespread interest not just in the terrain, but also in how it was mapped in the process of Britain's and then the Dominion's radical transformation of Indigenous, French colonial, and fur-trade territories.

Mapping with Words sketches a spatial imaginary shaped by the shift from water to land; from the spaces of imperial exploration and trade to those of colonial settlement and agricultural development; from the tracing of the earth's sinuous curves to the surveying of roads, boundaries, and property lines that cast a net of artificial grids over its surfaces. This shift introduced new dimensions to literary cartography as settlers became expressly concerned not just with navigation and trade, but also with property and habitation – with the transformation of space into a fixed place in which they could root themselves.[7] Cary's *Abram's Plains*, the poem that opens this study, conveys the feel of this transition from water to land and from imperial to colonial space, with descriptions that oscillate between the St Lawrence River system and the surrounding topography. The river and its tributaries remain paramount in the poem's spatial imagery: they were, after all, the only arteries through which resources and people could easily flow into and out of British North America at that time. But the changing character of the land, the appropriation of which was the primary objective of British colonial settlement, animates the poem's topographical descriptions.

The same can be said of *Talbot Road, Roughing It in the Bush, Studies of Plant Life in Canada,* and *Ocean to Ocean,* which each take their readers deeper into the spaces either of a single settlement or, in Grant's case, of an emergent Dominion stretching from sea to sea. Scott returns to waterways in his poem "The Height of Land" (as he does in a number of his northern wilderness and "Indian" poems, many of which are set in places only accessible by canoe). Yet, as the title of this poem suggests, he also assumes a degree of mastery over the land, and surveys a vast terrain to be imaginatively assimilated and, arguably, poetically incorporated into an ever-widening conception of settler space.

Cartographic Transformations

Beginning with a poem that commemorates the British victory over the French on the Plains of Abraham, and ending with another that has its roots in the negotiation of Treaty 9 in northwestern Ontario, *Mapping with Words* spans two periods of British colonial history: the Second British Empire (1783–1815) and what has been called the "imperial century" (1815–1914). Following the Treaty of Paris that marked the end of the Seven Years' War in 1763, a monumental land transfer subjected new parts of North America, the Caribbean, and South Asia to British colonial rule. After relinquishing its control over the thirteen colonies at the end of the American Revolution in 1783, Britain diverted much of its attention from the Americas to Asia and Africa, but Canada expanded dramatically, assuming something close to its current shape. A global phenomenon of unprecedented proportions, the movement of British settlers was compared at the time to "those earthquake convulsions, which change the entire geology of the earth."[8] In early Canada, places and territories were far from settled constructs. Proclamations and treaties continued to redefine the boundaries, political control, and uses of the land, while agricultural development, towns, roads, and railways radically altered its topography and ecological makeup.[9]

Cartographers played a crucial role in this transformation. In the decades immediately preceding the historical scope of this study, advances in navigational and surveying technologies facilitated Britain's appropriation of French-colonial and Indigenous territories in early Canada. In the 1750s, the clockmaker John Harrison perfected the marine chronometer, making it possible to accurately determine longitude at sea, and the astronomer John Bird developed the sextant, perfecting the measurement of latitude. The increasingly accurate maps that these technologies yielded were integral to successful colonial expansion. Not only did Britain's conquest of New France in 1759 depend upon detailed maps of the St Lawrence shoreline, but its subsequent control over the newly configured colonial provinces also relied upon surveys that gathered crucial information about the land and its inhabitants and abstracted it in ways that facilitated their exploitation and manipulation.[10]

Ontario (known as Upper Canada between 1791 and 1841, and Canada West from 1841 to 1867) became the westernmost hub of what James Belich refers to as "Canadian hyper-colonization" during this period.[11] In Rupert's Land and along the Pacific Coast, however, explorers and surveyors were also laying cartographic foundations not just for trade but also for the settlements that would eventually transform the geographical and social landscapes of the west. Between 1791 and 1795, George Vancouver surveyed the coastlines of much of the Pacific northwest; in 1793, Alexander Mackenzie reached the Pacific from Rupert's Land, becoming the first European explorer to cross the continent north of Mexico. The interior of the northwest, however, would remain unknown to Europeans until David Thompson completed his *Map of the North-West Territory of the Province of Canada* in 1814, around the same time that Peter Fidler was making the first organized property surveys of what would become Canada's western interior at Red River.

Moving ever further inland, surveyors worked to ascertain the colony's agricultural and commercial potential; to determine suitable locales for settlement; to chart navigational routes; and to lay the plans for farms, towns, and cities. They carved up land into tracts of property, displacing Indigenous peoples and transforming ecologies as they sought to define settler space in stark opposition to a shrinking wilderness. From the speculative "paper towns" that imposed arbitrary order on parts of Upper Canada in the 1820s and '30s[12] to the Dominion Lands Survey that remade prairie grasslands into the now-familiar patchwork quilt of farms, roads, and towns in the final decades of the nineteenth century, maps not only represented the land, but also created the lines of colonial occupation. To the extent that maps gave Canada its shape, both in the minds of map-readers and on the land itself, cartography is inseparable from the spatial experience and (to invoke Henri Lefèbvre) "production" of the country.

As Moodie's vignette underscores, imperial and colonial cartographers were not the first to chart this terrain. For as long as people have lived on it, there have been maps of the land and its waterways:

historians document a wide array of mapping practices among Indigenous peoples across the Americas, the materials for which included animal skin, bone, tusk, birch bark, wood, rock, sand, and ash, as well as oral record. These served a range of purposes, all of them pointing to the fact that the land was not just some static configuration of rock, earth, and water; rather, it was already part of a complex network of geographical places and relationships. While emigrants sometimes dismissed Indigenous cartography, surveyors relied heavily on it. As the historical geographer J.B. Harley emphasizes, the colonial expansion into North America would have proceeded much more slowly had the land that explorers encountered actually been, as they sometimes described it, "empty."[13]

Although dramatic in its effects, the cartographic reinscription of nineteenth-century Canada was a gradual process. If, as Traill suggests, individual tracts of land challenged the emigrant's geographical imagination, the larger contours of the expanding colony could be downright baffling. John MacTaggart, a British surveyor employed by Colonel By to plan the Rideau Canal in Upper Canada between 1826 and 1828, complained that at that time British North America amounted to "a large but ill-defined property, the nature of which we have yet failed to investigate, and respecting which the most erroneous ideas have been entertained."[14] As the colony and, later, the Dominion, expanded, so too did its *terra incognita*: "As late as 1890," writes the historian Carl Berger, "the director of the [Geological and Natural History] Survey, George M. Dawson, noted that of Canada's total territory of some three and a half million square miles, between one-quarter and one-third remained unmapped and unexplored even in the most superficial fashion."[15] Early Canadian writing is consequently full of references to "uncharted," "trackless," and "pathless" terrain and "tangled wilds," epithets that attest at once to the novel appearance of land with relatively few signs of human use (a scarce commodity in Europe), to a habitual unwillingness to acknowledge Indigenous habitation, and to the extreme disorientation that colonial settlement occasioned.

Settler writers did not just bemoan their lot; many endeavoured to change it. Working in various locodescriptive genres, from topographical poems and botanical inventories to narratives of exploration, travel, and settlement, early Canadian writers addressed a need for orientation and control; their writings betray a desire for the land to be ordered and encoded, for its boundaries to be set, for new paths to be drawn. While they seldom allude to cartography directly, they employ cartographic strategies to map with words the emerging spaces of settlement. How they negotiated this terrain, not just with the graphic maps to which they refer (the maps *in* texts), but also, and especially, through the verbal maps that emerge from their descriptions of topography and spatial experience (the maps *of* texts, or what Lisa Brooks, in the context of Indigenous cultural production, calls "text-maps"[16]) is this book's guiding question.

The Text-(as)-Map

Mapping with Words, then, is a work of what Robert T. Tally calls "literary geography": it offers a critical interpretation of the literary cartography that emerges from verbal descriptions of spaces and places.[17] The idea that writers map with words stems both from a keen sense of the paradigmatic power of maps as conceptual models during this period, and from an expansive, flexible understanding of mapping practices that range beyond the graphic. In *A History of Spaces: Cartographic Reason, Mapping and the Geo-Coded World*, the geographer John Pickles describes the pervasive influence of the surveyor's ways of seeing on our spatial experience. "The world," he underscores, "has literally been made, domesticated and ordered by drawing lines, distinctions, taxonomies and hierarchies," the nature of which are fundamentally cartographic: "Europe and its others, West and non-West, or people with history and people without history" are just a few of these spatialized orders that have had a powerful influence on how people determine their place in the world. Pickles goes on to demonstrate the myriad ways in which cartography undergirds our daily lives, forming "an integral tool in the structuring and functioning of what we take to be the everyday and the natural: the agricultural landscape, the modern city, the road along which we drive, the very rooms in which we sit and read ... are all products of the working of maps." Indeed, he argues, a "cartographic imagination" can be discerned in "the very structure and content of language and thought itself."

On this principle alone, we might add writing to the wide-ranging catalogue of mapping practices that, for Pickles, includes everything from landscape painting, panoramas, museums, and exhibitions to police surveillance, property development, and aerial photographs. While written representations are – to a literary scholar – conspicuously absent from this list, Pickles goes on to refer to "cartography in all its forms" as "earth writing" and as "a discourse that names the world,"[18] implicitly equating it with literature, for which both discourse and naming are central. A more explicit connection lies at the heart of one of Harley's enduring interventions in his field of critical geography: borrowing from literary theory, he calls for a "literature of maps" to deconstruct the apparent transparency of cartography, exposing the stories that maps tell.[19] *Mapping with Words* explores the corollary of this relationship, drawing upon the work of critical and cultural geographers in order to illuminate the ways in which literature, for its part, also maps the world.

There are, of course, fundamental differences between literary and graphic maps. As the geographer Yi Fu Tuan rightly points out, "language is better suited to the narration of events than to the depiction of simultaneous spatial relations."[20] Moodie's sketches, Traill's botanical guides, and Scott's poems orient readers in markedly different ways than would a conventional map with its decipherable legends, signs, and symbols – not to mention its ability to present sweeping geographies in a single visual frame (in other words, a map such as the one Moodie briefly describes in her vignette, and within and against which she writes much of her own spatialized narrative). Nonetheless, this book is not the first to connect writing and mapping. The events of narrative, after all, unfold in space as well as in time. Moreover, the cognitive processes to which literature appeals are frequently spatial as well as narrative. As Tally notes, literature can be broadly understood "as a form of mapping, offering its readers descriptions of places, situating them in a kind of imaginary space, and providing points of reference by which they can orient themselves and understand the world in which they live."[21] Writers create places in which we dwell and travel, if only in our minds, to powerful effect.

Lines of Occupation and Habitation: A Method of Reading

Reconceptualizing the study of early Canadian literature and land as a study of literary cartography, *Mapping with Words* builds on a rich body of scholarship on the relationship between writing and land in Canada. At least since Northrop Frye declared that the pressing question for Canadian writers has been not "Who am I?" so much as "Where is here?," scholars and critics have charted the literary-geographic imaginaries that define this place.[22] Only a handful, however, make more than passing reference to cartography. Of the more than forty illustrations in W.H. New's *Land Sliding: Imagining Space, Presence, and Power in*

Canadian Writing, for instance, just one is a map. The pioneering studies of Canadian literary cartography have mostly focused on contemporary writers. Explaining this preference in his pioneering work *Territorial Disputes: Maps and Mapping Strategies in Contemporary Canadian and Australian Fiction*, Graham Huggan points out "the relative infrequency of the map topos in early Canadian writing," and instead concentrates on the maps that "are prevalent in post-colonial literatures, often as symbols of imposed political authority or as metaphors for territorial dispossession."[23] Marlene Goldman operates in a similar vein in *Paths of Desire: Images of Exploration and Mapping in Canadian Women's Writing* (1997), and examines the ways in which contemporary women writers deploy maps as ironic metaphors in a critique of the imperial and patriarchal power structures that the Cartesian worldview has come to signify. Wendy Roy's approach in *Maps of Difference: Canada, Women, and Travel* (2005) anticipates mine in this study inasmuch as she points to writing itself as a form of mapping. Yet, like Goldman, whose writers largely use cartographic strategies in order to navigate and reconfigure a women's literary terrain rather than a geographical one, Roy remains primarily interested in other mapped subjects such as gender, authorial identity, language, and social relations. To limit our attention to maps that have been deliberately deployed or deconstructed as icons, motifs, and metaphors, however, is to elide the subtle but nonetheless significant ways in which writing and mapping overlapped in the production of the very spaces that so many contemporary writers seek to challenge. As Margery Fee makes abundantly clear in her recent book *Literary Land Claims*, "a diverse range of textual forms ... can be adapted to staking or resisting a land claim."[24] It is this connection between literary representations and physical spaces that this book explores.

Mapping with Words shifts the study of literary cartography in Canada both historically and generically from postmodern and postcolonial fiction to colonial nonfiction, and thus opens up important aesthetic and political dimensions of both familiar and less well-known texts from this period. These texts attest to a cartographic subjectivity that was expressed not just in maps, but in small gestures that arise from an impulse to map: tracing lines, naming places, and visually ordering spaces such that one might sense one's position in a larger (and largely invisible) geography. Examined through the lens of mapping, the strangeness of these gestures and their literary effects can be understood as a form of territoriality. Above all, literary geography foregrounds an experience of the physical world that is different from, and in many ways vaster than, landscape's more limited vistas. Huggan's distinction is instructive here: "landscapes express a vision of the land," he writes, but "maps conceptualize, codify, and regulate that vision."[25] The appeal of cartography is the appeal of a world made not just visible, but also orderly and navigable. We can understand the diagrammatic qualities of topographical descriptions not only as significant territorializing gestures, then, but also as expressions both of a desire for a cartographic subjectivity and of the pleasures of the map's spare designs.

Cartography and landscapes differ further still in both scope and object: in addition to delineating the contours of our immediate surroundings, maps also show what lies beyond them, allowing us to situate ourselves within a larger sense of geographical space that we could not otherwise apprehend (such as a township, province, bioregion, nation, or, indeed, the whole world). Literary geography attunes readers to the evocative power that derives not just from the visible scenes that writers describe, but also from the felt spaces and cognitive maps that they conjure. From the aerial perspectives that allow writers imaginatively to survey distant terrain, to the trajectories that either bring comforting feelings of connection or exacerbate lonely feelings of isolation, to the boundaries – natural and artificial – that order and contain places and communities, to the landmarks and features that give them meaning, "the geo-coded world" is everywhere in these written descriptions of land.

Finally, a map's object is not only spatial perception, but also spatial experience – lived, bodily, material. The map's lines reflect accommodation and movement: they help us to navigate physical geography and to delineate places and territories, telling us where we are and where we can and cannot go. Writers extended the work of map-makers by filling in "blank" spaces with their detailed descriptions, evincing their shared desire to know, understand, claim, control, and inscribe new meanings upon the land. With their distant and encompassing views, their intimations of wayfinding, and their demarcations of territory and personal property, writers, like cartographers, reinforced the colonial logic of claiming and dispossession. Their topographical descriptions endow spaces with value, marking areas as culturally and economically significant, and designating places as "ours" or "theirs," public or private, accessible or inaccessible, civilized or wild, God-given or forsaken.

Mapping is not only a metaphor: real, lived terrains lie beneath – and become intertwined with – the texts that this book explores. Following Jean Baudrillard (who coined the now well-worn phrase "the map precedes the territory"), Geoff King argues that "map and territory cannot ultimately be separated. Cultural mappings play a central role in establishing the territories we inhabit and experience as real"; and yet, "to blur this distinction between map and territory is to destabilize this relationship, to acknowledge the socially constructed character of the mappings within which our lives are orientated."[26] As critical geographers remind us, all maps, even of real places, are also fictions. Like the stories that maps tell, the topographical and spatial descriptions that this book discusses – descriptions that are in many ways motivated by a desire to be accurate – are rife with selective and subjective myth-making. In "Deconstructing the Map," Harley clarifies the implications of regarding the map as a text rather than a mirror of the world: "By accepting [the map's] textuality," he argues, "we are able to embrace a number of different interpretative possibilities. Instead of just the transparency of clarity we can discover the pregnancy of the opaque. To fact we can add myth, and instead of innocence we may expect duplicity ... we learn to recognize the narrative qualities of cartographic representation as well as its claim to provide a synchronous picture of the world."[27] The "interpretative possibilities" that Harley's deconstructionist map-reading practice opens up resonate with the poststructuralist model of Gilles Deleuze and Felix Guattari, who liberate both the map and the map-reader from the burden of singularity, completeness, and stability. A map, they point out, can also be an expression of "rhizomatic" thinking: it is "open and connectable in all of its dimensions; it is detachable, susceptible to constant modification. It can be torn, reversed, adapted to any kind of mounting – reworked by an individual, group, or social formation."[28] Acknowledging the nearly infinite possibilities for mapping any given region, Deleuze and Guattari prompt us to consider the extent to which, as Pickles puts it, "the counter-mappings we seek have been with us all along," and that cartography "is and perhaps has always been a multitude of practices ... lines of flight ... coded and recoded by forms of institutionalized power, but always with leakage."[29]

This theory of mapping has far-reaching implications for how we read and interpret Canada's colonial literary history. In *Literary Land Claims*, Fee stresses the need "to move away from narrowly nationalist histories and perspectives to those that better articulate the multiple dilemmas of colonization."As Papaschase Cree scholar Dwayne Donald asks, "How can we reread history to show that the actual interactions between Aboriginal peoples and Canadians were, and continue to be, more complex than colonial binaries can possibly recount?"[30] In answer, this book draws attention to the ways in which settler texts were themselves marked by this complexity. Rather than reading the literary cartography of this period as a simple process of territorial overwriting (and thus reinscribing the land claims of nationalist narratives), we might look to it for "leakage" through which readers can glimpse the alternate spatialities that have always been a part of colonial space and, indeed, its cartographic negotiation. While settler writers certainly worked to claim, erase, and reshape the land in strikingly cartographic terms, their text-maps often point not just to a singular, static, hegemonic order, but also to the variegated textures of a place that resist any single surveyor's claims, drawing attention instead to the tensions in the settler imagination as it confronted "the messy practice of actual colonial space" that, as the historian Adele Perry argues, "profoundly challenged imperial dreams and ideals."[31] Place names, to give just one example, appear as fragmentary histories that are not "lodged firmly in the landscape" (as Aritha Van Herk suggests in her reading of a map of Alberta[32]) so much as precariously inscribed across its surfaces: European names overwrite, mingle with, or are again supplanted by Indigenous ones, all of them unstable and shifting, claiming and reclaiming spaces and places and their cartographic meanings. To the extent that they reveal this layered "rework[ing]," these texts are not just maps, but also *about* mapping practices.

As those who have helped establish spatial and environmental history have shown (for instance, William Cronon in *Changes in the Land* and Paul Carter in *The Road to Botany Bay*), the land was never an inert backdrop against which colonial histories unfolded, but a dynamic context with which historical actors (literary ones among them) interacted in various complex ways.[33] The most interesting literary cartography is a record of the nuances of human responses to the earth. Maps are, after all, not just expressions of "knowledge and power," as Harley argues in his famous essay by that title; but also expressions of "the mutual and reciprocal shaping of human selves and material landscape."[34] The close readings that make up this study range across the spatial terrains that writers create to consider, among other things, the alternative mappings that emerge from their attempts to read as well as inscribe – to understand, not just to possess and control – the world that they encountered.

Mapping the Book

My examination of early Canadian literary cartography begins with Cary's *Abram's Plains* and Burwell's *Talbot Road*, two topographical long poems shaped by cartographic views of the country. *Abram's*

Plains, which commemorates Britain's victory on the Plains of Abraham in 1759, poetically surveys the new colonial territory from Lake Superior to Labrador. *Talbot Road*, which celebrates the establishment of the famous Talbot settlement and the surveying of its network of roads in what is now southwestern Ontario, registers the surveyor's impact on the changing landscape. While both poems are indebted to the picturesque aesthetics of topographical poetry, they also develop a cartographic aesthetic that appeals to the settler's desire for orientation, mobility, and accessibility. Reading these poems in the context of the ambitious survey initiatives that helped to secure British control over the colonies during this period, chapter 1 casts in relief the extent to which maps facilitated settler claims to and perceptions of the land, not as an obstacle or an object of terror so much as an extension of empire. The frameworks of toponyms and routes mitigate fears of isolation in an uncharted and impenetrable wilderness by extending the settler's limited scope of vision to a sense of colonial space as mappable and connected to the rest of the world. This first chapter draws attention, then, to the power of literary cartography as a form of imaginative surveillance, territorial appropriation, and control; and to the role of literary geography as a way to interpret the cartographic strategies through which writers helped to produce the lines of occupation that shaped the colonial spatial imaginary.

The cartographic strategies that Cary and Burwell employ resurface in other texts as well, assuaging their desire to contain and control the land and its inhabitants. Yet the other writers in this study underscore the extent to which the process of discursive mapping involved complex interactions between writers and a terrain that was far from a blank slate for the map-maker's designs. Chapter 2 examines Moodie's *Roughing It in the Bush* through the cartographic desire to at once understand and sharpen the boundaries of civilized space on the frontiers of settlement. While her clear interest in figures of containment and order reveals a spatial sensibility shaped by the kind of cartographic imagination celebrated by the likes of Cary and Burwell, she also demonstrates the limits of such perspectives. Read against these two poems, Moodie's literary cartography reflects not the privileged, aerial perspective of a Cartesian world view so much as the corrective vision of a woman struggling to orient herself and establish the bounds of home and civilized life on the ground. From the precariousness of private property to the physical and psychic implications of distance and isolation on the sparsely settled fringes of the colony, Moodie draws attention to some of the more bewildering features of Upper Canada in the first half of the nineteenth century. To return to the image that opens this introduction: the shock of recognition that delights Moodie's Indian friends as they gaze upon the map of Canada casts in relief her own tentative appropriation of spaces that, for her, possess few familiar routes and patterns. *Roughing It in the Bush* dramatizes her negotiation of a colonial space in the process of being transformed and remapped, but whose reinscription is far from clean or complete.

While Moodie interrogates what are primarily social spaces, her sister Catharine Parr Traill, who devoted much of her life to cataloguing and describing the native flora and fauna of the uncleared regions around her Ontario homesteads, charts the wilderness. Chapter 3 argues that Traill's botanical studies, particularly *Canadian Wild Flowers* and the more comprehensive *Studies of Plant Life in Canada*, work not only to fill in but also to redefine the significance of a complex ecosystem that cartographers left blank, and that settlers usually characterized as an obstacle or an impenetrable waste that awaited transformation into agricultural land. Traill perceives the wilderness as significant in its own right, complicating the meaning of waste spaces and providing an impetus for their conservation. In the process, she also blurs the boundaries between "wild" and "civilized" upon which Moodie, Cary, and Burwell (among so many others during this period) relied. Traill's natural history thus anticipates an ecological approach to wild nature, and maps a different kind of settler geography predicated on a more integrated relationship between agrarian culture and the Indigenous topography that the expanding settlements threatened to destroy.

Chapter 4 turns from the minutiae of forest ecology to the expansive spatiality of the emerging transcontinental nation. It reads Grant's *Ocean to Ocean* as a more complex meditation on Canada's expansion into the northwest than has heretofore been acknowledged. Anticipating the nation that would be shaped by the Canadian Pacific Railway, Grant's popular book weaves together topographical description; inventory; travelogue; political, poetic, and religious meditation; photography; and cartography to tell a new and multilayered story about Canada's geography. The first book of its kind to envision the country as a Dominion from sea to sea, *Ocean to Ocean* is as much about how land becomes territory – or how it is mapped and claimed as such – as it is about the land itself. As it juxtaposes narrative and graphic maps, *Ocean to Ocean* highlights the textual qualities of cartography in a way that exposes the open-endedness of any such encoding of land. While on the one hand a confident imperialist assertion of the Dominion's east-west trade route and political thrust, then, on the other hand it creates a layered text-map that complicates its own vision of the northwest as uninhabited and available for the taking. From Grant's fragmentary record of Indigenous presence to his impassioned defence of treaty promises, an image of the northwest begins to take shape that is alive with rich history and diverse cultural meanings. *Ocean to Ocean* thus draws attention to what was at stake with colonial expansion, charting the northwest as a space of competing narratives and claims that needed to be carefully negotiated.

Treaties are a chief concern of chapter 5, which brings the discussion back around to poetry and its unique relationship, in Scott's work, to the negotiation and appropriation of Indigenous territory. Scott's lyric poem, "The Height of Land," has many features of a topographical poem, although its physical setting has predominantly been read as symbolic rather than literal. Examined through the lens of literary cartography, however, the topographical descriptions that anchor the poem in the territory of Treaty 9 reveal a poet negotiating a particular kind of colonial landscape. Like Cary and Burwell, Scott produced what is, in effect, a poetic appropriation of space. And yet, as a treaty commissioner he was intimately aware of the competing interests and claims that could unsettle such spaces. "The Height of Land" thus brings together a number of issues that surface over the course of this book, the most important of which is the instability of any map, cartographic or textual, that ignores the full implications of treaty space.

Literary cartography highlights the complexity of colonization as a process that involved not just inscribing, but also attempting to read, a terrain that for settlers as well as Indigenous peoples included overlapping and frequently conflicting layers of meaning. Reading these texts as maps points to both the erasures and the territorial negotiations that informed how the land was experienced, imagined, and written. While this book focuses primarily on settlers' future-oriented textual mappings, its conclusion takes up the work of the nineteenth-century explorer, cartographer, and writer David Thompson – who blurs the line between imperial exploration and colonial surveying – in order to foreground the counter-maps that, to return to Pickles, have "been with us all along" and that can be read as part of the texture of colonial space rather than as distinct from it. While Thompson's maps anticipated Canada's expansion across the northwest to the Pacific, they also throw into relief the fictions upon which colonial conceptions of this territory were founded. An exploration of the literary cartography of Thompson's *Narrative*, first published in 1916 (the same year that Scott's "Height of Land" appeared in *Lundy's Lane*), leads us to contemplate the complex and contradictory resonances of the cartographic imagination in early Canada, where the desire to grapple with and record the realities of these spaces and places frequently collided with the desire to erase or transform them, and where all maps are therefore partial and provisional.

Mapping with Words does not offer the comprehensiveness of a literary atlas. Just as a large-scale map must sacrifice a wider view of the terrain for a richer yet more narrowly focused exploration of the surface textures of the land, it sacrifices an exhaustive treatment of an incredibly rich and varied literary-cartographic landscape (if such a treatment is even possible) for close readings that bring more attention to the particular nuances of each text-map. It thus offers a useful supplement to sweeping studies such as New's *Land Sliding*, which necessarily fragments individual texts in order to make its broad literary-historical arguments. Alongside such treatments, we need close readings, not to provide a discussion of each text that is in any way complete (for, like Borges' fabled map drawn to the scale of the territory itself, any such thing is illusory) so much as to grapple with their peculiarities and tensions. A single text rarely does a unified thing. Like the lands it attempts to chart, its meanings shift and, sometimes, contradict one another.

Like the maps that it critiques, then, *Mapping with Words* is by necessity also a selective work of literary criticism. In order to focus on the dynamics of settler space as they emerge in nonfiction writing, it leaves many spatial narratives out of its primary discussion, from exploration literature to novels and short stories. Interested in literary geography as a means of opening up the dominant spatial metanarratives of place to the counter-maps that lie beneath and between their lines, it does not purport to undertake a sustained examination of either Indigenous or French colonial text-maps. Rather, it aims to expose the extent to which colonial texts are themselves complex stories of encounter through which other perspectives might emerge, and so to destabilize the apparently firm foundations upon which the settler's spatial imaginary rests. To read these texts closely is to dwell in the difficult spaces of colonization and the multilayered imaginative negotiations that created them. To a great extent, these spaces endure. From the roads we travel, to the patches of ground we think of as ours or not, to the national parks that continue to divide "wilderness" from "civilization," to the treaties that demand to be reread with greater consciousness of their negotiation of shared land, we live among the legacies of colonial mapping practices that – despite the many ways in which the physical and social landscapes of this country have changed and continue to change – still inform our perceptions of the land, its inhabitants, and the relationships between them. Literary geography ultimately reveals that each map is itself a text: a story about the land and about how people ought to conduct themselves upon it. As well as opening a window onto past spatial imaginaries, these literary records of fraught negotiations share much with present-day text-maps. They are part of a larger literary-cartographic texture that writers weave, mapping and remapping our relations with the earth, with territory, and with each other.[35] Where there is one story, there are always others that have been, or might be, told. Map-makers' work is never complete.

Chapter One

Illuminating the Horizon: The Cartographic Aesthetics of Two Early Long Poems

In the first line of the preface to his long poem *Abram's Plains* (1789), Thomas Cary appeals to the reader's desire for a literature that maps the world: "literature," he writes, "seems to be emerging from the closet to illuminate our horizon."[1] Heralding the growth of an Anglophone literary tradition in eighteenth-century Canada, Cary also signals his concern with its physical spaces, his metaphor anticipating the connection between writing and the surveying of land that animates both *Abram's Plains* and early Canadian literary cartography more broadly. Originally published by subscription in Quebec,[2] the poem addresses colonial readers for whom Canada's "horizon" was dimly conceived rather than vividly known. Cary describes the west-to-east trajectory of the St Lawrence River system and many of its tributaries, generating a poetic survey of a vast terrain that few would have seen with their own eyes – a terrain that, in the wake of the Conquest of New France the poem celebrates, was in the midst of being reimagined as British colonial territory. This chapter explores Cary's poetic mapping of this territory alongside another long poem that showcases the affinities between writing and surveying: Adam Hood Burwell's *Talbot Road*. In a metaphor reminiscent of Cary's, Burwell celebrates the bringing "to light" from "geographic night" of the remote Talbot settlement along the north shore of Lake Erie in what is now southwestern Ontario.[3] First published in the *Niagara Spectator* in 1818, and possibly read aloud at the Talbot anniversary that year, Burwell's poem – like Cary's – primarily addresses a local audience eager to have their presence on the land legitimated by maps and literary maps alike.[4] Together, these poems exemplify a literary-cartographic impulse in early Canadian writing that links the work of writers and map-makers in the imaginative delineation of settler space.

A former East India Company employee, Cary emigrated in the 1770s from Britain to Quebec, where he worked as a merchant and Tory government clerk, eventually opening a lending library in 1797 and founding a newspaper, the *Quebec Mercury*, in 1805. Burwell was born in Canada near Fort Erie and lived as a young man in the Talbot settlement before moving to Kingston. An author, journalist, and eventually clergyman, his investment in the colonial project extended, as Cary's did, to an interest in expanding its literary culture. Indeed, Michael Williams describes a young writer inspired by a "vision in which an oracle foretold the birth of a great poet in Upper Canada," which Burwell concluded was in reference to himself.[5] *Abram's Plains* and *Talbot Road* represent pioneering efforts to poeticize early Canadian spaces – to "cultivate" them not just with ploughs but also with English verses. Equally concerned with the proliferation of British colonial rule through clearing and cultivating the soil and with the establishment of an orderly, well-governed society thereon, they also work to shed light on the land's contours, features, and, most importantly, its changing geographic and demographic character, in order to lay claim to it.

Literary cartography encompasses processes of representing and poeticizing – or ascribing literary value to – the land. Many writings by early Canadian settlers accomplish both of these aims to varying degrees and effects, not least the many long poems that render in verse the landscapes of early Canada. Cary and Burwell join a long line of poets who would interpret these landscapes through the structures of eighteenth-century English topographical poetry,[6] including J. MacKay in *Quebec Hill* (1797), Cornwall Bayley in *Canada: A Descriptive Poem* (1806), and Charles Sangster in *The St Lawrence and the Saguenay* (1856). *Abram's Plains* and *Talbot Road* also follow in a tradition that, in English Canada, began with the explorer and fur trader Henry Kelsey's "Now Reader, Read ..." (c.1693–4), a poem that names and describes features of the eastern prairie not just for their own sake, but as part of a proprietary gesture of claiming land for the Hudson's Bay Company and the British Crown. Kelsey's poem is a "literary land claim" (to borrow the evocative title of Margery Fee's recent book): a poetic extension of the wooden "[c]ross" that he describes erecting "[a]t deerings point" (which scholars speculate is near present-day The Pas, Manitoba) "in token of [his] being there."[7] Cary and Burwell's poems also anticipate others – including the Canadian Oliver Goldsmith's "The Rising Village" (1825), Adam Kidd's *The Huron Chief* (1830), and Joseph Howe's *Acadia* (1874) – that share their concern with colonial property, possession, and dispossession.

What is unique about *Abram's Plains* and *Talbot Road* is the evocative presence of colonial maps behind their poetic renderings of land as British territory, and their apparent interest in cartographic strategies as a way to orient and locate. These poems thus lay an important foundation for thinking about the relationship between literature, cartography, land, and colonization. Their literary cartography dramatizes maps as agents of space-discipline, territorial appropriation, and – especially significant in poetry that has not unfairly been deemed derivative and amateurish – aesthetic design. Finally, their cartographic vision develops a poetics of early Canadian space that eschews the inward-looking perspective of the isolated garrison that, according to Northrop Frye, characterized so much early Canadian writing: through the framework of the map, these poets imagine Canada as a place defined by accessibility, mobility, and connection to the world. Theirs is a poetics of toponymy, of routes, of an expansive, even transnational, sense of space – of "[c]ities and plains extending far and wide," as the Canadian Goldsmith would write in "The Rising Village," "[a]s o'er the world their widening views extend."[8] These authors clearly attach such "widening views" to maps.

Commemorating the victory of the British over the French on the Plains of Abraham in 1759, and Colonel Talbot's pioneering settlement project and the surveying of its famous network of roads, respectively, these poems are concerned with events that were not only social and political, but also cartographic. The conquest of New France would have been impossible without detailed marine and shoreline surveys charted by Samuel Holland, James Cook, and J.F.W. Des Barres. In the following decades, British North America became the object of a number of mapping projects that "fixed and arranged the geographic space of northeastern North America in preparation for colonial settlement," which would grow exponentially in the years to come.[9] Most notably, the *Survey of Canada* (1760–3), which comprised more than forty large-scale maps of the settled parts of the former New France, and the *Atlantic Neptune*, a collection of coastal surveys compiled by Des Barres between 1774 and 1781, were (and remain) astonishing feats of cartographic surveillance that demonstrate the close connection between cartographic knowledge and territorial control. Further inland, settlement initiatives such as Colonel Talbot's were facilitated by Mahlon Burwell's large-scale surveys, with the names of settlers inscribed (in pencil, so that they could be erased if they failed to maintain roads and clear land) in the rectangular land grants that imposed a geometrical grid over the irregular terrain (see figure 3). Subsequent decades saw the development of county maps and atlases throughout the colonial provinces that were detailed enough to include the names of landholders, industries, churches, inns, and taverns. In short, it was a busy time for map-makers.

A desire for comprehensive and detailed knowledge about the world and its inhabitants defined the era of colonial and imperial expansion known as the Second British Empire. This desire was fuelled by a combination of curiosity and confidence that expressed itself in ambitious global initiatives such as Jonathan Carver's *The New Universal Traveller* (1779), a compendium of geographic and ethnographic information that, according to its title page, contains:

> *a Full and Distinct Account of all the Empires, Kingdoms, and States, in the Known World. Delineating, Not only their Situation, Climate, Soil, and Produce, whether Animal, Vegetable, or Mineral, But comprising also an interesting Detail of the Manners, Customs, Constitutions, Religions, Learning, Arts, Manufactures, Commerce, and Military Force, of all the Countries that have been visited by travellers or navigators, from the Beginning of the World to the Present Time. Accompanied with a Description of all the celebrated Antiquities, and an accurate History of every Nation, from the Earliest Periods. The Whole being intended to convey a clear Idea of the Present State of Europe, Asia, Africa, and America, in every Particular that can either add to useful Knowledge, or prove interesting to Curiosity.*[10]

A bold aim indeed. In its boldness, however, *The New Universal Traveller* epitomizes the late-eighteenth-century imperial outlook, particularly its robust confidence that the world could be contained, examined, understood, and placed at the armchair traveller's fingertips. Despite obvious knowledge gaps – Canada, for example, is "bounded ... on the west by parts unknown"[11] – its claims to accuracy and comprehensiveness do not waver. Even the blank spaces on its maps seem to imply that whatever remained unknown at that time was merely waiting to be discovered. On the "Accurate Map of North America" that appears between pages 574 and 575, for instance, "Parts Undiscovered" (which refers to all of what is now western and northwestern Canada) is printed in the second-largest font on the page – it was, after all, possibly the most exciting section of the map, and embodied the tantalizing possibility of exploration.

If maps' spatial emptiness invited settlers in, their spatial knowledge made other parts of the land appear legible and thus accessible.

Cary and Burwell's poetic treatments of the land deploy cartographic strategies that foster feelings of familiarity with a terrifyingly vast and alien country. Reducing unfathomable distances to a scale that could be apprehended with a single glance, they place their readers in a position of omniscient mastery and shed light into the dark areas of the settler's geographical imaginaries. The surveyor's panoptic gaze and the map's all-encompassing order, among other cartographic effects, shape their approach to the land, providing the sight-lines from which Canada could be imagined as an accessible, resource-rich colony increasingly under Britain's control.

A cartographic sense of space, for example, allows each poet to reach beyond the geographical limits of the picturesque prospects through which landscapes usually emerge in topographical poems. While each author follows the conventions of a prospect poem by describing views that an observer can see from an elevated position, each also creates impossible panoramas, conjuring a sense of space that fits within the limits of the imagination's elastic walls but extends beyond the sight-lines of the actual world – unless the observer happens to be looking at a map. A striking feature of the sweeping view of the waterways and terrain from Lake Superior to Labrador that Cary's speaker describes in *Abram's Plains* is that, even from the commanding height of the famous battleground on which he is perched, he cannot possibly see it. The thousands of miles of lakes, rivers, forests, and fields that he invites readers to envision rely upon, and reproduce, a cartographic God's-eye view. Similarly, *Talbot Road* ranges across a tract of territory too vast to be surveyed from any promontory, inviting readers to imagine that they can "see, as on a single sheet, / The Talbot Road unbroken and complete" – in other words: a map.[12]

Such visions would have been impossible without cartography. Indeed, in his extensive research of these two poems, D.M.R. Bentley identifies Carver's *New Map of North America, from the Latest Discoveries* (1778) as a likely model for Cary's versified survey of the Great Lakes and other St Lawrence tributaries (figure 2), and proposes that Burwell, for his part, was influenced by his brother Mahlon's surveys of the Talbot settlement (figure 3).[13] These suggestions point to the importance of cartography as a conceptual framework for the poets' relationships to and depictions of the land. The maps that Bentley identifies, along with the wider surveying culture of which they were a part, arguably had as profound an impact on Cary and Burwell's representations of Canada as did the eighteenth-century British topographical poems that their verses also echo. Such maps not only provided the knowledge and orientation necessary to write about these places, but also modelled a way of seeing that permeates the very structure of these poems.

To read these poems as literary cartography is to recognize the extent to which they poetically manifest not only the knowledge, but also the order, of mapped space. It is to consider the cartographic ambitions and desires that shape their spatial elements, from the toponyms that anchor their landscapes and the routes and geographical trajectories that carry readers imaginatively across them to the ways in which they confer value to particular tracts of land. Literary geography draws attention, too, to the territorializing imperatives of these poems and the extent to which, like the maps that anticipated empires and facilitated their expansion, their words transform the land into a text: a legible diagram of British territorial values rather than a source of fear and terror – an accessible place rather than a hostile space.

Abram's Plains

If, as Susan Glickman observes, "the very title of *Abram's Plains* demands our engagement with history,"[14] it also demands our engagement with geography. *Abram's Plains* refers to a site where history and geography intersect: on the Plains of Abraham, outside Quebec City on 13 September 1759, General Wolfe and his British army defeated the French under Montcalm – a defeat that dramatically reconfigured colonial territories across eastern North America, leading to the transfer of New France to Britain in 1763. At the geographical heart of Cary's poetic remapping of the new province of Quebec, the site of this battle underscores the poem's territorial themes. It also supplies the panoptic vantage point from which the poet presents his "comprehensive view" of his surroundings.[15] However, despite the poet's elevated position on the plains, the poem does not begin with a conventional picturesque prospect – that is, a landscape apparently observed directly and organized into foreground, middleground, and background in the manner of eighteenth-century landscape paintings. Instead, it opens with a description of the poet's immediate surroundings and then moves into a poetic survey that carries him far beyond his physical range of vision.

What the poet can actually see of the land itself from where he "sit[s] and court[s] the muse" is limited to the pastoral "shades" of the plains, with their "green sod," "grazing herds," "shy songsters," and "shyer squirrels," with perhaps a glimmer of the St Lawrence River beyond.[16]

His confined view nonetheless facilitates a kind of claim to the land on which he immediately appears right at home: what thirty years before had been a bloody battleground is now a restful scene in which the poet appears to fit so naturally that he is taken "for some native of the wood, / Or else some senseless block thrown from the flood."[17] This apparent congruence with his surroundings conceals his colonial relationship to the land. By equating himself with a "native" of this place, he asserts his, and by extension Britain's, belonging in a land once inhabited and controlled by others.

From his shady seat on the plains, the topography of Quebec emerges largely through his imagination, embodied in the apparently unbounded flight of his "muse" (whose inquiring gaze neither "arched gates" nor "walls" nor "wide-surrounding ditch" can keep from penetrating even a fortified town).[18] If only in his mind, the poet assumes a surveyor's stance, perspective, and authority, his muse supplying the wide-ranging vision of the map-reader. Cary's cartographic surveillance sharpens as he charts the extent of the territory from the Great Lakes to the Gulf of St Lawrence that had come under British control in 1760. Following the course of the St Lawrence and its tributaries from Lake Superior in the west to Labrador in the east, and naming rivers, lakes, and several towns along the way, *Abram's Plains* might well be read as the poetic analogue of Carver's map illustrating Canada and "New Britain" in his *Travels through the Interior Parts of North America in the Years 1766, 1767, and 1768* (1778) – a book from which, Bentley observes, Cary borrowed liberally.

Formally, the heroic couplets that guide the reader through this terrain organize a sequence of geographical views into a linear pattern that at once unifies the region and draws prospective settlers – imaginatively, at least – deeper into a colony whose emigrant population remained concentrated in the east. These views are marked by toponyms of lakes, rivers, and towns that provide the geographical and linguistic frame upon which the poem is built. Propelled forward by Cary's rhymed iambic pentameter, the poem moves quickly through certain places and pauses in others, ultimately subsuming the layered history of Indigenous and French habitation that the toponyms convey, from "Huron" to "Montmorenci" to "Lorette," under what arguably remains the most significant toponym in his poem: *Britannia.*

In the eighteenth-century spirit of buoyant confidence in the reach of human (and in particular, British) knowledge and ingenuity, Cary is unstinting in his veneration of Britain's expanding colonial and commercial empire. Glossing over such impediments as the American Revolution – which, despite threats to Quebec and Montreal in 1775 and 1776, he reduces to a "storm of civil broils" significant only in that it brought "loyal sufferer[s]" to Canada – he looks back instead to the British victories and the "magnanimity" that strengthened and expanded its imperial strongholds.[19] With the decisive battle of the Plains of Abraham at its centre, the poem celebrates a period of unprecedented British influence in North America. The Peace of Paris that ended the Seven Years' War in 1763 extended Britain's control over all French territories in North America with the sole exception of Louisiana. *Abram's Plains* echoes many of the ambitions embodied in the Royal Proclamation of 7 October 1763 that transformed a French colony into an English one. The proclamation articulated King George III's desire "that all [Britain's] loving Subjects, as well of Our Kingdoms as of Our Colonies in America, may avail themselves, with all convenient Speed, of the great Benefits and Advantages which must accrue [from the 'extensive and valuable Acquisitions in America'] to their Commerce, Manufactures, and Navigation."[20] In 1783, when America won its independence, the remaining British colonies that are now part of Canada had only about 200,000 colonial inhabitants, most of whom were French, and aspects of French culture (including civil law and the seigneurial system of landholding that accompanied it) were protected under the Quebec Act of 1774; yet, as the geographer Cole Harris underscores, "power had changed hands. Colonial officials, officers and troops, and most of the principal merchants were now British."[21]

The poetic map that emerges in *Abram's Plains* reinforces this shift in authority, and casts in particular relief the connection between land and imperial economic development. Cary shares King George's concern with "commerce, manufactures, and navigation" as expressed in the Royal Proclamation: these serve, in *Abram's Plains*, as beacons of progress, converging in the survey of the St Lawrence river system and thus making his poem into a versified map of the colony's commercial potential. The orderly list of the Great Lakes begins the poem's shaping of an extensive inland navigational system that is connected to the world. From Lake Superior – "as *Asia's Caspian* great, / Where congregated streams hold icy state" – it proceeds quickly through the lakes, each of which is contained by a rhyming couplet:

Huron, distinguish'd by its thund'ring bay,
Where full-charg'd clouds heav'n's ord'nance ceaseless play.

Thee *Michigan*, where learned beavers lave,
And two great tribes divided hold thy wave.
Erie for serpents fam'd, whose noisome breath,
By man inhal'd, conveys the venom'd death.[22]

While Cary's heroic couplets evoke the "relatively enclosed physical shape" of each lake,[23] the ease with which they propel the reader swiftly through the Great Lakes to the St Lawrence recalls the tracing of a route on a map, the effortlessness of which belies the impediments of both foul-smelling venomous serpents and obstacles such as rapids and falls. The poet pauses only once to draw out the sublime sight and sound of Niagara Falls that "echo[es]," first in an additional rhymed hexameter, and then in an extended comparison to Handel's "Messiah" (which creates a geographical and aesthetic connection between "New" World and "Old").[24] Although each of the Great Lakes is marked by a defining feature (such as "learned beavers" or "serpents fam'd"), the parallel structure of the couplets in which the lakes are represented anticipates, in verse, the unimpeded "chain of river navigation and navigable inland seas" that later settlers such as Susanna and John Dunbar Moodie would appreciate as ever more effectively connecting the interior of the continent to its eastern settlements with the aid of canals.[25]

As cartographers would often do to attract settlers and investors to the colonies, Cary lends value to his survey of the St Lawrence by mapping exploitable resources into its surrounding geography. Catalogues of the region's natural history and the east-to-west survey of the river become intertwined in the poet's vision of Canada's resource potential and commercial routes. Together, the poet claims, they offer riches equivalent to the most profitable mines: "What," he asks of the St Lawrence,

tho' no mines their gold pour through thy stream,
Nor shining silver from thy waters gleam;
Equal to these, the forests yield their spoils,
And richly pay the skillful hunter's toils.
The beaver's silken fur to grace the head,
And, on the soldier's front assurance spread;
The martin's sables to adorn the fair,
And aid the silk-worm to set off her air.
Gems of *Golconda* or *Potosi*'s mines,
Than these not more assist her eyes' designs.

The jetty fox to majesty adds grace,
And of grave justice dignifies the place;
The bulky buffalo, tall elk, the shaggy bear,
Huge cariboo, fleet moose, the swift-foot deer,
Gaunt wolf, amphibious otter, have their use,
And to thy worth, O first of floods! conduce.[26]

Notwithstanding their eventual function in "adorn[ing] the fair" of the imperial elite, these fur-bearing animals are catalogued for their "use" rather than their aesthetic or ecological value. In other words, this is a list of "spoils" that, comprehensive though it might seem, identifies only those features of the Canadian wilderness that contribute to the "worth" of the St Lawrence and, by implication, of the colony as a whole. A few lines later Cary makes it clear that the St Lawrence itself is not just valuable as a highway conducting resources from the interior out of the colony; "thy own resources," he stresses, must not "be past by, / Resources that within thy bosom lie."[27] The catalogue of fish and the description of whaling that follow associate further riches with the river, and contribute to an emerging sense in the poem that both land and water in the colony are bursting with exploitable natural resources, much like the Canada depicted in Henri Chatelain's *Carte Particulière du Fleuve Saint Louis* (c. 1719) (figure 4), which is framed by a similarly resource-driven catalogue of the area's natural history. Culling the depths of wild nature for knowable and exploitable features, and then proceeding to categorize and order them, Cary's only identifiably "Canadian" nature appears carved up and compartmentalized for colonial and imperial consumption, underlining the role of natural history in the reconfiguration (and appropriation) of the land as commercial resource.

In addition to underscoring its economic value, natural history also renders the land less threatening in this poem. Cary uses knowledge of local plants, for instance, to assuage emigrant fears of the wilderness such as had been powerfully expressed in the Anglo-Irish poet Oliver Goldsmith's *Deserted Village* (1770). Lamenting the enclosure of common pasture lands in the English countryside that forced many British peasants to emigrate to America, Goldsmith decries Georgia's "matted woods" and "poisonous fields," which he contrasts with the comforts of home, such as "[t]he cooling brook, the grassy vested green," and "[t]he breezy covert of the warbling grove" of the idyllic, but now deserted, landscape.[28] His speaker finds in North America a terrifying wilderness "with rank luxuriance crowned,"

Where the dark scorpion gathers death around;
Where at each step the stranger fears to wake
The rattling terrors of the vengeful snake;
Where crouching tigers wait their hapless prey,
And savage men, more murderous still than they;
While oft in whirls the mad tornado flies,
Mingling the ravaged landscape with the skies.[29]

Invoking Goldsmith, Cary gives the "[t]hick-matted woods" of Quebec their own brand of "rank luxuriance":

Where branch entwines with branch and roots with roots;
Where flies, in myriads, borne on filmy wings,
Unceasing teaze, with tumefying stings.
Where the dark adder and envenom'd snake,
In curling folds, lurk in the shelt'ring brake.[30]

Direct echoes of Goldsmith in this passage at first suggest a landscape as impenetrable and inhospitable as the wilds of Georgia. Yet Cary diverges from Goldsmith, and revulsion is supplanted by optimism, as his poet locates, in among the vegetation of the Canadian wilderness itself, the cure to any ills therein: "nature good and wise," he assures his readers, "[w]here poison shoots its antidote supplies."[31] Local knowledge drawn from Carver of the therapeutic Rattlesnake Plantain, a species of orchid native to eastern North America,[32] defuses the threat of wilderness and ensures survival.

While in some parts of Cary's poem natural history helps to anchor the scene in North America, in other parts the specific topographical imagery and information with which he orients and acclimatizes the reader to an identifiably North-American wilderness dissolves into generalized and imitative description. As Bentley notes, "in many places" the poem reads as "little more than a pastiche of phrases from *Windsor-Forest* and *The Seasons*."[33] In these moments, Cary disengages from the particulars of the land, and the reader's sense that they are reading about Canada fades. Yet its stock imagery and diction does more than simply make *Abram's Plains* into a poetic "repository of monuments" to Britain, as Smaro Kamboureli characterizes the early Canadian long poem more broadly.[34] While they momentarily obscure the uniqueness of the topography, these echoes of English verse establish Canada's territorial, mnemonic, and cultural continuity with Britain. Working in tandem with his expansive toponymy and lists of natural resources, Cary's derivative and generalizing descriptions help him transform Canada into a habitable "place": compatible with the British imagination, it becomes, in effect, a "perceived or felt space, space humanized, rather than the material world taken on its own terms."[35] If this is lazy poetry, it is also a territorial gesture that is, ironically, as deeply invested in the formation of this place as any inscription of its unique features and character. Cary charts poetic *routes* (rather than roots) that connect the poem, and the land from which it springs, to the same imperial centre to which the colony was directing its resources.

To similar effect, Cary gives the landscape of Quebec a new layer of literary significance by populating its geography with figures from Classical myth. Circe, the Greek enchantress, inhabits the poem alongside Indigenous figures with their tomahawks, all of them yielding to Cary's bid for "moderation" and "moral virtues."[36] Echo and Ceres dwell along with Naiads and Dryads in the "caves," "wild deserts," and "yellow harvests" of a "new" world that resonates with the cultures of the "old" European one, while supplanting the Anishinaabe tricksters, Thunderbirds, Waindegoos, and Little People, among others, that had long populated the lands from Lake Superior to Lake Ontario.[37] Cary thus conducts an imaginative appropriation and cultivation of spaces that were, as he amply describes, being physically transformed as well.

Not surprisingly, he celebrates this transformation at the hands of British colonists: "How blest the task," he confidently exclaims, "to tame the savage soil, / And, from the waters, bid the woods recoil!"; the clearing and cultivating of land is admittedly "hard," and "yet," the poet assures the reader, "bare the soil shall lay, / And, unobstructed, shine the lamp of day."[38] Echoing the metaphor that opens the preface, here Cary links the clearing of wilderness with the literal "illumination" of landscape. To clear and cultivate land is, he suggests, to release it, as God does the world in *Genesis*, from darkness to light. Indeed, Cary's "British spirits" stand "bold" and God-like before nature:

> Such is the ardour of the British breast,
> If of that liberty it loves possess'd,
> At their command floods back their billows heave,
> And a bold shore their oozy bottom leave:
> ...
> Tall forests their high-waving branches bow,
> And yield, submiss, to lay their honors low.[39]

Whether as God or as Moses, man lords over nature, with water and land retreating and yielding in accordance with his desires.

The agricultural settler's shaping powers in this passage parallel the poet's cartographic reconfiguration of Quebec/New France as well as territories occupied by displaced Huron-Wendat communities into "our infant world" that, he confidently maintains, "asks but time's fost'ring hand" such that "[i]ts faculties must by degrees expand."[40] In both cases, the manipulation of the land is represented as a fulfilment of its preordained purpose. Under the Loyalist farmer's care, for instance, the "earth" becomes "unclog'd" and "responsive."[41] All who help to clear the wilderness contribute to the quasi-mythical transformation of "deserts" to fertile fields, a process praised by Cary's "Naiades,"

> Who, in full chorus, vocal, join their lays,
> To chant, in chearful carols, Ceres' praise:
> Whose yellow harvests, nodding, glad the shore,
> Where Dryades, midst wild deserts, reign'd before.
> Where prowl'd the wolf, the bear and fox obscene,
> Now grateful kine, loud lowing, graze the green.[42]

In full embrace of the deep-rooted Western idea that forests were antithetical to civilization, the poet interprets the conversion of wild forests into cultivated fields and pastures – which replace "obscene" wild animals with "grateful" domestic ones – as the topographical manifestations of the "blessings" of "peace" in the colony.[43] Attributing the land's fertility to the stability and order that the colony enjoys under British rule, the poem's territorial vision supports its commemoration of General Wolfe, who symbolizes Britain's successful conquest of New France, and Lord Dorchester, who symbolizes Britain's stable and continuing influence in Quebec. Cary's versified survey identifies British improvements as evidence that "*Britannia's* conquering sword" has been not a violent force, but a benevolent forerunner of progress and material advantages – something for which even French Canadians should "[b]e thankful."[44] Juxtaposing the "unkind soils" that surround the vestiges of a French colonial village with the "rich meadows" and "fat[tened] ... meads and groves" that flank the St Charles River (which he represents as emblematic of British wisdom and moderation), he sets up a paradigm in which land "beneath a GEORGE" is more productive than land under the "small tyrants" of seigneurial New France.[45]

The various ways in which Cary confers meaning and value onto parts of the land and, indeed, different kinds of landscapes in this poem exemplify the extent to which mapmaking is, in J.B. Harley's words, "an art of persuasion" rather than a neutral representation. Harley underscores that even the most seemingly accurate maps are products of "selection, classification, standardization, and the creation of mappable hierarchies" – processes that are all "inherently rhetorical" and guided by their makers' desires and ideologies. "The surveyor," he reminds us, "whether consciously or otherwise, replicates not just the 'environment' in some abstract sense but equally the territorial imperatives of a particular political system."[46] To a certain extent, then, all maps are fictions that, as Mark Monmonier bluntly puts it, "lie" about the land and the people who occupy it in order to further the map-maker's agenda.[47] Not unlike the imperial maps that inspired its geographical structure and themes, *Abram's Plains* represents the land neither neutrally nor mimetically, but rather in ways that selectively reflect the values and aspirations of an imperial "Britannia" whose economy depended on colonial expansion and resource extraction.

As powerful as the rhetorical force with which maps speak through symbology, order, and toponymy are the silences that conceal other histories and ways of seeing the land. A common, and particularly egregious, silence in many topographical poems about early Canada in particular obscures Indigenous knowledge and habitation. As we shall see, Burwell omits Indigenous peoples entirely from his account of the Talbot settlement. Other poets at once memorialize and marginalize them as noble or ignoble savages – or sometimes both – who may once have held dominion over these regions, but are now exiled to "far distant wilds," as the Canadian Goldsmith would put it in "The Rising Village."[48] Cary does not entirely elide Indigenous peoples' presence in the terrain he surveys. Yet, as he does with the French *habitants*, he locates them in places where they appear to pose no impediment to the Anglo-colonial transformation that his poem charts. Echoing Carver, he attributes control of Lake Michigan to "two great tribes divided," but only on this frontier and in the northern wilds of "bleak Labradore" does he so much as hint at Indigenous possession. Where they do appear in his settler landscape, they are receptive subjects of assimilation. In keeping with the Enlightenment definition of culture that metaphorically linked the cultivation of soil and people, Cary parallels the transformation of wilderness into farmland with the conversion of warriors into farmers. While the wilderness is characterized as "savage" and in need of "tam[ing]," "a task of more exalted kind," writes Cary, is

To arts of peace, to tame the savage mind;
The thirst of blood, in human breasts, to shame,
To wrest, from barb'rous vice, fair virtue's name;
Bid tomohawks to ploughshares yield the sway,
And scalping-knives to pruning hooks give way.[49]

Cary later adds that, like the earth, "man is but moulded clay" and can be altered, along with the landscape, to conform to British colonial ideals.[50] As Bentley observes, not only does the poet betray his "actual or willed ignorance of the fact that the Hurons had practised agriculture for thousands of years in what is now Ontario," but, when writing about the French settlements later in the poem, he also ignores "the fact that under the terms of the Quebec Act (1774) the seigneurial land-tenure system was ... retained and consolidated for the benefit of colonial entrepreneurs."[51] Rather than carefully approximating the actual state and organization of people on the land at that time, Cary maps land use in a way that legitimizes the growing influence of the British upon it. His poem, then, registers desire more than reality.

His depiction of the Huron-Wendat villagers of Lorette (Wendake) is another case in point. Here, he applauds the changes that have apparently already occurred under the apparently benevolent influence of European civilization:

Here, of the copper-tribes, an half-tam'd race,
As villagers take up their resting place;
Here fix'd, their household gods lay peaceful down,
To learn the manners of the polish'd town.[52]

By describing the Huron as "half-tam'd," Cary invokes stereotypical hierarchies of progress and civilization that privilege, among other things, a "fix'd" or settled way of life over the migratory hunter-gathering practices that racist conventions of the day equated with savagery. Moreover, as they "peaceful[ly]" give up their own "gods" and ways, the Huron people appear as willing converts to the way of life that European settlements offer, though he neglects to characterize this conversion as primarily a fact of their assimilation with French rather than British settlers.

The literary cartographer also registers toponyms that convey a fragmentary narrative of the area's human history. Along the St Lawrence, the land's heterogeneous social texture is preserved in a way that in Burwell's Talbot settlement it is not. Names such as Niagara (of disputed Neutral, Haudenosaunee, or Mohawk origin), Ontario (from the Huron-Wendat word for great lake), Oswego (the Mohawk word for a small waterway flowing into a larger one), and Masquinongi (from the Algonquin word for a species of fish), along with the French names Montreal, Champlain, Charlebourg, Beauport, and Orleans, among others, inscribe diverse histories, habitation, and colonial contest into Cary's text-map.

Yet Cary also dramatizes the erasure of Indigenous signifiers from the land itself in a moving description of the "piteous groans of rending firrs" from the mill at Malbay:

> Within whose rind, I shudder while I tell,
> Spirits of warriors close imprison'd dwell,
> Who in cold blood, butcher'd a valiant foe,
> For which, transform'd to weeping firrs, they grow:
> Down their tall trunks trickling the tears distill,
> 'Till last the ax and saw groaning they feel.[53]

Cary does not mourn the people whom he characterizes as cold-blooded murderers in this image, which may also derive from the Anishinaabe belief that trees could feel pain (according to Peter Jones in his *History of the Ojebway Indians*, this was why "they seldom cut down green or living trees"[54]). Yet this passage all but conceals the losses incurred during this period, when both the forests and the First Nations who inhabited them were under assault across what is now eastern Canada. Unlike some other early writers (e.g., Goldsmith, who in "The Rising Village" describes "the hideous yells" of "savage tribes" asserting "[t]heir right to rule the mountain and the plain"[55]), Cary is not interested in documenting Indigenous resistance to colonial expansion in his poem. Yet, as Harris underscores, resistance was not uncommon: "At the beginning of the modern settlement of the Ottawa Valley," for instance,

> Native chiefs told American settlers that the land belonged to them. The settlers, they said, were driving away game and threatening the way of life of their people. Other chiefs probably said as much, but small scattered populations of hunters and gatherers had no power to stop the advance of capital and settlers into their territories. For the most part, the Native

> presence was ignored and virtually invisible. Their land was wanted and taken. It was assumed to be uninhabited, or inhabited so thinly by wandering people that their land uses were inconsequential – common, legitimating tropes worldwide of settler colonialism ... They usually had no choice but to move away, in so doing encroaching on the territories and compounding the problems of other struggling Native peoples.[56]

In light of this history, the Indigenous toponyms that survive in Cary's text-map ring almost as hollowly as the "Indian Place-Names" that tell "but tales of ghosts" in Duncan Campbell Scott's 1905 poem.[57] The few Indigenous and French communities that are given a place in the text-map of *Abram's Plains* are cast under the formidable shadow of Britain and – like a British flag planted on the site of its victory – the Tory poet and his cartographic muse.

Recognizing the panoptic power that he wields, the poet reassures the inhabitants of a French-Canadian town that his muse "comes no foe [their] streets with blood to fill, / Her only weapon is a grey-goose quill. / ... Tho' [their] extended works she curious scan, / She comes no spy to draw the secret plan."[58] Alluding to lingering anxieties among the French population in Quebec about surveillance in the aftermath of the war, these lines recall a time of intense scrutiny of the land and its diverse populations – a time when Governor Murray's survey of Canada included "a census of each parish, [with] information on population and the number of men able to bear arms," to prepare the British in the event of "future war with the French for Canada."[59] While the poet claims that his intentions are benign, his "grey-goose quill" reminds us that in the hands of a cartographer the pen can indeed prove mightier than the sword. Cary wields his pen with confidence and optimism, mapping a knowable, navigable, and, above all, unthreatening territory that, in its apparent newness, heralds the beginning of an empire ranging from Lake Superior to Labrador.

Talbot Road

Perhaps no early Canadian poem showcases the manner in which colonial maps became "dictators of a new agrarian topography" that imposed their "space discipline" throughout "the 'wilderness' of former Indian lands in North America"[60] in greater detail, or with greater conviction, than does Adam Hood Burwell's *Talbot Road: A Poem*. While the literary cartography of *Abram's Plains* remains loose and suggestive, in *Talbot Road* the connection between poetry and mapping is as strong as the blood-bond between the poet and his surveyor-brother, Mahlon. Colonel Talbot's land-surveyor-in-chief, Mahlon Burwell was responsible for surveying the extensive network of roads collectively referred to as "the Talbot Road" that his brother's poem celebrates. To read *Talbot Road* closely is to witness the surveyor's transformation of the topography into orderly tracts of private property efficiently linked by a communications network that was unprecedented in British North America at the time.

My reading of *Talbot Road* extends from and elaborates on Bentley's characterization of the poem as "the product of a geometric caste of mind, a formatively spatial way of thinking that Burwell shared, not only with his surveyor-brother Mahlon, but also with many others who were responsible for the organization of Upper Canadian space in the nineteenth century. Like the Talbot settlement itself ... *Talbot Road* was shaped by a survey mentality, by a mind that delighted in straight lines, 'proper angles' (200), and 'cross-way[s]' (450), in geometrical designs, architectural plans, and comprehensive schemes."[61] Burwell appeals to a cartographic imagination when, in the introductory "Argument," he indicates that the poem will culminate in "a connected survey of Talbot Road, from its eastern to its western extremities."[62] Like *Abram's Plains*, *Talbot Road* employs visual and spatial descriptions to generate not just a set of picturesque prospects, but also a cumulative text-map of the region, until by the end of the poem the reader is urged to "see, as on a single sheet, / The Talbot Road unbroken and complete."[63] Moving between text-maps of its past, present, and future geographies, *Talbot Road* charts the settler landscape's changing features, emphasizing as it does so the surveyor's role in the creation of colonial space.

Burwell dedicates his poem to Colonel Talbot, a native of Malahide, Ireland, who established a considerable reputation as one of British North America's most ambitious and efficient colonizers when his plan for the settlement of what is now southwestern Ontario reversed a period of declining emigration to Canada.[64] Yet *Talbot Road* does not offer much in the way of a portrait of this formidable figure – whether heroic or misanthropic and dictatorial (Talbot supposedly embodied each of these traits). The topography, the emerging settlement, and the road take precedence over individual people in the poet's attentions. Burwell's primary objective is to show the region as it changed over time from a fertile but disorderly wilderness to an orderly patchwork of agricultural townships connected by the network of roads. As he does so, he implicitly commemorates Mahlon, whose name remains linked with Talbot's and with the region's geographical history. The "confidential friend" of the settlement's founder, Mahlon was considered "the strongest personality in the settlement after Talbot himself"; in fact, it is said that "none of the original settlers stood higher in the estimation of the community than Colonel Burwell, who possessed the respect of all."[65] The interplay of real and imagined topographies that gives this poem its unique spatial texture showcases the creative power of Mahlon's surveying as much as that of Talbot's planning and governance.

The central figure and unifying principle of Burwell's poem is the road itself, which relates both materially and conceptually to the motif and perspective of the survey. Just as colonial settlement depended upon the accessibility and connectivity that roads provided, so too the "practices and technologies of vision" of modern mapping "depended on being able to range far and wide across space."[66] The particular character of the settlement sustains less attention than the question of how it got there and how it will continue to grow and change, with the road serving as index and instrument of the territory's (re)inscription. The prominent place that Burwell gives to the road (as well as to the natural "highways" of rivers and streams) throughout the poem registers his concern with the infrastructures that helped to transform the Talbot tract from wilderness into agricultural land. With its many intersections, the Talbot Road becomes a symbol not so much of mobility as of accessibility, the settlement emerging as a network of destinations inviting emigrants *in* rather than *through*. The pattern of orthogonal lines that the road generates in the reader's mind underscores the mapping over of "a wilderness, and scarcely known" with a neat grid of towns and farms, the symmetry of which readers are encouraged to associate with the virtues of "greatness," "providence," "reason," "order," "industry," "[p]rosperity," and "[c]ommerce" that the poem celebrates.[67]

The Talbot Road furnishes the settlement with what the anthropologist Tim Ingold defines as "lines of occupation." These lines, Ingold explains, include the frontiers that delineate territory and property as well as the routes that "facilitate the outward passage of personnel and equipment to sites of settlement and extraction, and the return of the riches drawn therefrom. Unlike paths formed through the practices of wayfaring" (an example of which might be the "bridle path" that the Talbot Road, as Burwell observes, replaced in Bayham, or the Indigenous trail that another part of the road conceals, and which Burwell similarly erases), he continues,

> such lines are surveyed and built in advance of the traffic that comes to pass up and down them. They are typically straight and regular, and intersect only at nodal points of power. Drawn cross-country, they are inclined to ride roughshod over the lines of habitation that are woven into it, cutting them as, for example, a trunk road, railway or pipeline cuts the byways frequented by humans and animals in the vicinity through which it passes. But lines of occupation do not only connect. They also divide, cutting the occupied surface into territorial blocks.[68]

Formally, the heroic couplets that both Cary and Burwell employ parallel the abstract geometrical lines of occupied space. In *Abram's Plains*, for instance, the St Lawrence is experienced not for its own sake but rather as a conveyor from point to point, connecting destinations at which resources can be collected and redistributed. With even greater force, the Talbot Road network emerges in Burwell's poem as an imposed pattern of lines that thread together a new order of colonial space by linking destinations and cutting up the earth's surface into agricultural property.

Burwell foregrounds the surveyor as the creative agent of this transformation. Near the beginning of the poem, he accordingly asks not who built the Talbot Road but "what master hand / This work *projected*, and its order *plann'd*?" Burwell's primary interest – and the foremost element of his poem's "noble ... theme" – is not the physical construction of the settlement and its network of roads (although he devotes considerable attention to clearing land), but their imaginative conception.[69] Having "canvass'd" the land, "its importance weigh'd / And, in his mind, its future state survey'd," Talbot is celebrated as the progenitor of a newly habitable region, his map a mental construct that reflects the surveyor's prophetic designs.[70] Throughout the poem, Burwell's emphasis on the future – an emphasis that becomes especially prominent in his "Apostrophe to Hope and Anticipation" – highlights the power of imagined plans in charting the way for territorial development. He underscores that before it was ever a real place the Talbot settlement was a "[g]reat scheme" that "spontaneous flow'd" from Talbot's "mind."[71]

This creative power is not given to Colonel Talbot alone; the paradigmatic settler also forms mental maps that anticipate what his land will look like in the future: formulating "[n]ew schemes for future happiness," he "dwells" on "each prospect" in his mind,

And portions out, for the ensuing year,
A barn to build, or some new land to clear;
Or plants an orchard on the sunny hills,
And with judicious hand a garden fills;
Rich waving harvests reaps from off the fields,
And all the golden treasures Ceres yields.[72]

The settler's visions do not reflect the present state of his land; they are, rather, a series of imagined future "schemes," superimposed upon the present-day "cabin rude, of humblest form" and the surrounding "dubious maze" of "tow'ring pines,"[73] much as township plans laid their designs over the wilderness. Far more than idle speculations, such schemes provided and maintained the impetus for land development, anticipating the man-made environment that would, someday, follow. Capitalizing on the map as a design that precedes the territory that it purports to represent, the settler stands alongside the surveyor in Burwell's poem as a God-like figure who redesigns the world and makes a garden of the wilderness.

In the opening lines of the poem, Burwell's image of Talbot as part God, part Adam forging a new Eden in Upper Canada not only conveys the creative power of the map, but also fosters a "myth of entitlement" through which, as J. Edward Chamberlin notes, settlers claimed an original relation to the land and, by implication, a sense of rightful possession of, it.[74] This myth "match[ed] their myth of discovery" that, Bentley adds, represents one of "three principles of land ownership that had – and have – immense consequences for Canada and all its peoples: (1) the right of first discovery; (2) the right of first possession; and (3) the right of annexation through labour."[75] Crediting Talbot with having "found" a land "[r]emote from man," Burwell legitimizes his presence as the discoverer of an uninhabited region – the "first who trod this desert ground."[76]

No trace remains in this poem of the area's significance to the Indigenous peoples from whom the British Crown purchased the tract in the early 1790s, and who had created the original trail along which the first part of the Talbot Road was constructed. The region's history includes the Iroquoian-speaking nation that Samuel de Champlain called "the Neutrals" because of their neutrality throughout the Iroquois-Huron wars in the seventeenth century and the Mississauga Anishinaabe, who expelled the Neutrals in 1700. Like the Hurons to the north and east, the Neutrals practiced agriculture as well as fishing, hunting, and gathering. Moreover, Don W. Thomson mentions "Indian assistants" (presumably Anishinaabe) who helped with Burwell's surveys, and occasionally left "abruptly to attend tribal pow-wows."[77] Accentuating Talbot's pioneering efforts, Burwell erases this history, along with that of the Loyalist settlers who began to arrive in the 1780s (before Talbot) and had already surveyed some of the townships and farm lots along the shores of Lake Erie.

Instead, Burwell depicts a vacant, virgin territory that is, for Talbot and his settlers, quite literally a blank slate. Here the "rudest forms" of nature lie in wait as raw materials from which the colonizer, characterized as a kind of artist, will create "beauty."[78] The "wild woods" and "hoarse and hollow" winds that at first seem to be the only features of this unsurveyed landscape deepen its apparent loneliness, and help to abstract the region from any social or historical significance.[79] Drawing on the map's capacity to "foster the notion of a socially empty space" and thus "lessen ... the burden of conscience about people in the landscape," Burwell is also silent on the mistreatment of Indigenous peoples by colonists in the region that Anna Brownell Jameson would describe, not many years later, in *Winter Studies and Summer Rambles in Canada*; nor does he mention the Six Nations Reserve on the Talbot settlement's eastern border, or the Huron Tract to the north. His brief account of the War of 1812 also neglects Tecumseh (whom Jameson regards as the region's "historical hero" and Adam Kidd would memorialize, among other Indigenous figures, in *The Huron Chief*), although it celebrates the "dauntless spirit" of Tecumseh's white ally, General Isaac Brock.[80] Travellers through, rather than inhabitants of, the settlement, writers such as Jameson and Kidd could represent the fraught demographics of settler territory without personally addressing the consequences. Burwell appears to have avoided this problem altogether by simply rewriting history, using literary cartography as a rhetorical device rather than a documentary tool.

In the interest of inviting emigration, Burwell fills in the apparently blank slate of his "desert" wilderness landscape with images of "a land, by nature's bounty blest," and, almost immediately, references to its "[p]ure ... waters" and "the best" "soil" begin to codify the landscape as, like Cary's, ideal for agricultural settlement.[81] Talbot's territory is vast – "[f]rom east to west," it comprises "full fifty leagues or more" – flanked by two significant waterways: Lake Erie and the Thames, and "divide[d]" by "some thousand rills" that provide additional possibilities for transportation and commercial activity.[82] Relying upon an expansively cartographic sense of space, the surveyor's "careless eye" "roves" "[u]ninterrupted" over scenes of apparently inexhaustible beauty and fertility:

Productive nature smiles o'er all this land,
And strews her bounties with a lavish hand,
In wild profusion – soft meand'ring rills,
Deep woods, rich dales, smooth plains, and sunny hills,
Sylvan recesses, dark o'erhanging groves,
Where vocal songsters tune their throats to loves;
Where lurks the fox in crafty, sly career,
And in light gambols bounds the wary deer.[83]

Although still "wild," this land is lush, variegated, and "[p]roductive," and thus "invit[ing]" to prospective settlers.[84] The proliferation of plurals and superlatives throughout this passage, and in several others like it, suggests almost limitless prospects and advantages for the men and women that Talbot predicts will soon "swarm the ground" and turn it into a "beauteous zone" of farms and townships.[85]

The poem itself partitions the land into increasingly navigable "zones" by situating and naming township sites and beginning to distinguish the "some thousand rills" that "divide" the expansive landscape into "vales," "banks," and "margins."[86] Otter, Catfish, and Kettle creeks, for instance, are named or, more accurately, renamed: the place where Talbot first settled near the mouth of Kettle Creek, for instance, was first called "Skitteewaabaa" – a name that inscribes a history of Anishinaabe habitation onto the land – and other major waterways have deeper toponymic histories as well: the Thames, for example, was called "Askunesippi" (or "antlered river") by the Iroquois, and then (as at least one of Mahlon's maps records) "La Tranche" by early French explorers. Burwell's poem exemplifies how "the naming of the country, the Englishing of half a continent and its contents, including its native peoples, altered and even destroyed what had been here before."[87] Shifting the reader's attention from general to more specific characteristics of the terrain, the poem penetrates the land and clarifies its inscription of territorial claims.

As idyllic as the landscape appears in these early descriptions, Burwell wastes little time before describing its dramatic transformation under the apparently benevolent influence of colonization. The first ninety lines of the poem, which trace the region's "general outline before settlement" (thus generating the first layer of Burwell's poetic map) depict the wilderness prior to colonization as appealingly picturesque and fertile, and, at the same time, a "desert" of "rugged wilds" awaiting the improving influence of human industry.[88] The poet invites the reader to share Colonel Talbot's eager anticipation of the moment when "[e]arth shall resign the burden of her breast, / And wear a richer, variegated vest," with the comparative effect of this image registering the change that is about to take place as unequivocally felicitous, not just for the settlers, but also for the land itself: what else, after all, could be expected from a "noble" and "philanthropic" plan ordained by both God and nature?[89] The language of religious generosity couches Talbot's colonial enterprise – including the "pierc[ing]" of the woods by Talbot and his "thronging bands of men," and the reduction of the wilderness, under the settler's axe, to "a scene of terror" – in a providential mission that absolves the colonizer of any guilt associated with his invasive destruction of what was there before.[90]

Like the rhetoric of philanthropy, Burwell's characterization of the settlers' land-clearing efforts as "Herculean labors" glorifies the work of transfiguring the landscape from wilderness to inhabited territory, while also confirming that:

> [u]nderlying the various signs of progress in the settler colony – in demography, social structure, economy, communications, and urban germination – was the rhetoric of struggle with a vigorous, long-standing natural environment. In many ways, this rhetoric was the product of a technologically aggressive, exploitative culture, reaping resources in many parts of the world. It gave voice to the prevailing view that the changes wrought in Ontario between the 1780s and 1853 were the products of an epic victory of human ingenuity and effort over a challenging wilderness.[91]

As *Talbot Road* demonstrates, such rhetoric was also a product of the common view that wilderness, no matter how much life it supported, was merely "neglected ... waste" until it could be cleared, inhabited, cultivated, and thus rendered useful to an agrarian society: "untenanted," declares Talbot to his settlers, productive "nature work[s] in vain."[92] The trope of vacancy combines, here, with the fiction of wasted productivity to justify colonization. Once again, this strategy was not new: as Chamberlin notes, "the classification of land as idle – land that is not used for agricultural purposes or owned by someone – has provided the basis for countless colonial adventures in the settlement of aboriginal territory; and it is still invoked to justify the encroachment on so-called wilderness lands."[93]

"Encroachment" is not an inappropriate term for the impact of Burwell's "swarming settlers" who, "in eager bands, / Sought out, and took, the unlocated lands," ultimately leaving "no vacant ground."[94] If the poem's subsequent mapping of farms, roads, and townships onto the landscape shows the literal effects of Talbot's metaphoric reclothing of idle waste with productive farms, it also evidences a swift and aggressive assault on the wilderness. Despite its idealization of the natural world, *Talbot Road* lends support to the claim that during the pioneering period "the general ethos in rural North-America was anti-nature"; indeed, the laborious task of clearing trees fuelled what Catharine Parr Traill describes in *The Backwoods of Canada* as a "war" between men and the wilderness.[95] In *Talbot Road*, that "war" – waged as much against the "hills, and logs, and brooks" that make "conveyance rough" as against the forest – is "charm[ed]" by the "hope of reward" that allows the settler to transcend his present "drear confines" and dwell instead in his imagined visions of "future happiness."[96] Such visions do not eradicate trees altogether, but replace wild forest with a domesticated woodland that assumes the forms of the cultivated "orchard," the "stately row / Of shady trees" that will someday flank the road, and the "arching arbor" and "willow grove" that will inspire future poets and lovers.[97] The containment and symmetry of these highly regimented, man-made plantations suggests the equivalent in landscaping of Mahlon Burwell's surveys, such as his 1810 map of Delaware (figure 3), which diagrams the subjection of wild land to artificial designs. Like his brother's maps, Burwell's poem illustrates formally and thematically the extent to which settlers were transforming the organic spaces of forests, meadows, and wetlands into "an open landscape that was regimented by the straight lines and right angles of the geometry imposed by humans."[98] In addition to the symmetry of planned arbors and orchards, the geometrically exact "cross-way[s]" and "connect[ions]" that the Talbot Road lays over the Upper Canadian topography (captured in a rigidly linear and symmetrical verse form) illustrate how the "dubious maze" of a wild, organically variegated forest was replaced with a navigable man-made pattern "dropped like a horizontal portcullis on the landscape."[99]

Further guarding against the potential for chaos that Burwell's "swarming settlers" introduce into the landscape, *Talbot Road* traces a cartographic process by which the wilderness was reorganized not only into neatly readable territory, but also into clearly defined tracts of private property. To read this poem is to witness the transformation of a "wilderness ... scarcely known" into an "animating scene" of pioneers staking their claims on every navigable tract of land:

Now, ceaseless, crowd the emigrants along,
And moving families the country throng;
The fertile banks of Otter Creek, some take;
Some Talbot Road, and some prefer the lake;
While others claim'd a midway space between,
And all produced an animating scene.[100]

With each tidy quadrant of property inscribed with the name of its resident settler, Mahlon Burwell's map of Delaware "animat[es]" the land with families much like the ones described here by his poet brother. Staking their claims on each available piece of ground, the "ceaseless" stream of emigrants that "crowd" the landscape of *Talbot Road* suggest limitless expansion. Dividing settlers among distinct geographical areas (such as "[t]he fertile banks of Otter Creek," "Talbot Road," "the lake," and "a midway space between"), he neatly arranges and contains the crowd, finding a place for everyone.

The war that the poem wages against chaos is paralleled and interrupted by the War of 1812, an event that stalls the settlement's progress by turning Talbot's "wood[men]" into "soldier[s]" and exposing it to invasion and devastation. Like the American Revolution in *Abram's Plains*, the interruption is only briefly described; the lasting effect of post-war devastation is to spur each settler to work with renewed vigor and pride to complete Colonel Talbot's designs.[101] Given the area's vulnerability during the war, it is perhaps surprising that Burwell's representation of the settlement bears scant resemblance to one of Frye's garrisons. Its distance from more populous parts of the colony in 1806 was great enough to inspire surprise in Cornwall Bayley that "cultivation even travels *there*!" yet the settlement as Burwell portrays it shares few, if any, characteristics with those "small and isolated communities" of which Frye writes, which are "surrounded with a physical or psychological 'frontier,' separated from one another and from their American and British cultural sources," and "confronted with a huge, unthinking, menacing, and formidable physical setting."[102]

In its insistence that every remaining piece of ground be surveyed, Burwell's poem downplays this "formidable ... setting" by effectively pushing its "frontier" well beyond the margins of the textual map. Largely missing the signifiers that mark a region's instability as much as its self-containment and protection, *Talbot Road* runs against the grain both of the "garrison mentality" and also of other fictions by which territories are so often defined. According to Edward Said: "A group of people living on a few acres of land will set up boundaries between their land and its immediate surroundings and the territory beyond, which they call 'the land of the barbarians.' ... Yet often the sense in which someone feels himself to be not-foreign is based on a very unrigorous idea of what is 'out there,' beyond one's own territory. All kinds of suppositions, associations, and fictions appear to crowd the unfamiliar space outside one's own."[103] Readers can sense this kind of "unfamiliar space" looming at the edges of many poeticized landscapes – of Goldsmith's portrait of "the lonely settler" "amid a wilderness of trees" in which lurk everything from "savage beasts" to "savage tribes," for instance, and Howe's settler in his "lone cottage" surrounded by "the wild covert of the forest shade" in which "[t]he Micmac" lie in "ambush."[104] Like *Abram's Plains, Talbot Road* ultimately charts a uniform and homogeneous territory against which neither wilderness nor barbarians appear to pose a threat. This effect contrasts with Michael Smith's framing of the same terrain in his *Geographical View of the Province of Upper Canada* (1813), a book with which Burwell must have been familiar, as he appears to have pasted a clipping of his poem into a copy of Smith's text.[105] Smith specifies that the London District "is bounded east by Indian land, on Grand River, [and] north by the wilderness."[106] The only boundaries that Burwell mentions in his poem are Lake Erie and the Thames, both of which also happen to be important natural conduits and, as such, facilitate movement into the territory as much as they mark its limits. Published in the same year that the British government purchased the Huron Tract (an area of more than a million acres east of Lake Huron) from the Chippewa (Ojibway) nation, the frontier was literally retreating, and it may be no coincidence that it does not figure at all in Burwell's poem. On David William Smyth's *Map of the Province of Upper Canada* – the second edition of which was also published in 1818 – the Huron Tract is neither "[w]ilderness" nor "[h]unting country," such as that much further north, but rather a "Great Tract of Woodland" that appears coterminous with "London District" (figure 5).

Like Cary's, Burwell's model of colonial space is open to the world, not isolated from it. References to shipping on Lake Erie and to a "copious tide of Emigration" that supplied the settlement's population connect the territory to international markets and places of origin.[107] Eliding the notorious dangers and expense of boat travel on the lake, and ignoring altogether the immense natural obstacle of Niagara Falls, which was only made navigable by the Welland Canal in 1827 (the construction of which did not begin until six years after the poem was written), Burwell anticipates the easy communication of goods and people via unimpeded navigational routes. Exploiting a cartographic sensibility that transcends the narrow concerns of place or region, Burwell positions the settlement within a larger imperial geographical imaginary.

The incoming tide of emigrants generated a redesigned landscape that Burwell charts in the most map-like section of his poem, which traces the network of roads along an "order[ed] ... list" of counties and townships.[108] These are named, oriented according to the division of the Talbot Road into east and west sections, and occasionally distinguished by landmarks and topographical description. The list begins with "Norfolk county," in which

> first the Talbot Street
> East, marks its course thro' Middleton complete;
> Thence, into Middlesex, thro' Houghton Gore,
> And thence, thro' Bayham, (where was mark'd before
> A bridle path) – thence Otter Creek comes down
> From Norwhich, lengthwise, nearly thro' the Town[109]

The passage continues in like manner, arranged by a series of "thences" and "nexts," indicators of sequence that propel the reader along a determined route through the country. To a more precise effect than that achieved by the customary "heres" and "theres" of picturesque description, Burwell specifically locates portions of the Talbot Road and townships and landmarks along it, sustaining an illusion of travel in much the same way that a map-reader makes an imaginative journey by tracing a finger from point to point on a map:

> Next Aldbro' – now the reader must be sent
> From Middlesex into the County Kent:
> Then follows Orford; Orford, Howard join,
> Harwich and Raleigh range along the line;
> Tilb'ry, and Romney East and West, which past,
> Mersea remains, on Talbot Road the last.
> Mersea's in Essex County[110]

The skeletal spareness of this list, particularly in these final lines, is part of its cartographic effect. While some locations in the poem are fleshed out by descriptions of particular features of the landscape or of certain towns, here that flesh falls away, leaving only the bare place names along the stark frame of the road.

The abstract quality of this "line" belies the tremendous labour, time, and difficulty of road construction and maintenance. Moreover, as Bentley argues, it strings together a series of undifferentiated towns devoid of "local colour" or "uniquely Canadian specificity."[111] Yet this very failing also strengthens two aspects of the poem that relate to its cartographic inscription of the land. First, Burwell's adoption of a wider perspective that unites the townships under the generally approving conclusion "[t]hey all are beautiful, they all are good" abstracts particular places to individually named but otherwise identical points, lines, and bounded areas, much as they would appear on a map.[112] What the reader is finally invited to see is not this or that place, but the many places that together – and equally, in the poet's estimation – have prepared an expansive and otherwise apparently blank ground for human occupation. Second, as is also the case with Cary's derivative poetics, Burwell's "stock, eighteenth-century diction" inscribes a British aesthetic and identity into the landscape (as, of course, do the place names he identifies, such as "Norfolk," "Middlesex," "Norwich," and "Kent," which would have gone far to prod American settlers in the area to remember where the country's loyalties lay).[113] Echoing through the poem's landscapes, these names remind readers that the "immediate world" of the Talbot settlement was in the process of being written over in the image of Britain. It is this reality that *Talbot Road* seeks to map.

This landscape's geometrical frame recalls the straight roads and hedgerows that divided the British countryside into private landholdings after the Enclosure Acts rather than the idyllic rural world that, as many eighteenth-century landscape poets lamented, enclosure had destroyed. In the Talbot settlement, however, every settler is a property owner, each tract of land a "little Eden that he calls his own." Nor is private property constrained by primogeniture, as it was in England: the "[n]ew schemes for future happiness" on which the settler meditates include plans "[t]o buy a farm for each deserving son." Burwell thus distinguishes elements of land occupancy in Canada that differ from British systems and the attendant "structures of feeling" that Raymond Williams traces through its topographical poetry.[114]

More than a picturesque sensibility or even a broadly literary one, *Talbot Road* appeals to a cartographic imagination. Burwell's "survey mentality" not only preferred the symmetries of eighteenth-century design to the asymmetries of untenanted nature, or desired navigable roads in place of labyrinthine woods, but also entrusted maps, both graphic and literary, with the creation of such spaces. Burwell's poem conveys no doubt that Talbot's designs, though incomplete at the time of its publication, will be fulfilled. Solitary though they may be, there is a measure of certainty in the smooth, regular lines of the Talbot Road as they appear in the poem: their very existence points confidently to the future, their seductive geometry emblematic of the new order of mobility, accessibility, and a culture rooted in commerce. Adding his own vision to the legacies of his various "surveyors," Burwell superimposes over their mappings an imaginary landscape, a possible world whose prosperity is signalled by the architecture of commercial progress:

> The Town, the Village shall be seen to rise;
> The stately mansion, and the costly hall,
> The labell'd office, neat, convenient, small,
> The ample warehouse, and the clean fireside,
> Where friendship, love, and harmony reside.
> The bustling town, the morn shall usher in,
> And close the evening with a constant din,
> The din of business – Wealth already stands,
> And drops profusion from his open hands.[115]

Gone from this scene are the crude log cabins and rugged pioneer clearings that appear earlier in the poem. The wilderness has been replaced by a "constant chain of cultivated farms, ... waving fields, ... [a]nd orchards" that reflect the surveyor's orderly patterns, ultimately suggesting no end to his designs.[116] Perhaps most important, the blank slate of unmapped land has given way to a mapped territory that is perpetually surveyable by each farmer who "commands" the "surrounding fields" from his own "stately mansion."[117] Everyone becomes a kind of surveyor in this poem: the emigrant and farmer, the poet, and, ultimately, the reader all join Colonel Talbot in imagining and understanding the region from the encompassing perspective of a cartographic gaze.

In Western thought, notes Harrison, the clearing of forests was considered "the first decisive act, religiously motivated, which would lead to the founding of cities, nations, and empire"; many early Canadian settler writings – Burwell's among them – represent this "original deed of appropriation" as one "that ... open[s] the space of civil society." Certainly, this was the view of the Scottish Nova Scotian settler John Young, who wrote in his *Letters of Agricola on the Principle of Vegetation and Tillage* (1822): "The wilderness is a term of cheerless import, and involves whatever is repugnant to the human heart. When the lineaments of the country have become distinct and visible, it will win our affections, and consolidate our patriotism."[118] Following Harrison, we might indeed interpret the desire to "illuminate the horizon," as Cary put it – or, in Burwell's words, to bring the land to light "from geographic night" – as the expression of "a civilization of sky worshippers" and forest-clearers extending back to Greek and Roman times.[119] But these poets also worship maps. In both poems, the land remains an abstraction, with the particularities of place obscured by the generalities of a descriptive mode whose main interest is not, in the end, the physical experience of clearing and settling the land, but rather the cartographic claiming and creation of navigable territory. The visibility these poets seek comes above all from the surveyor's sweeping gaze, and resonates, as we shall see, with desires that would extend this vision across the unforested prairies as well as the deepest recesses of thick forests and mountain streams. As chapter 2 suggests, however, this visibility was also a fiction, if a powerful one.

Chapter Two

The Land up Close: Mapping Disorder in *Roughing It in the Bush*

Among the writers included in this study, Susanna Moodie may be the most well known. Students of Canadian literature cannot get very far without encountering her collection of sketches, *Roughing It in the Bush* (1852), whether in its original form or as a ghostly presence in more contemporary texts such as Margaret Atwood's poetic adaptation, *The Journals of Susanna Moodie* (1970). Born Susanna Strickland in Suffolk, England, in 1803, Moodie emigrated to Upper Canada in 1832 with her husband John W. Dunbar, a retired British Army officer, and their young daughter. There they eventually joined her brother Samuel Strickland, a surveyor and homesteader, and her sister Catharine Parr Traill. Unlike the Stricklands and the Traills, however, the Moodies bought a cleared farm near Cobourg before taking up their land grant in the backwoods of Douro Township in 1834. The sketches in *Roughing It in the Bush* follow this geographical trajectory, beginning with their overseas journey and ending with their departure from the backwoods for Belleville in 1840. Although it contains one of the most compelling descriptions of a map in early Canadian writing, this book might not immediately spring to mind as an exemplar of literary cartography. Few of its chapters orient readers in the ways that Thomas Cary's and Adam Hood Burwell's poems do, and the book as a whole contains very little of their optimism. Written as a corrective to the many emigrant guides that promoted colonial settlement, *Roughing It in the Bush* sets out, through a range of stories centred around the author's own "painful experience," to undermine the very kind of glowing advertisments that Cary and Burwell provide.[1] In addition to chastizing the "dealers in wild lands" who profited from "the folly and credulity" of their "fellow men," Moodie criticizes those "pamphlets, published by interested parties, which prominently set forth all the *good* to be derived from a settlement in the Backwoods of Canada; while they carefully concealed the toil and hardship to be endured in order to secure these advantages."[2] Chief among Moodie's implicit targets was William Cattermole, an agent of the Canada Company who had influenced her husband's – and doubtless many others' – decision to emigrate with his assurance that "there is no place in the known world where individual exertions are so well requited by the bounties of nature as in Upper Canada."[3] In contrast with the easy accommodation that Cattermole's description promises, Moodie's sketches convey (sometimes with humour, other times with bitterness) experiences of profound hardship, homesickness, and disorientation.

Moodie's relationship to maps (and, indeed, into her own mapping practices) is revealed in her description of the map of Canada and the exchange that it occasions. To return to that passage, with which this book began: the map as Moodie depicts it, with her "Indian friends'" eyes and fingers ranging over its contour lines, their animated voices declaring its verisimilitude, establishes a material connection between body and land, text and topography. There is little in her account of the soaring distance, the abstraction of generalized and ordered cartographic space, that appears in *Abram's Plains* and *Talbot Road*. Rather, the map interests her as part of a multisensory, embodied experience of the land. To the extent that it does provide the kind of schematic surveillance and orientation that Cary and Burwell celebrate, Moodie effectively writes herself out of its sphere of reference. When she refuses to part with the map, even after Peter Nogan offers "[c]anoe, venison, duck, fish, for it; and more by-and-by," she does so in a way that diminishes her own singular presence in the equation between cartography, settler, and land: she must retain the map, she tells us, not for her own use, but because her husband consults it "daily ... in reference to the names and situations of localities in the neighbourhood."[4]

It is not altogether surprising that Moodie aligns the map with John rather than with herself. As Laura Smyth Groening reminds us, women tended to occupy different colonial spaces than men, and although the separations between them may be less stark than Groening suggests,[5] in this moment Moodie delineates distinct geographical spheres for herself and her husband. While these spheres overlap frequently throughout the book (which, after all, mingles sketches and poetry written by both Susanna and John), Moodie's passing remark about her husband points to certain differences between how women and men related to early Canada as a mapped space. As she makes clear at other points in *Roughing It in the Bush*, John enjoyed greater mobility than she did, and his wide-ranging travels through the province frequently contrast with her more restricted movements around their homesteads. Consequently, Cary and Burwell's confident poetic surveys have more in common with John's contributions to the book – especially his "Canadian Sketches" in the second edition – than they do with Moodie's intimate descriptions of settler life.

Indeed, many descriptions of settler space in *Roughing It in the Bush* present significant challenges to the literary-cartographic models with which this study opened. This is not to say that Moodie did not long for the security and order of their mapped spaces. Following reviews that accused her of creating "counterfeit pictures of Canadian life" that were as exaggeratedly critical as Cattermole's were positive, in her introduction to the 1871 edition (the first Canadian edition), titled "Canada. A Contrast," she celebrates the transformation of the Upper Canadian landscape into something akin to Burwell's linear order.[6] Echoing Luke 3:5, she writes: "The rough has become smooth, the crooked has been made straight, the forests have been converted into fruitful fields, the rude log cabin of the woodsman has been replaced by the handsome, well appointed homestead, and large populous cities have pushed the small clap-boarded village into the shade."[7] In Upper Canada in the 1830s, however, the full effects of this conversion could not yet be felt. Moodie's account of this period conveys the messiness of a settler geography in which the "order of the land survey," while clear on paper, was (as it would remain until the middle of the nineteenth century) "largely hidden" on the ground.[8] To read *Roughing It in the Bush* as a literary geographer, then, is to grapple with the limits of the cartographic order that Cary and Burwell exploit. Moodie charts the frailty of the mapmaker's lines, and documents the difficulties of colonial reinscriptions of the land. From the illusions of panoramic views, to the badness of the roads, to the precariousness of private property and personal space, to the looming threats of the wilderness, she exposes the inadequacies of cartographic lines against the heterogeneous reality that they seek to control.

This does not mean, however, that *Roughing It in the Bush* is without a literary cartography of its own. While it may well be the case that "very little of *Roughing It in the Bush* is about nature,"[9] a great deal of it is about space. Moodie has much to tell us about the contours and characteristics of settler space as she experienced them – not from the privileged elevation of a map's aerial views, but from up close. Although in a markedly different way than did Cary and Burwell before her, she labours to make colonial geography *visible* to her readers. She too attends to the routes, boundaries, and other lines of spatial communication, containment, and order that define her relationship to the terrain and to the people who inhabit it. Instead of a navigable order, however, she charts a complex spatiality woven through with the desires and disappointments of a genteel emigrant woman struggling to orient herself and establish the bounds of civilization, first around her farm near Cobourg and, later, in the newer and sparser clearings of Douro Township.

Moodie's literary cartography is simultaneously limited and enabled by her physical encounter with the land, its imaginative reach shaped by a profound sense of what it was to actually live on and move through the spaces of the Upper Canadian frontier. If picturesque prospects and wide-angled surveys occasionally relieve the more restricted sight-lines of her largely domestic settler space, *Roughing It in the Bush* is nonetheless the product of a narrator unable to maintain such perspectives. Charting a loss of control over her surroundings, Moodie provides a moving record of the disorientation and consequent vulnerability that was surely a common, if underappreciated, part of emigrant experience. In so doing, she paradoxically also maps her world: reinforcing its boundaries, drawing new ones, and charting her own passage through it. This chapter argues for greater attention to the spatiality of Moodie's most famous work, and seeks to clarify the literary-cartographic imprint of her expectations and observations of space, property, demographics, and the meanings she attributes to cultivated and wild land.

The Problem of Seeing

Animating the sense of space that emerges in *Roughing It in the Bush* is a problem of perception that Moodie succinctly describes in her later companion collection, *Life in the Clearings versus the Bush* (1853). Here Moodie complains about the heavily wooded landscapes of Upper Canada, where, she writes:

> One wood is the exact picture of another; the uniformity dreary in the extreme. There are no green vistas to be seen; no grassy glades beneath the bosky oaks, on which the deer browse, and the gigantic shadows sleep in the sunbeams. A stern array of rugged trunks, a tangled maze of scrubby

> underbrush, carpetted winter and summer with a thick layer of withered buff leaves, form the general features of a Canadian forest.
>
> A few flowers force their heads through this thick covering of leaves, and make glad with their beauty the desolate wilderness; but those who look for an Arcadia of fruits and flowers in the Backwoods of Canada cannot fail of disappointment.[10]

Her palpable desire for not only the harmonious variety, but also the visual depth, of picturesque landscapes is an extension of the frustrated longing for home that also undergirds *Roughing It in the Bush*. Devoid of "green vistas" and "grassy glades," the Canadian forest appears, to her eyes, a monotonous space where, like the longed-for flowers that cannot compete with the thick underbrush, her memories of the picturesque Suffolk countryside – not to mention the other European "Arcadias," real and imaginary, that shaped her aesthetic sensibilities – find no purchase. The land appears to her almost wholly without aesthetic and mnemonic value, evoking not only an oppressive sameness, but also a profound loneliness.

Even more disconcerting than the discomfort of unfamiliarity that inflects Moodie's description, however, is the fact that unlike a picturesque prospect, this landscape is impervious to her gaze: she can see neither into nor through it. Unlike vistas and glades, the "stern array of rugged trunks" and "tangled maze of underbrush" cannot be visually penetrated. Neither, then, can it be mapped. The sense of disorientation that this passage elicits is literal: if every forest looks the same, Moodie suggests, it is difficult to know precisely where you are; in effect, you are lost. The problem that she identifies was practical and cartographic as well as aesthetic. Before it was cleared of trees and brush, much of Canada did not offer the sight-lines necessary for proper land surveys, let alone picturesque prospects; hence the surveyor John MacTaggart's lament as he worked to map the Rideau Canal between 1826 and 1828 that in "a dark dense wood, the surveyor has to change his home system altogether: for instance, if we get upon a hill or other eminence in Britain, we may see the natural lead of the land; but in Canada, owing to the wilderness, you have to grope for this like blind men."[11] The bold lines of colonial maps conceal this laborious process of trudging blindly through thick underbrush and cedar swamps in order to make the land visible.

Published a year before *Life in the Clearings*, *Roughing It in the Bush* delineates Moodie's first encounters with a landscape that similarly resists her own designs upon it, and that proves at once a geographical and social wilderness impervious to the aspirations of ill-prepared settlers who by "stern necessity" and "severe duty" sought accommodation within it.[12] The first two sketches dramatize, in a manner that is different from but related to her description of Canadian forests in *Life in the Clearings*, the failure of a way of seeing and the impossibility of gaining optic command over her surroundings. In these opening skeches, Moodie describes the unnerving experience of having her initial impressions of a place prove to be little more than a fantasy, the distant mastery of space a chimera that dissolves when the land is encountered up close. She recalls her first views of the colony first seen from aboard the *Anne*, the ship that brought Moodie, along with her husband and baby daughter, across the Atlantic and up the St Lawrence to Quebec City. From the deck, before beginning her life as the wife of a backwoods pioneer, Moodie enjoys sweeping, panoramic vistas that (with the exception of "A Trip to Stony Lake," where she describes the land as seen from a canoe) are otherwise rare in her spatial experience of the colony. These early glimpses of Canada echo the mastery and optimism of Cary and Burwell's wide-ranging surveys, but also expose the limits of such views. Moodie's literary cartography marks the disparity between what can be seen from afar and what is revealed up close.

As other critics have remarked, Moodie's initial descriptions of the St Lawrence are not the careful observations of someone who knows the land well; rather, they are the kind of "panoramic vistas" that "belong to genteel sightseeing – and a quick, unimplicating view of foreign sites."[13] The product of distance, these views yield only bland abstractions that, replete with clichés drawn from the imported conventions of the sublime and the picturesque, attest that Moodie "can barely see the New World."[14] As the author herself comes to recognize, the "perfect paradise" of Grosse Isle at first sight, the "fairy vision" of its surrounding islands, and the "astonishing panorama" of Quebec that causes her to "melt ... involuntarily into tears" of "unalloyed delight" register, more than anything else, their author's "absor[ption] into ... one sense of seeing" that springs as much from her hopes for the new world (and faith in Providence to guide her through it) as it does from an accurate perception of the place that she and her family will inhabit.[15]

These views are more properly defined as panoramic than cartographic. As Michel de Certeau underscores, however, these two perspectives share the "voluptuous pleasure ... of 'seeing the whole.'"[16] For Moodie, the world seen at a distance becomes a sequence of beautiful images, a "magnificent scene" "composed" of "stupendous objects," a "picture" of "cloud-capped mountain," foaming "cataract," "wood, and rock, and river" that unfurls before her as though by divine design. She revels in this feast for the eyes, impelling her readers (much as Cary does) to "look at the St Lawrence, that king of streams, that great artery flowing from the heart of the world, through the length and breadth of the land, carrying wealth and fertility in its course."[17] Moodie's panoramic impressions of the St Lawrence and Cary and Burwell's literary-cartographic descriptions are, in effect, the kind of "imaginary totalizations" that de Certeau argues produce a "simulacrum, in short a picture" – indeed, this is also Moodie's word for it – "whose condition of possibility is an oblivion and a misunderstanding of practices" on the ground.[18]

At best, the result is a "fiction of knowledge."[19] While Moodie's initial views of the country from afar do some work to locate the emigrant in her new surroundings, they serve less to convey the shape and character of the land than to establish a contrast between perception and reality. As the ship captain says, "many things look well at a distance which are bad enough when near."[20] His warning is quickly borne out when the "ark of safety" from which Grosse Isle looks like a "second Eden just emerged from the waters of chaos" can only temporarily protect her from the "revolting scene" of Irish emigrants on its shores, for example, or conceal the "filthy hole" of a cholera-ravaged Quebec.[21]

The repeated contrast between distance and closeness lends a certain rhythm not just to the first two chapters, but to *Roughing It in the Bush* as a whole, which derives much of its dramatic tension from the kind of disillusionment that John Howison describes in his 1821 *Sketches of Upper Canada* (with which Moodie was almost certainly familiar[22]):

> The first view of a new settlement excites pleasing emotions. It is delightful to see forests vanishing away before the industry of man; to behold the solitude of the wilderness changed into a theatre of animation and activity; and to anticipate the blessings which a bountiful soil will lavish upon those who have first ventured to inhabit its bosom. A new field seems to be opened for human happiness; and the more so, as those who people it are supposed, by the casual observer, to have been the victims of poverty and misfortune while in their native land. But a deliberate inspection will destroy all those Arcadian ideas and agreeable impressions. He who examines a new settlement in detail, will find most of its inhabitants sunk low in degradation, ignorance, and profligacy, and altogether insensible of

> the advantages which distinguish their condition. A lawless and unprincipled rabble, consisting of the refuse of mankind, recently emancipated from the subordination that exists in an advanced state of society, and all equal in point of right and possession, compose, of course, a democracy of the most revolting kind.[23]

Moodie counters her own idealized first impressions with a sobering scrutiny of their imperfections, and so establishes a theme of deceptive appearances that plays out geographically as well as socially over the course of the book.

While not explicit targets of Moodie's criticisms – and while not, strictly speaking, "first view[s]" of the kind Howison describes – the cartographic prospects that Cary and Burwell provide in their topographical poems contain all the hope-inspired superficiality of such facile glimpses. Their God's-eye perspectives are tantamount to flights of fancy that register only the harmonious order and progress of their settlement landscapes, and downplay the struggles and failures on the ground. Moodie's text-map challenges the mastery that Cary and Burwell give settlers over their idealized visions of the social and geospatial landscapes of early Canada. If panoptic elevation enabled such men to "cast themselves as giants in a drama of imperial superiority,"[24] the lack of such certainties of surveillance compromises Moodie's ability to dominate the landscape in which she lives, much though she might desire to do so. To read *Roughing It in the Bush* after *Abram's Plains* and *Talbot Road* is to descend, as de Certeau does, from the pleasures of the cartographic view from above into the disorder that exists below.

Moreover, it is to contradict the easy mobility of Cary and Burwell's routes through the colony with a more harrowing experience of space that resists travel as much as it does visual mastery. As the Moodies make their way up the St Lawrence and then onto the land itself, the author's attention to roads points not to accessibility but to the challenges of creating a stable and easily negotiated settler space. The road that leads to the Moodies' first temporary dwelling, for instance, dwindles into a trail of "black stumps" barely distinguishable from the surrounding woods.[25] Located a mere eight miles west of Cobourg (in other words, in the "clearings" rather than the "bush"), this road is typical of the unfinished quality of a landscape in which roads are as likely to lead settlers astray as to guide them into the colony. Impassable in certain seasons, they were barely navigable at the best of times. Corduroy roads (so named for their surface of side-by-side logs perpendicular to the direction of the road) may well have prevented travellers from sinking in mud and bog in the warmer, wetter months, but the price of more efficient travel was nearly being "jolted to death" by the bumps. Along with the "miserable, insecure log bridge" over Herriot's Falls "where darkness and death raged below," Moodie's roads are an index of the emigrant's physical isolation and vulnerability.[26]

Accordingly, roads tend not to stand as symbols of civilization's triumph over wilderness, as they do in Burwell's poem, so much as sites of an ongoing battle between humanity and nature. This battle takes on heightened emotional significance when, en route to their uncleared land grant in Douro, Moodie watches their sleigh laden with household items overturn due to a log that has fallen across the road. The image of "all [her] household goods and chattels ... scattered over the road" along with her broken crockery and stone china is poignant and awakens readers to the deprivation that emigrants faced in the woods.[27] Signs of the refinement and ease of the life that the Moodies left behind, the crockery and china are also a material connection to home that is literally shattered by their arrival in the bush. Moreover, the word "chattels" invokes the language of property law, signalling the loss not only of a symbolic link to her home, but also of its material security. A reminder of the significance of objects that could not easily be replaced, this scene represents colonial roads not as harbingers of civilization in the wilderness so much as tenuous passages that conduct people ever farther from the civilized world and its possessions and protections.

The landscape Moodie describes here hardly anticipates the orderly reinscription of the country that both she and her husband celebrate at later points in the book. In "Canadian Sketches," a final chapter added to the 1871 edition, John applauds the "plank and macadamised [crushed stone] roads [that] have branched out in all directions from the various central county towns, stretching their ramifications like the veins of the human body, conveying nourishment and prosperity throughout the country, increasing the trade and the travel, connecting man with man and promoting intelligence and civilisation."[28] His arterial network lauds the emergence of roads as apparently organic elements of an increasingly humanized terrain. His bodily metaphor erases the antagonism between civilization and wilderness, closing the gap between humans and nature by showing how people, like God, can redesign the land in their own image. Perhaps even more successfully than does Burwell's geometrical grid, John's organic network also naturalizes the appearance of the new infrastructure: it is as though his roads have "branched out" of their own accord, growing as part of an animate body from the land itself, as Adam did from dust.

Although even the roughest roads were precursors of those "veins" to which John alludes in his concluding sketch, throughout much of *Roughing It in the Bush* they appear, rather, as fragments of an unfinished series of disjointed and unreliable routes – dotted lines that loosely stitch together a territory defined by "numerous detached, feeble, and unprogressive settlements."[29] Many descriptions suggest that, while along the shores of Lake Erie Colonel Talbot was efficiently implementing his plans, other parts of the province were assuming a more disorderly shape effected more by speculators' whims and follies than by any organized design. Indeed, John bemoans the extent to which the sly operations of "land-jobbers," or speculators, "retarded the natural progress of the country," as well as how steamboat proprietors prematurely directed settlement westward before the necessary population and infrastructures could catch up.[30] From Moodie's observations, it appears that the interiors of settlements were as haphazardly arranged and difficult to navigate as was the wider settler geography of Upper Canada, a point which belies the regular gridded space of the "Partial Map of Hamilton Township" that Carl Ballstadt includes in his edition of *Roughing It in the Bush.*

Like her roads, Moodie's clearings occupy a far more chaotic middle ground between regulated and unregulated space than this map suggests. Instead, she describes what Heather Murray calls "pseudo-wilderness": a liminal space that (often uncomfortably) blurs the boundary between wild and artificial, or "civilized."[31] This liminality defines both interior and exterior spaces. The "miserable hut" that serves as the Moodies' first residence in the colony, for instance, stands in a clearing that, though not far from the growing town of Cobourg, is "scarcely reclaimed from the bush." A "small dilapidated log tenement" in a "broken hollow" and "surrounded on all sides by the dark forest," this dwelling underscores the frailty of human constructions in the face of inclement weather and an imposing landscape.[32] With no door, a leaky roof and walls, and only one remaining pane of glass in the window, the house is an architectural expression of the incompleteness, imperfection, and fragility of human designs on the colonial frontier.

The permeability of the house's roof and walls also anticipates the dissolution of familiar social boundaries and hierarchies that the control of private property regulates. In their farming community near Cobourg, the governing order upon which the Moodies have always relied is turned on its head. Not only does this "established society ... refuse ... to accommodate their desires for hierarchy and deference,"[33] but the geographical boundaries and demarcations that would reinforce this social order are also revealed to be largely ineffectual. Moodie's descriptions of this terrain reflect the colonial surveyor's attention to property, but only to show that on the edges of settlement private ownership holds little authority or meaning. Indeed, the breakdown of her own firmly held notions of private property begins almost immediately: the Moodies are reduced to renting a small cabin on their own land, because by some bureaucratic oversight they have failed to secure "right of possession" to their legally purchased farmhouse.[34] This leaves the Moodies at the mercy of Joe H(arris) and his family, who promise to vacate the property but do so on their own (lengthy, manipulative, embittered) terms, leaving a dead skunk in the cupboard as a final exertion of control over the place. This episode reveals the fraught and highly individual sense of territoriality that governs settler space against which established laws dictating ownership have little power.

Indeed, in the environs of the Moodies' first farm, squatters appear to have a firmer hold on the land than do landowners, which adds to the apparent lawlessness of the colonial landscape. Chiefly made up of "the lower order of Americans" who "had spied out the goodness of the land, and *borrowed* various portions of it, without so much as asking leave of the absentee owners," these occupants contribute to the erosion of a spatial order that the Moodies hold sacred.[35] Moodie observes first-hand what was in fact a widespread phenomenon in Upper Canada that added a messy layer to the cartographic inscription of its spaces. As MacTaggart explained a quarter of a century earlier, "instead of being pointed out farms on *diagrams*, where, probably, no such things exist, or, if they do, are not worth the cultivating, [squatters] go forth their own surveyor into the wilds, and where they meet with a fine river, a fertile valley, and cool spring well, squat in contentment."[36] According to the historian Gerald M. Craig, "[These] land seekers had a remarkable capacity for ignoring the property rights of absentee owners and the edicts of a distant government. The land was there, and they often used it without asking anyone's leave. To a very considerable extent, Upper Canada was settled by squatters, and it was never practicable to evict very many of them; the speculators and the government simply had to make terms with them."[37] The squatters' disregard for Moodie's personal space and abode highlights the connection between property, propriety,[38] and privacy. "They entered your house without knocking,"

Moodie writes, "and while boasting of their freedom, violated one of its dearest laws, which considers even the cottage of the poorest labourer his castle, and his privacy sacred."[39]

Such characters pose a problem for Moodie because they challenge what Henri Lefebvre would call her "spatial economy." Concerned with how places accumulate meaning that guides behaviour, Lefebvre defines this "economy" as a practice that

> valorizes certain relationships between people in particular places ... and thus gives rise to connotative discourses concerning these places; these in turn generate "consensuses" or conventions according to which, for example, such and such a place is supposed to be trouble-free, a quiet area where people go peacefully to have a good time, and so forth. As for denotative (i.e., descriptive) discourses in this context, they have a quasi-legal aspect which also works for consensus: there is to be no fighting over who should occupy a particular spot; spaces are to be left free, and wherever possible allowance is to be made for "proxemics" – for the maintenance of "respectful" distances. This attitude entails in its turn a logic and a strategy of property in space: "places and things belonging to you do not belong to me."[40]

Description certainly has a disciplinary function that might be described as "quasi-legal" in Cary and Burwell's poems. For Moodie, whose settler geography is marked by the breakdown of both tacit and explicit forms of consensus, the situation is more complicated. Few maintain the respectful distances upon which her spatial economy relies. Property laws are broken in many senses, and the squatters' disrespect for landowners parallels the sham system of "borrowing" (which she describes as "a system of robbery") that depletes their limited supplies.[41] In this chaotic terrain, personal space and possessions are threatened, unprotected by a rudimentary territorial order that is, it seems, eroded almost as quickly as it is inscribed.

A defining feature of Moodie's settler space is the permeability of boundaries of all kinds. This permeability is far from liberating. On the contrary (and rather paradoxically), the breakdown of the spatial economy that leaves Moodie feeling exposed and unprotected only contributes to her sense of confinement. Her observation that "there is no such thing as privacy in this country" is an important part of her characterization of her new home not as her "castle" but as her "prison."[42] Nosy neighbours join forces with an oppressive wilderness (that "dark prison of ... boundless woods") to make her feel not unlike "a condemned criminal" in "his cell," unable properly to survey her surroundings and yet under almost constant surveillance by others.[43] Replacing comforting boundaries with confining ones, the prison trope reiterates the loss of control that makes this settler neighbourhood such a difficult space for her to negotiate. Although throughout *Roughing It in the Bush* she frequently turns her pen to scrutinize and judge her neighbours, the theme of imprisonment positions Moodie not as a powerful observer but as a vulnerable captive. Indeed, her homes at times feel like the colonial settler's version of Jeremy Bentham's Panopticon, a prison designed to give inmates the feeling that they are "always ... under inspection."[44] The intrusions of "Mrs Joe" and her offspring therefore take the form of optic as well as bodily invasions of the Moodies' home. Moodie recalls that when asked to leave her house, "they would range themselves upon the door-step, watching my motions, with their black eyes gleaming upon me through their tangled, uncombed locks." Removing their bodies but not their penetrating gaze from her house, the boundary between interior and exterior that her "door-step" represents remains broken, the home it supposedly protects invaded by the "black eyes" in which she detects a sinister mixture of "idle curiosity, not unmingled with malicious hatred."[45] Even after Joe and his family finally move away, Moodie is rarely, if ever, free from the feeling of ruthless scrutiny, her gossiping neighbours apparently collectively holding the power of surveillance and judgment.

In line with the problems of seeing to which she draws attention earlier in the book, Moodie, in contrast with her neighbours, experiences what John Thurston describes as a "loss of the objectifying mastery of the gaze, even in her own home." Thurston refers to the vignette in which a neighbour's cat makes off with Moodie's only remaining candle while she is watching over a sick child at night. An apt instance of the hazy boundary between domestic and wild, the cat's mischief-making also tightens the link between the motif of invasion (the cat breaks in through a window) and Moodie's precarious visual control over her space.[46] The link between the loss of her own powers of vision and the threat of home invasion emerges even more clearly in "Brian, the Still-Hunter." Perhaps none of Moodie's sketches register the oppressiveness of the settler landscape more acutely than does this chapter, with its account of a night spent anxiously waiting for her husband's delayed return from a distant neighbour's farm. Its opening poem, which refers to "the tangled mazes of the forest," plants an image of impenetrable opacity in the reader's imagination – an image that intensifies when the night "close[s] in cold and foggy" and Moodie, unable to "distinguish any object at more than a few yards from the door," fears that her husband and hired hand have "lost their way in the woods." Her fears are as much for herself as they are for her lost men: the perceived threat of "rude wayfarers" and wolves forces her to bar the door with "a heavy box," and still she contemplates the possibility that the wolves "should break through the frail windows, or come down the low, wide chimney, and rob [her] of [her] child."[47] Although Moodie does not always represent herself as the "one woman garrison" that Northrop Frye memorably calls her, in this sketch, she recalls, "for the first time in my life I found myself at night in a house entirely alone."[48] The solitary guard of her cabin, she acutely senses the frailty of its walls and the absence of a lock on the door.

Here, as in the episode Thurston discusses, the loss of candlelight both accentuates and allegorizes Moodie's powerlessness over her surroundings. The permeability of boundaries that are supposed to keep the inside separate from the outside, the uncertainties of the route that is meant to guide her husband home, and the cabin's darkness all combine to reinforce the connection between her fears and the conditions of disorientation. Until Brian, an emigrant from Lancashire and a reclusive hunter who has become a friend of her family, brings assurance that all is well and her husband is on his way, even "the pure air of the early day" with its "solemn and beautiful repose" fails to allay the anxiety that the wilderness has instiled in her.[49]

Despite the emotional force of such scenes, the terror of nature that critics such as Frye and Atwood influentially associate with Moodie is only one part of her response to this terrain. Her relationship to this environment is more complex than Frye's garrison theory or Atwood's gothic reading (and, in *The Journals of Susanna Moodie,* rewriting) suggest – at the very least, it has as wide a range as the bifurcated narrative persona that Moodie creates in *Roughing It in the Bush.* Moodie periodically reminds readers of the differences between her past self (the struggling newcomer who is the protagonist of many of these sketches) and her present one (the older and more settled Canada-booster who narrates them): "Now," she explains, "when not only reconciled to Canada, but loving it, and feeling a deep interest in its present welfare, and the fair prospect of its future greatness, I often look back and laugh at the feelings with which I then regarded this noble country."[50] The meanings that she ascribes to the land are also as varied as her roles and experiences within it; what readers see will shift subtly depending on whether they focus on Moodie as a mother, writer, wife, gardener, or literary cartographer.[51] The aforementioned sketch that on the one hand displays her fear of the woods, for example, on the other hand references her practice of painting wild flowers, her first successful cow milking, and her husband's hearty laughter at her fear – all of which hint that "this one idea [that] had taken such strong possession of [her] mind that [she] could admit no other" was by no means the only idea that she held about her environment.[52] The reader witnesses her recoiling from her surroundings while also accommodating herself both in and to the land by adapting to its particular demands.

In certain moments in *Roughing It in the Bush*, Moodie is able to dream a new territory into being. On Lake Katchawanook, near their bush farm in a less settled part of the colony, for example, she can imagine that she and her husband are "the first discoverers of every beautiful flower and stately tree that attracted our attention"; "we gave names to fantastic rocks and fairy isles," she writes, "and raised imaginary houses and bridges on every picturesque spot which we floated past."[53] For a brief interlude, Moodie solves her problem of seeing by not seeing the land itself. At the farthest edge of her colonial frontier, she looks not at but, in the words of Edward H. Dahl, "*through*" the wilderness "to the time when it will serve their wants, and supply them with the comforts of civilization."[54] In a gesture of imaginative appropriation common to surveyors tasked with planning new settlements, she maps her immediate experience of the land in a way that continually looks beyond it to its future potential.

To similar effect, when John names their first farm "Melsetter" after his family home in the Orkneys, he inscribes their small piece of the colony with a British heritage, and so contributes to the "Englishing" of Canadian space. Yet Moodie frequently draws attention to the conflicts beneath such overwriting. Threats of spatial confusion in *Roughing It in the Bush* extend beyond incidents of physical disorientation – such as the possibility of losing one's way or becoming stranded in the woods – to include difficulties negotiating a social wilderness. The vulnerability, disorientation, and lawlessness that Moodie experiences in this place derive from the fact that, as a member of the British upper-middle class, she was not in the demographic majority. Lured to their first farm by a land-jobber, who hoped that they might serve as "decoy duck[s]" that would draw other "respectable settler[s]" to the neighbourhood, the Moodies are categorized from the outset as outsiders in what largely remained, in the 1830s, a "Yankee front."[55] Strategically planted to attract a different class of settlers to the region – and so, by implication, to displace its current residents and gentrify the area – they occupy the uncomfortable position of being agents of demographic and cultural change in an established community with a prior history and sense of place, no matter how recent. Their neighbours regard the Moodies with suspicion and resentment because they threaten their own relationships to, and ways of being on, the land.

Despite her contempt for Joe Harris and his family, Moodie is not insensitive to the poignant human impact of the shifting demographic landscape. In a scene that turns into a meditation on this other family's displacement, she watches the funeral of Phoebe, Joe's daughter, who had "only survived the removal of the family a week; and at her own request had been brought all the way from the [Rice L]ake plains to be interred in the burying ground on the hill which overlooked the stream."[56] The girl's request that she be buried on the farm, combined with the distance that the family travels to fulfil her wish, reveals the depth of their attachment to the land on which the Moodies now reside. Phoebe's burial recalls the bittersweet words with which her grandmother, in an earlier chapter, establishes her family's connection to this place by remembering other loved ones who are literally part of its soil:

> There is not an acre in cultivation but I helped to clear it, nor a tree in yonder orchard but I held it while my poor man, who is dead and gone, planted it; and I have watched the trees bud from year to year, until their boughs overshadowed the hut, where all my children, but Joe, were born. Yes, I came here young, and in my prime; and I leave it in age and poverty. My children and husband are dead, and their bones rest beneath the turf in the burying-ground on the side of the hill. Of all that once gathered about my knees, Joe and his young ones alone remain. And it is hard, very hard, that I must leave their graves to be turned by the plough of a stranger.[57]

From the cleared fields to the planted trees to the turf on the hillside, the farm's geography is inextricably tied to another family's toils and triumphs. By incorporating the old woman's words into her own narrative of the region, Moodie acknowledges both Joe's ancestral claim to the land and, by implication, the role of late Loyalists – even with what she regarded as their "doubtful attachment to the British government" – in the creation of Upper Canada.[58] Although the Moodies desired, and very much believed in, the transformation of these spaces by an educated and genteel class of British emigrants, *Roughing It in the Bush* notes, and to a certain extent mourns, the erasures that occur when land is transferred and its significance redrawn.

Such scenes militate against the Moodies' own inscriptions of place in this book by pointing to the subjective, contingent, and fragile nature of one person's understanding of a given locale. While on the one hand Moodie seeks to forge her own sense of belonging, on the other she highlights her nonbelonging in a place that has already been defined by other people's stories and claims. Once again distinguishing herself from writers such as Burwell, for whom the creation of colonial territory is akin to writing on a *terra nullius*, she defines the colonial experiment of which she is a part as a palimpsestic process. Even the backwoods clearing where the Moodies are the first to build a house and farm the land does not provide them with a blank slate; Moodie's descriptions include the Mississauga who inhabited the area. Unlike Cary, she resists idealizing the assimilation of Indigenous peoples to colonial agrarian society; rather, she attempts to provide an accurate – albeit personally inflected – portrait of an enduring culture. As the Mississaugas' discovery of John's map of Canada shows, the wilderness had already been named and defined by people who still called it home. The area had long been inhabited by these Anishinaabe peoples, whose stories are written on the land itself in petroglyphs that can still be found throughout the region.[59] Moodie gestures to the area's Indigenous significance by identifying specific locations with their stories, the meaning of which she only partly grasps. In "A Trip to Stony Lake" – a sketch that charts in precise topographical detail a canoe route near their clearing – she writes of a "small lake, perfectly round in form, and having in its centre a tiny green island, in the midst of which stood, like a shattered monument of bygone storms, one blasted, black ash-tree." She moves from her own topographical description to speculations about the Indigenous meaning of the place: "The Indians call this lake *Bessikakoon*, but I do not know the exact meaning of the word. Some say that it means 'the Indian's grave,' others 'the lake of the one island.' It is certain that an Indian girl is buried beneath that blighted tree; but I never could learn the particulars of her story, and perhaps there was no tale connected with it."[60] Her uncertainty, both about the meaning of the name and also about the story attached to the place, marks her own foreignness as it points to Indigenous meanings beyond her own knowledge. Recalling her allusion to lakes and rivers "haunt[ed]" by the souls of the drowned, this anecdote – fragmentary though it may be – points to the value of the area for the Mississauga and complicates an earlier (and frequently cited) observation that "[t]he country is too new for ghosts."[61]

The Indigenous significance that Moodie attaches to the land reflects ongoing as well as historical habitation, however. In a classic colonial contradiction, she repeats the myth of the dying Indian, writing elegiacally that "a mysterious destiny ... hangs over them, pressing them back into the wilderness, and slowly and surely sweeping them from the earth," while showing her Mississauga neighbours – many of whom were valued friends and community members – continuing to practice their traditional economies of hunting and fishing as they traverse and camp around her bush farm.[62] Treaty 20 (also known as the Rice Lake Treaty) had opened the area to colonial settlement in 1818, but many Mississauga communities resisted moving to reserves until the 1830s, and then continued to hunt, fish, and use lands not ceded in the treaty. The historian Donald B. Smith explains that "at the treaty council, held in Ojibwe, the Mississauga believed that they retained all islands, points, and land at river mouths. ... The surviving council minutes, in English, indicate this understanding, but the treaty text, in English, does not."[63] Their ongoing land use cuts across the property lines of Moodie's settler map. Of a "dry cedar-swamp" near their bush farm that "had originally been an Indian sugar-bush," for instance, Moodie writes, "although the favourite spot had now passed into the hands of strangers, they still frequented the place, to make canoes and baskets, to fish and shoot, and occasionally to follow their old occupation."[64] The Mississaugas' continuing presence, captured sporadically by Moodie's pen, combines with their eager reading of her husband's map of Canada to create a partial but nonetheless dynamic and living map of Indigenous habitation that overlaps with her delineation of settler space.

As Smith recounts (drawing from the writings of Moodie's brother, Samuel Strickland, among others), relations between settlers and the Mississauga in the area were not always as harmonious as Moodie and her sister, Traill, suggest. From the injustices of the treaty to the desecration of burial sites, the Mississauga had good reason to view the newcomers as "intruders whom they cannot expell," as one emigrant put it in his diary.[65] That Moodie was aware of such feelings is apparent in her account of the Mississauga who hunted and gathered around Stony Lake. As her guide tells her, "[t]hey are very jealous of the settlers in the country coming to hunt and fish there, and tell many stories of wild beasts and rattlesnakes that abound along its shores" to deter them.[66] But for Moodie, the Mississauga are first and foremost respected neighbours and friends. They do not just come and go, casting in relief her own tentative appropriation of spaces that possess few familiar routes and patterns; they belong to her community. At the very least, Moodie's portraits show that the dispossession of Indigenous peoples to make way for the new colonial order was – like other aspects of the land's reinscription – far from complete. In the bush, as in the pseudo-wilderness of their first farm, Moodie's literary cartography is criss-crossed with stories that resist a simple transformation from rough to smooth, from wilderness to civilized, from lower to upper class, from Yankee or Mississauga to British territory.

The Problem of Wilderness

Not surprisingly, the precariousness of the colonial map is most acutely felt on the fringes of settlement. On the one hand, the move from the clearings to the bush that takes place halfway through *Roughing It in the Bush* implicates the Moodies even more clearly in the project of colonial expansion as they retreat from the realm of squatters and Yankee loyalists to the domain of "The Wilderness, and Our Indian Friends" (as Moodie affectionately titles the first chapter of the second volume) with the purpose of transforming it. On the other, as is the case in the pseudo-wilderness of their first farm, in the wilderness the settler's reinscription of space is difficult and fraught. For Moodie the woods are the geographical embodiment of the problem of seeing, and as she moves deeper into them, the failure of surveillance has more severe consequences. The wilderness is a reminder of the fragility of colonial culture as she understands it; the boundary between civilized and wild is permeable, especially with people living too close to the woods, who become vulnerable to mental as well as geographical disorientation. Moodie's literary cartography in the second half of the book represents an attempt to solidify that boundary.

From the beginning, the wilderness is associated with instability. Moodie's anxieties about "removing" to John's land grant in the bush reflect her reluctance to interrupt the process of accommodation through which, no matter how painful, she has formed a growing attachment to their first farm. Despite their inauspicious beginnings and relatively brief residence at Melsetter, as they prepare to leave it Moodie recognizes the fullness of the life that they built there. As "the birthplace of

[her] little Agnes," the farm is associated with the expansion of her family, and she admits that, after all, she "had learned to love it" and "it was much against [her] wish that it was sold."[67] The move to the backwoods signals an unnerving new beginning in the colony that, at least at first, exacerbates the "highly unsettling and unfinished process" of emigration "whereby one life is abandoned and another new life begun" – sometimes more than once.[68] As Moodie puts it, "removing ... is apt to give the emigrant roving and unsettled habits."[69] In *Life in the Clearings*, she would elaborate that the "roving ... habits" of emigrants had geographical as well as social consequences: "In old countries, where landed property often remains for ages in the same family, the present occupant plants and improves for future generations, hoping that his son's sons may enjoy the fruit of his labours. But in a new country like this, where property is constantly changing owners, no one seems to think it worth their while to take any trouble to add to the beauty of a place for the benefit of strangers."[70] The distinction that Moodie draws here between old and new world relationships to land resonates with her husband's claim in *Roughing It in the Bush* that a new country is like an undeveloped "language" whose patterns of "thought, metaphor, and ingenuity" have only begun to form.[71] The effects of prolonged habitation as yet unrealized, the contours of settler space remained, in some fundamental way, unmappable because their final shape was still uncertain.

While John seizes on the creative potential of such uncertainty and heralds the colonist as an "energetic" innovator, a creature of "original thought," Moodie registers only the dangers of disorientation and consequent mental and emotional dissolution.[72] Against John's hopes that they would find a more congenial society of British emigrants in the backwoods, Moodie's fears about the implications of moving to an even more remote geographical region reverberate through her descriptions of this space. Located on a thin line of new settlements stretching north towards the Canadian shield – perpendicular to the more popular east-west path of settlers along the southern expanses of arable land – the Moodies' 360-acre tract of bush is far more isolated than their first farm. Beyond Peterborough and Lakefield, it borders on a wilderness that remained at the margins of settlement until well into the 1850s – even today, the area is cottage country: an escape from the main hubs of urban culture. Here, too, speculation influenced emigration: the Moodies, among many others, were lured to the Trent-Severn river system in anticipation of its being opened up to navigation by canals that would connect Lake Ontario with Lake Huron. Although a survey of the canal route was completed by 1835, construction was delayed until almost a century later. An original footnote to *Roughing It in the Bush* registers the economic consequences of stalled development in the area: "After a lapse of fifteen years, we have been glad to sell these lots of land, after considerable clearings had been made upon them, for less than they originally cost us."[73]

The couple's disappointment doubtless colours Moodie's account of the journey from the cleared farm near Cobourg to the bush, which takes them deep into a forest that is characterized by silence. The journey resembles a descent into a wintry underworld: "the clearings began to diminish, and tall woods arose on either side of the path; their solemn aspect, and the deep silence that brooded over their vast solitudes, inspiring the mind with a strange awe. Not a breath of wind stirred the leafless branches, whose huge shadows – reflected upon the dazzling white covering of snow – lay so perfectly still, that it seemed as if Nature had suspended her operations, that life and motion had ceased, and that she was sleeping in her winding-sheet, upon the bier of death." In the frozen stillness of early February, the Moodies' removal from their "picturesque" farm to this sublime place takes on the aspect of a beautiful but hauntingly silent still life.[74]

I am not the first to remark that Moodie's representation of the wilderness is mercurial, to say the least. Within a dozen pages or so, the reader can be convinced – along with Moodie herself – that "[t]he farther in the bush" one resides, "the farther from God, and the nearer to hell," and that the wilderness is a sacred place where "the soul draws nearer to God, and is filled to overflowing by the overwhelming sense of His presence."[75] Her capriciousness is understandable given her multifaceted experience of hardship, triumph, pleasure, and failure in this place (not to mention the fluctuations of weather that alternately pleased, defied, and endangered them). While there is certainly a great deal of evidence that, over the course of her life, Moodie explored the woods around her frontier homes with a "growing comfort and ease of movement in the wilderness," in *Roughing It in the Bush* she seems more interested in conveying the feeling of dwelling in an unknown space rather than a mapped place.[76] Referring only in passing to activities such as exploring the woods, painting flowers, and gardening, she gives a hazy and fragmented textual shape to an environment with which she was in fact becoming reasonably well acquainted. In other words, while she oriented herself in the wilderness, she does little in this book to orient her readers. Indeed, her overwhelming concern seems to be with how settlers lose their way, both geographically and psychically, in the bush. This concern at once highlights the need for cartographic order and, in effect, begins to instil that order by distinguishing one kind of space from another. Defining the wilderness as not only antithetical to reason, but also able to bring about the complete breakdown of humanity, Moodie both polices its boundaries and organizes early Canadian space and society according to a kind of environmental determinism.

The otherworldly motif that emerges in the above passage describing the Moodies' journey into the woods is part of this spatializing strategy. As they continue towards Douro, their driver tells them of the "discovery" of the nearby site of Peterborough, which lay beyond a "great swamp" through which only a decade earlier "not a settler had ever passed" for fear that it led to "the end of the world." The driver's story places the Cavan swamp (which then still separated Peterborough from other nearby clearings) on the farthest edge of the emigrant's mental map: unexplored, this tract of wild land would quite literally have signified the end of his known world, although the Anishinaabeg knew the location as Nogojiwanong.[77] As he continues, the driver blends this unknown with an even more mysterious and potentially deadly "other world" in which hapless farm animals "fell a prey to the wolves and bears, and were seldom recovered."[78] The tale of epic heroism that ensues – describing a brave old Scotsman conquering the swamp's bush, bog, mosquitoes, blackflies, and snakes to discover a beautiful and fertile land on the other side – at first seems to lend the Moodies' own journey a note of courage and optimism. The Scotsman's successful negotiation of the swamp results in a triumphant revelation that "instead of leading to the other world, it had conducted him to a country that would yield the very best returns for cultivation. His favourable report [that good land had been found on the other side of the swamp] led to the formation of the road that we are about to cross, and the settlement of Peterborough, which is one of the most promising new settlements in this district."[79] Recounted as the Moodies begin their own colonizing quest in the backwoods, this story serves as a parable of pioneering, with the courageous Scotsman modelling the perseverance required to conquer a wild country.

The scene that directly follows it, however, ironically undermines the story's resonance in a book that, as a whole, stages a tale not just of accommodation and adaptation, but also of fear and failure. No sooner does the driver finish his story than they cross paths with an ox-sleigh, the occupants of which shock Moodie with their horrifying appearance: "during the whole course of my life I never saw three uglier mortals collected into such a narrow space. The man was blear-eyed, with a hare-lip, through which protruded two dreadful yellow teeth that resembled the tusks of a boar. The woman was long-faced, high cheek-boned, red-haired, and freckled all over like a toad. The boy resembled his hideous mother, but with the addition of a villanous obliquity of vision which rendered him the most disgusting object in this singular trio."[80] Although quickly dismissed with covert laughter and mockery, there is something sinister in the sudden appearance of this "singular trio" at the end of the driver's inspiring tale of pioneering courage and discovery. In their ugliness and deformity, the three occupants of the ox-sleigh belie once again the sureness of the emigrant's triumph over the wilderness, providing a foreboding glimpse of the degenerating effects of life in the bush that becomes a recurring source of anxiety for Moodie in this book. Their unnervingly bestialized physiognomy raises the possibility that the wilderness turns people into animals. Moreover, the boundary between civilization and wilderness – which suddenly seems able to conquer as readily as be conquered – appears disarmingly permeable.

This scene vividly introduces the pervasive and deeply unsettling motif of degeneration in the second half of *Roughing It in the Bush*. The connection that it draws between the land and moral and physical corruption, however, is hinted at much earlier. Moodie's first chapter, "A Visit to Grosse Isle," foreshadows the way in which she will interpret the threats of the Canadian wilderness later on. This sketch describes Moodie's disillusionment when what appears at a distance to be a picturesque "second Eden" yields, up close, the "revolting scene" of a "motley crew" of quarantined Irish emigrants who are washing their clothes along the shore of the island.[81] In addition to "the confusion of Babel" that animates the scene, part of what makes it appear so "savag[e]" and "barbar[ic]" to Moodie seems to be the way in which their bodies merge with the geographical setting. "The men and boys," she writes, "were *in* the water, while the women, with their scanty garments tucked above their knees, were trampling their bedding in tubs, or in holes in the rocks, which the retiring tide had left half full of water."[82] Her own propriety and foreignness is marked by the way in which the land literally repels her: she finds the rocks "so hot that [she] could scarcely place [her] foot upon them," while the Irish emigrants walk with bare feet – indeed, many are "almost naked," with little demarcation between their bodies and the world. With no man-made structures and few clothes to keep bodies and land separate, this scene is emblematic of a collapsing distinction between geography and people in *Roughing It in the Bush.*

Moodie portrays people and land as, in effect, mutually polluting. When the Moodies retreat to a sheltered spot on the island, it is the lower-class Irish emigrants who, in keeping with the author's oft-repeated prejudice against them, "sully ... the purity of the air and water with contaminating sights and sounds."[83] But when the Moodies' travelling companions debark, it is the place itself (now full of the contagion of people) that appears to "infect" them: "our passengers, who were chiefly honest Scotch labourers and mechanics from the vicinity of Edinburgh, and who while on board ship had conducted themselves with the greatest propriety, and appeared the most quiet, orderly set of people in the world, no sooner set foot upon the island than they became infected by the same spirit of insubordination and misrule, and were just as insolent and noisy as the rest."[84] Examined in light of later descriptions of the land, the sketch of Grosse Isle sets up a paradigm of geographical determinism that ensures that the land will be much more than just a backdrop in these sketches – instead, it is a shaping force that needs to be carefully monitored.

Before they remove to the woods, Moodie's sympathetic portrait of Brian the Still-Hunter strengthens the association between wilderness and moral and mental dissolution. She describes Brian, whose in-depth knowledge of the Canadian wilderness directly contrasts with her fear of it, as a "harmless maniac."[85] Yet, although he becomes a valued friend, Brian's alcoholism and eventual suicide make him a cautionary figure. Ultimately, his retreat from human society to the woods helps Moodie to demarcate the wilderness as a space that threatens the emigrant's mental stability, and thus the very fabric of civilized society. Brian is the first of several people who illustrate what was then a widely shared belief among European settlers, sparked by the eighteenth-century French naturalist Comte de Buffon, that the North American geography caused animals and people "to 'degenerate' from their original types." As the historian Suzanne Zeller remarks, due in part to Buffon's influence, throughout the first half of the nineteenth century in Canada "life in the backwoods was widely seen as detrimental to the health and even to the physique of European immigrants, who were likened to plants stifled by forest overgrowth."[86] Among Zeller's many sources is Strickland, who would write in *Twenty-Seven Years in Canada West* (1853): "Buried in the depth of a boundless forest, the breeze of health never reaches these poor wanderers; the bright prospect of distant hills, fading away into the semblance of clouds, never cheered their sight; they are tall and pale, like vegetables that grow in a vault, pining for light."[87] Strickland's description of a population "buried" in a stifling landscape returns us to the idea that to live on the frontiers of settlement was to succumb to a death-like existence characterized by isolation and darkness, and that the wilderness was a landscape in need of the illuminating powers of surveyors and land clearing.

Captain Lloyd joins Brian as a cautionary example of the way in which topography and space – including the distribution of military land grants – are implicated in a dehumanizing colonial experience that, in the very process of building a new society, threatens its breakdown. Like John, Captain Lloyd is a half-pay officer lured to Canada by emigration's opportunities. Lloyd differs from John, however, by settling in Dummer, which, Moodie notes, "might not inaptly have been termed 'The *last* clearing in the world.'"[88] She adds that "the bait that has been the ruin of so many of his class" was "a large grant of land" in this "remote and untried township": "These government grants of land, to half-pay officers, have induced numbers of this class to emigrate to the backwoods of Canada, who are totally unfit for pioneers; but, tempted by the offer of finding themselves landholders of what, on paper, appear to them fine estates, they resign a certainty, to waste their energies, and die half-starved and broken-hearted in the depths of the pitiless wild."[89] A disconnect between land "on paper" and the land itself engenders the disorientation that Moodie describes. In effect, the map lies: Captain Lloyd's land proves "barren and stony" and his failure to raise crops on it, combined with "[t]he want of society" and "the total absence of all the comforts and decencies of life," drives him to "inaction, apathy, and at last, despondency." Resorting to drink and eventually abandoning his family in despair, he succumbs to the dehumanizing influences of the backwoods until a neighbour describes him as "the filthiest beast in the township" (using a metaphor that recalls Moodie's bestialized characters in the ox-sleigh several chapters earlier).[90] If at Grosse Isle it is the emigrants who appear to pollute the landscape, here it is clearly the other way around: geography is responsible for a human being's complete disintegration.

Captain Lloyd's story appears in a chapter called "The Walk to Dummer," the narrative of which draws attention to the threats of disorientation that Moodie and her companion, Emilia, face on their mission to bring aid to the lonely family. This title, as Helen Buss notes, "draws attention not to the woman [the Captain's wife] she and Emilia go to rescue, but to the 'walk,' the long cold journey through the 'tangled maze of closely-interwoven cedars,' through the 'interminable forest' on a frigid winter day when they fear, as Emilia confesses, they may die of hunger while trying to bring food to a starving woman."[91] Dummer represents the frontier's farthest edge, and Moodie stresses that she does "not know of any [clearing] in that direction which extends beyond it." Her journey, then, takes her to the brink of "*terra incognita*"; with nothing but a "lonely, blazed path" to guide them the "nine long miles to the first clearing," the threat that the women "will be lost in the woods" generates much of the sketch's tension.[92]

Framing the Captain's story in the narrative of her own journey that is remarkable for its physical strain, Moodie reinforces the parallel between geographical and moral way-finding. As she later makes clear, to become lost physically is tantamount to becoming lost spiritually: "There are few trifling failures more bitter in our journey through life than that of a tired traveller mistaking his road. What effect must that tremendous failure produce upon the human mind, when at the end of life's unretraceable journey, the traveller finds that he has fallen upon the wrong track through every stage, and instead of arriving at a land of blissful promise, sinks for ever into the gulf of despair!"[93] As if to safeguard against such "tremendous failure," Moodie details the route of her own "Quixotic expedition" with noticeable precision: the beaver meadow, the rapid and "icy cold" creek, the swamp, and the maple wood that she and Emilia must traverse are landmarks in a narrative that is as geographical as it is psychological. Despite the methodical care with which she outlines her journey's topography, the threat of getting lost hangs over her efforts to chart the terrain. Few landmarks characterize either the "great swamp" – a "tangled maze of closely-interwoven cedars, fallen trees, and loose-scattered masses of rock" – or the "interminable forest [that] stretched away to the right and left, before and behind" them.[94] Roads are not much help either: as they approach their destination, the women turn down the wrong one and are forced to retrace their steps. Their navigational difficulties help to explain the geographical circumstances that have defeated the Captain and endangered his family. Geography is not merely a metaphor: it is an actor in their drama.

Moodie's description of the Lloyds' house leaves little question that the configuration of settler space is not just a geographical manifestation, but also a primary cause, of their deplorable state. Its immediate environment, from the "black pine-forest" that "stretched away to the north of the house, and terminated in a dismal, tangled cedar-swamp," to the "steep, bleak hill" on which the house stands, is isolated and unwelcoming. Moodie's description of it echoes Thomas Moore's "The Lake of the Dismal Swamp," a ballad from his *Poems Relating to America* (1806) that also hauntingly equates wild and inhospitable landscapes with madness. The poem recounts a young man's vain search for his lost love in the Great Dismal Swamp – a real place in Norfolk, Virginia – in language that resonates throughout Moodie's descriptions of wilderness in *Roughing It in the Bush*:

> Away to the Dismal Swamp he speeds –
> His path was rugged and sore,
> Through tangled juniper, beds of reeds,
> Through many a fen, where the serpent feeds,
> And man never trod before.[95]

Finally, the fact that the house has been built to face away from the road emphasizes its disconnection from human community as well as a lack of panoptic command, both of which suggest the settler's vulnerability in this landscape rather than dominion over it.

Such stories help Moodie to build up the meaning of wilderness as threat, and thus to reinforce its supposed separateness from civilization. More than just evaluations of space, however, they are also part of a powerful case for environmental determinism. Moodie suggests that particular classes and cultures are suited to particular new world geographies. As much as the genteel Englishman does not belong in the wilderness, "the Indian" is revered (in the stock terms of the noble savage) as "one of Nature's gentlemen"[96] and finds his natural home and identity there. Moodie underscores this idea in *Life in the Clearings*, where she observes that "[t]he red man is out of his element when he settles quietly down to a farm ... He never appears to advantage as a resident among civilized men; and he seems painfully conscious of his inferiority, and ignorance of the arts of life. He has lost his identity, as it were."[97] Moodie's critique of assimilation – which contrasts with Cary's endorsement of it – is premised on an essentialist view of the ways in which geography and spatial practices shape identity and culture, an idea that much of *Roughing It in the Bush* explores.

How and where Moodie positions herself in relation to this landscape and its troubling "spectre of madness" is more difficult to ascertain.[98]

While she manages to maintain her own sanity, she is also physically and psychologically marked by the bush: "I looked double the age I really was," she writes; "I clung to my solitude ... I was no longer fit for the world ... I was contented to live and die in obscurity."[99] As she prepares to leave her bush farm for Bellville, Moodie appears as a prematurely aged woman who retreats from the "world" at the very moment that she would reenter it. While she has worked to give shape to her spaces, establishing homes and gardens, clearing a bush farm, cultivating fields, and (to perhaps the most lasting effect) redefining the meaning of these places by writing about them, so too have these spaces worn and reshaped her former self, as they have done for so many others featured in her sketches. In the end, rather than being the one who maps the land, in some fundamental way Moodie is mapped by it.

As her husband's "Canadian Sketches" suggests, the ultimate trajectory of *Roughing It in the Bush* as a whole – at least by 1871 – would direct its readers towards the disciplined spatial order for which Moodie longs throughout much of her book. On the whole, however, her sketches tend to illustrate the complexity and heterogeneity that such an order conceals. Moodie's literary cartography is at once limited and enabled by her direct encounters with the land; its imaginative reach is shaped by her unique impressions of what it was to actually live on and move through the spaces of the Upper Canadian frontier, and to contend with the places not yet governed by the map. Indeed, the most interesting parts of *Roughing It in the Bush* are those that map this concealed experience of space. On some level, the book is itself a map, the collection of sketches formally reproducing the messy incompleteness of the geography that the Moodies encountered, with its diverse peoples and interests colliding, all struggling for definition and to define their own space.

Chapter Three

The Intimate Geography of Wilderness: The Spatiality of Catharine Parr Traill's Botanical Inventories

While Susanna Moodie carefully navigated the edge of the wilderness, reinforcing the boundary between wild and civilized space, her sister, Catharine Parr Traill, ventured into its depths. She did not recoil, either in her writings or in her everyday life, from those "interminable forests through which the eye can only penetrate a few yards."[1] She sought neither to tame these spaces, nor to push them off the edge of the map, as Adam Hood Burwell does in *Talbot Road*. Nor did she simply reduce them, like Thomas Cary in *Abram's Plains*, to economic resources. Instead, Traill explored the wilderness with the eager curiosity of the field naturalist, looking to it as a source of endless interest and pleasure. This chapter examines how her botanical writings in particular challenged narrow conceptions of the wilderness and its value in the settler landscape. Complicating the idea that the land needed to be improved in order to become meaningful as a place, Traill's botanical writings point to the wilderness itself as significant: not antithetical to settlement, but threatened by it.

These writings have an important literary-cartographic dimension. While some theorists draw a sharp distinction between inventories of natural history and the more overtly "*spatial* discourse" of, for instance, exploration narratives,[2] Traill's work blurs the line between these modes of topographical description. Natural history was, for Traill, a geographical practice that amounted not just to a form of classification and inventory, but also to a way of mapping her world. Blending the eighteenth-century Linnaean taxonomic model of classification with folk methods focused on locating, identifying, and naming specimens in their habitat, her botanical writings suggest a way to move through and come to know the forests, meadows, and bogs around her homesteads differently than many settlers were inclined to see them. Rooted in geographical experience, her botanical writings are a sustained meditation on how settlers might dwell in a place that offered much more than just arable land concealed beneath obstructive forests. The settler's imperative, Traill suggests, ought to be not to wage war against the wilderness, but rather to treat such spaces as gardens in which indigenous species, and indeed whole ecosystems, might interpenetrate cultivated ones.

As the reader of Traill's best-known work, *The Backwoods of Canada* (1836), learns early on, Canada ignited an already keenly developed geographical curiosity in its author. Towards the end of the Atlantic crossing, her interest in the ship captain's maps and her eagerness to "learn ... the names of the distant shores and islands" reveal an imagination sensitive to the way in which cartography and topography interact to engender a sense of place.[3] But even more than she desired to know the land's toponymy, Traill longed to set foot on it, to know it by touching it, to see it up close. Hence her disappointment when she is kept from disembarking at the Isle of Bic, the Traills' first stop in the new country. As a substitute for the direct exploration she is denied, her husband Thomas brings her "a delightful bouquet" of wild flowers, a consolatory gesture that she receives with noticeable pleasure.[4] Marking Traill's first direct, tactile encounter with her newly adopted land, this moment foreshadows the most prominent way in which she would continue to relate to the land for the rest of her long life in Canada: not so much by way of its geography, but rather by way of its natural history, and botany in particular.

So strong was Traill's impulse to engage with her surroundings in this manner that in *The Backwoods* the reader finds her collecting plant specimens before she even has a home to call her own.[5] She was introduced to natural history as a girl in England, where the activities of observing, collecting, and classifying natural objects were widely popular among experts and amateurs alike. Her father and older sister Elizabeth were avid naturalists who, with the help of exemplary texts such as Gilbert White's *Natural History of Selborne* (1789) and Izaak Walton's *Compleat Angler* (1653), instructed Catharine in the practices that would serve her so well in Canada, where she quickly perceived a need for the kind of knowledge and, especially, appreciation that natural history could provide to settlers.[6]

During the era of imperial and colonial expansion, natural history had a profound impact on how Europeans viewed the biological makeup of the planet. Like those of cartography, its methods of ordering the environment comprised part of the mental equipment that emigrants imported to the colonies. Through natural history, they could not only gain a measure of control over their surroundings, but also express their passion for both science and religion. That the practice required little in the way of supplies or training only enhanced its appeal for colonists who lived in relative isolation with limited resources. It was doubtless with many of these factors in mind that Traill encouraged other women to take up the activity, "especially to those who, living in the bush, must necessarily be shut out from the pleasures of a large circle of friends, and the varieties that a town or village offer."[7]

Because natural history failed to gain widespread momentum or institutionalized support in Canada until the 1850s, however, settlers such as Traill, who arrived in the Katchawanook region of Upper Canada in 1832, found many gaps that required filling. According to Thomas R. Dunlap, "so little had been done, particularly in the early nineteenth century, that new species or new facts could be found almost anywhere."[8] The surveyor John MacTaggart emphasized the need for a botanical inventory in his impassioned call for a "Society for the Promotion of Natural History," published in the *Montreal Herald* in 1826: "What are the names of the trees, briers, shrubs, plants, herbs, flowers, mosses, &c., which are or have been found in this country? Let the local names be given, as *prickly ash, spotted alder, pitch pine, curly maple, winter green,* &c. Let the reasons for such names be expounded, and their qualities told."[9] A natural history society was formed in Montreal shortly thereafter, but when Traill arrived in the colony there was still very little local knowledge from which she could draw. She appears to have been ignorant of Thomas Nuttall's important botanical catalogue *The Genera of North American Plants* (1818), which addressed parts of Canada, as well as of other writers who included natural history in their accounts, as did Jonathan Carver in his *Travels through North America* and MacTaggart in his *Three Years in Canada*. Instead, she made what use she could of Frederick Pursh's *Flora of North America* (1814) – for a time the only botanical text available to her in the backwoods and, as she would write in the opening of *Canadian Wild Flowers,* "the only work that treated in any way of the Wild Plants of Canada" – navigating its Latin descriptions via her knowledge of Italian.[10] For the intents and purposes of most settlers, however, the colony's botanical record remained as opaque and inaccessible as the wilderness itself.

Traill was among the first Canadian settlers to penetrate the tangle. Detailed descriptions of flora and fauna are central to her writings, both fictional and nonfictional. Woven into the narratives of such popular works as *The Backwoods of Canada* and *The Canadian Crusoes* (1852), these descriptions support (and sometimes interrupt) Traill's stories to draw readers deeper into their natural settings. In other texts, natural history supersedes narrative elements to provide readers with a more comprehensive and focused picture of the Canadian landscape. Several of the sketches that she published in the *Anglo-American Magazine*'s "Forest Gleanings" series, for instance, assemble clear and detailed topographies of the Katchawanook and Rice Lake regions by way of extensive inventories of their flora and fauna;[11] and her children's book, *Lady Mary and Her Nurse; or, A Peep into the Canadian Forest* (1856), is structured around a series of instructive conversations about the unique characteristics of Canada's wilderness. Her most significant contributions to Canada's natural history, however, were those volumes devoted entirely to botany – books that offer a sustained, intimate view of the Canadian wilderness through a methodical yet imaginatively engaging inventory of its vegetation, which she compiled in collaboration with her neice, Agnes Moodie Fitzgibbon, who contributed the illustrations. It is on these unassuming yet important works that the proceeding discussion is focused, with concern lying especially with *Canadian Wild Flowers*, which at the time of its publication was "the only widely accessible scientific botany book on Canadian plants,"[12] and the more comprehensive *Studies of Plant Life in Canada; or, Gleanings from Forest, Lake and Plain* (1885) that followed it.

Broadly, this chapter builds on David Jackel's observation that Traill succeeds (where Moodie fails) in "see[ing]" nature with remarkable clarity.[13] The practice of natural history, which relied upon close observation and precise description, provided Traill with a motivation and a lens through which to encounter her backwoods environment directly, to make it visible to others, and thus to inspire a fresh regard for wild regions that many settlers – her sister included – were looking only to transform. Over the course of nearly sixty-seven years in the sparsely inhabited area between Rice Lake and Lake Katchawanook, near Peterborough, Traill revealed the contents of the wilderness one plant at a time. From the heights of the impressive old growth pines down to the most delicate fronds of moss that clung to their trunks, natural history carried her past the stark "monotony" of woods seen at a distance to the infinite variety of "objects to charm and delight the close observer" that lay hidden within.[14] The intricate worlds that emerge in Traill's sketches of these objects invited emigrant readers to reimagine a terrain that many held in fear, antipathy, or simply ignorance as they destroyed it with utilitarian efficiency.

Traill's natural history, then, has a territorial dimension. Although markedly different in scope and intent from institutionalized inventories (such as John Macoun's reports for the Geological and Natural History Survey, which helped chart resource-rich areas; see chapter 4), her descriptions fill in spaces that most colonial maps left blank. In the process of revealing the contents of the wilderness, Traill also reconfigured its boundaries. This reconfiguration has two facets that appear to work in contradictory ways but are not necessarily at odds. First, her botanical writings trouble the distinctions that many – including her sister – drew between the wilderness and settler civilization, instead presenting the two as compatible. The highly ordered arrangements of specimens in *Canadian Wild Flowers* and *Studies of Plant Life in Canada,* for instance, invite settlers in by making the terrain not only comprehensible, but also navigable. Drawing from the legacy of natural theology, Traill also appeals to settlers' religious sensibilities by representing the wilderness as part of an unambiguously Christian world. More subtly, but no less significantly, she connects the wilderness to Canada's emerging culture. Mingling her own fresh, concrete language with fragments of poetry, Traill's inventory traces an affinity between the natural world and a young nation's aesthetic and literary concerns. These elements of Traill's natural history domesticate the wilderness by decorating it with the imported trappings of civilization. At the same time, her descriptions challenge the supposed preeminence of civilization – and of cultivation – over wild nature. She urges readers to see the two as compatible, but equally to recognize undomesticated wilderness as unique and valuable. Mitigating the more anthropocentric elements of her natural history is a rich impression of a complex ecology that Traill felt was worth preserving from the onslaught of settler civilization. As aware as she was of the problems that the wilderness posed for settlers, she ultimately depicted it as far more threatened than threatening. If in books such as *The Backwoods of Canada* and *The Canadian Settler's Guide* (1855) she celebrated the expansion of settler space, in *Canadian Wild Flowers* and *Studies of Plant Life in Canada* she charts the vulnerable topography that it was replacing, encouraging emigrant readers to appreciate the terrain in its present state rather than for its agricultural potential.

Wayfinding

Traill was accutely aware of the disorientation that settlers experienced in the wilderness. As Carl Ballstadt points out, the story of children lost and found in the great "maze and enigma" of the Canadian forest became "the most significant theme in her fiction," and also appears regularly in her nonfiction.[15] Although some critics argue that Traill's writing reveals an evasive or paranoid response to this wilderness,[16] the intense, physical encounter with nature that the pursuit of natural history demanded suggests otherwise. Traill respatializes the wilderness by inviting settlers in.

Naturalist texts opened windows through which readers could see nature's composite elements up close without actually having to set foot in the woods or bogs, but the field naturalists who produced such texts faced quite another prospect. In order to create a thorough account of a region's flora and fauna, an intrepid naturalist had to slog through "Cedar swamps, Cranberry marshes, Poplar swales, and Peat bogs,"[17] braving the depths of the woods in order to see all they contained. Traill not infrequently reminds her readers of the physical confrontation with nature that was necessary if its treasures were to be discovered; the botanist, as she put it, must often "plunge ... amid the rank, tangled vegetation, [to] bring ... beauties to the light."[18] As important as it was for her to document Canada's native vegetation, her ultimate object seems to have been to similarly lure her readers away from the pages of the book and into the forest – in other words, her inventory encourages contact with wild nature itself. Like Sir Walter Scott, whose words she quotes in *Studies of Plant Life in Canada,* she invites us to "[h]ie to haunts, right seldom seen, / Lovely, lonesome, cold, cold and green" to see them up close.[19]

An eclectic combination of elements helps each volume transform the wilderness into a more comprehensible, and correspondingly less alien and bewildering, landscape. "[N]ot," as she put it in *Studies of Plant Life in Canada,* written "for the learned,"[20] Traill's botanical guides addressed a popular audience, making the wilderness more accessible to settlers in a language and form that they could easily understand. *Canadian Wild Flowers* and *Studies of Plant Life in Canada* each present a tidy catalogue of specimens: the first is restricted to flowers, while the second includes flowering shrubs, trees, and native ferns. These Traill identifies one by one by both their common and Latin botanical names, before describing, in careful detail, their appearance, the environments in which they are commonly found, and their known uses (which include what could be eaten and what could not, and what medicines could be extracted from which plants and how). Such instructions do not dominate her descriptions, however. Anecdotes, local folklore, fragments of poetry, and moments of personal religious contemplation soften the rigid order and practicality of her botanical texts, offering aesthetic, cultural, and religious interest as well.

The feeling of navigability created by the untangling of dense vegetation is also sustained by the form of the botanical guide. This form has a soothing regularity: the shape of each entry soon becomes predictable, and consequently the reader moves ever more comfortably and easily through the material until, species by species, the contents of the woods are not only made known, but also arranged into an orderly collection. In this manner, Traill, like the naturalists to which Michel Foucault alludes in *The Order of Things* (and, indeed, like a surveyor), lays an imaginary "grid ... out over the entire vegetable or animal kingdom."[21] Reproducing what Derek Gregory describes as an "'optics' of plant morphology in which nature [appears] as a table and *spatialized*," enabling the observer to imagine the world "as an ordered totality,"[22] Traill's careful and efficient arrangement of specimens fills in the blanks that remained on maps such as the one that oriented readers of *The Backwoods* to Newcastle District and the Otonabee River (figure 6). Within the "grid" or "table" that natural history's system of classification provides, each of Traill's botanical descriptions builds an exquisitely detailed yet manageable and usable layer into regional topographical knowledge.

The formal and practical aspects of Traill's botanical writings achieve on a local scale the material appropriation of nature that Mary Louise Pratt identifies in the practice of colonial natural history more broadly. What is true of the map is also true of natural history: as many scholars point out, it is by no means a benign medium, objective though its stance and language profess to be. Especially in the colonial context, its way of seeing the world has been connected to identifiable political and material consequences. For instance, Pratt argues that natural history's method of itemizing the world by dissecting it into parts – in the process cutting each specimen off from its surrounding environment – eased the imperial and, later, colonial appropriation of lands and resources. Locating natural history's foundations in "the period of 'primitive accumulation' [1500–1800] in which ... European bourgeoisies were able to accumulate the capital that launched the Industrial Revolution," Pratt emphasizes its utilitarian and materialist rationale. In her view, "the systematizing of nature" epitomized by Carl Linnaeus' taxonomic method (outlined in his *Systema Naturae* in 1735), "models the extractive, transformative character of industrial capitalism." In the end, she writes, "natural history asserted an urban, lettered, male authority over the whole of the planet; it elaborated a rationalizing, extractive, dissociative understanding which overlaid functional, experiential relations among people, plants, and animals. In these respects, it figures a certain kind of global hegemony, notably one based on possession of land and resources."[23] In the Canadian context, as Suzanne Zeller elucidates, natural history served the aims of Britain's expanding imperial and colonial economy. The parent of the "inventory sciences" (botany and geology, among others) that spurred Canada's territorial and economic expansion, natural history served a utilitarian purpose as it was increasingly counted on to supply "the missing link between potential and reality."[24] The practice and discourse of natural history thus hovers between the map's speculative and representational dimensions, with explorers, settlers, and developers alike benefiting from its systems of describing the terrain and cataloguing its resources and agricultural capabilities.

Pratt and Zeller highlight natural history's anthropocentric (and conventionally male) approach to the wilderness, which organizes the natural world in terms of usable parts for human consumption. They also underscore its penetrating and dissecting impulses that tend to draw the observer into an ever-narrowing field of vision. Not infrequently, Traill's record conforms to this model: in her patient, meticulous delineation of one species of flowering wintergreen's "smooth, dark-green leaves, delicately fringed with soft, silky hairs, tinged with a purplish hue," of flowers "slightly drooping from among the shining leaves on thread-like pedicels," and in her precise counting of their "stamens ... six; sepals of the calyx, five; [and] petals, three," as in her brief yet vivid rendering of the mandrake's "broad umbrella-like leaf ... closely folded round the simple fleshy stem," she remains focused on minute details to the exclusion of their larger context.[25] Like the illustrations that accompany them, these descriptions fragment the natural world into a series of portraits artfully exhibited on a background that remains, for all intents and purposes, blank. As Christoph Irmscher remarks, intricate and beautiful as they are, Fitzgibbon's lithographs, hand-coloured for *Canadian Wild Flowers*, "serve to civilize the wildflowers, bending them into frames and patterns that are no longer those of nature herself."[26]

And yet, while she revels in close observation of individual plants, Traill resists natural history's tendency to itemize nature object-by-object at the expense of the interconnected whole in which each plant is an integral part. Like traditional "folk taxonomies" that strive "to understand and explain the workings of ecosystems, or at the very least biological communities,"[27] Traill's descriptions also attend to the wider environment in which her specimens are found. In the tradition of Gilbert White's attention to the "chain of nature,"[28] she is just as likely to pull back from the minutiae in order to convey the larger scene in which many plants interact. Emblematic of this more comprehensive and holistic view, her description of a peat bog emphasizes the interconnected environment in which individual plants thrive:

> A beautiful carpet of white Peat Moss *Sphagnum cymbifolium* is spread over the surface, nearly a foot deep; on this we see wreaths of the graceful low-bush Cranberry, trailing its slender branches with their dark green glossy myrtle-like foliage and delicate pink revolute flowers, as well as berries in every stage of progress, the tiny green immature fruit – the golden – the mottled and the deep red ripe berry. ... There the slender leaved Sundew mixes its white flowers with the fringed Orchis, and sends up from the watery soil its modest flowers in the midst of a bed of the grand blossoms of that rarely constructed plant the "Pitcher Plant."[29]

This economical yet strikingly lucid description weds detail with detail until what amounts to an intricately enmeshed ecosystem comes into view. Her disposition towards narrative and "word painting"[30] rather than drily enumerative lists untangles the wilderness not by artificially separating its features, but by drawing attention to their relationships in an organic composition. Such passages are not uncommon, and their presence throughout Traill's botanical inventory reminds the reader that each apparently isolated specimen exists as part of a complex whole.

Traill's habit of moving from the narrower parts of nature to wider landscapes endows her natural history with a proto-ecological perspective. She emphasizes harmonious balance, but while she paints each plant and flower with a certain poise and fullness of character (rendered by such metaphors and adjectives as "carpet," "wreaths," "slender," "delicate," and "grand"), she rarely succumbs to idealization. Rather, as products of many painstakingly observed elements layered together to form a picture in which the details remain crisp, these word paintings underscore her direct and careful encounter with nature.

Their narrative presentation, moreover, enhances the reader's ability to imagine Traill's experience of walking through the woods and viewing it from many vantage points. Traill mapped her terrain from the ground up and offers tangible evidence that, contrary to views of wilderness as "empty," "in nature there is no space left unoccupied."[31]

The order of Traill's inventory also reflects the lived "experiential relations" (to return to Pratt) of the settler discovering the natural world geographically and, in so doing, preserves a sense of the wilderness as a physical milieu. Although she groups her plants "somewhat in families," Traill departs from traditional scientific taxonomy to arrange them "as a general rule, in the order in which they appear in the woods" – an order that mirrors her rambles through the wilderness rather than artificially dissecting it.[32] In addition to cataloguing its features, then, Traill's natural history captures a sense of the backwoods as an expansive interconnected world of flora and fauna in which the naturalist lived and moved as a relatively insignificant observer. While emphasizing every benefit and pleasure this natural environment offers to humankind, Traill also encourages her readers to meditate upon the wilderness as a unique environment defined by its nonhuman elements. It is not uncommon to find her asking, as she does in *Canadian Wild Flowers*, "[f]or whom are [its] solitary objects of beauty reserved?"[33] On the one hand, this serves as a rhetorical question inviting people in to witness first-hand the splendours of Canada's more isolated landscapes. On the other hand, it is a subtle acknowledgment that the significance of its hidden treasures may in fact lie beyond the realm of human experience – that the beauty of such hidden places exists "[j]ust for itself and God."[34] Or, it may serve more humble living things; as she remarks of certain "native Rannunculus flowers" whose uses are not known to her: "doubtless even the lowliest among them has a part to perform, though not apparently for man's sole benefit but also for the support or shelter of some of God's creation among the insect tribes or smaller animals or birds which find nourishment in their seeds, leaves or roots."[35] While most maps left wild spaces blank, filling in only those areas that had some human significance, Traill's inventory conveys time and again that life extends well beyond human meaning and perception: "[s]omething fills up all vacancies, either in vegetable or animal life," she famously writes; "unseen organisms, too subtile and too fine to become visible to our unassisted vision, have their existence though we behold them not."[36]

While the emigrant remains a central figure in her botanical descriptions, Traill's "consumption" of nature takes many forms, only some of which participate in the kind of appropriation that Pratt and Zeller attribute to colonial natural history. In the opening pages of *Studies of Plant Life*, Traill recalls the fascination and solace she discovered in the backwoods as a recent emigrant: "I soon found beauties in my forest wanderings in the unknown trees and plants of the forest. These things became a great resource, and every flower and shrub and forest tree awakened an interest in my mind, so that I began to thirst for more intimate knowledge of them. They became like dear friends, soothing and cheering, by their sweet unconscious influence, hours of loneliness, and hours of sorrow and suffering."[37] The "resource" value of nature in this passage is spiritual, intellectual, and aesthetic, rather than practical – something that Fitzgibbon's artfully curated illustrations cement. The experience of exile that colours Traill's recollection hints that the motivation for her investigation comes from something more than rational, scientific, or utilitarian interest: she has an emotional need for the wilderness, as well as a material one. Images of comfort and security throughout her botanical writings point to this need, and reverse expected paradigms of wilderness as inhospitable. Significantly, it is the woods rather than clearings that offer Traill respite from the challenges of her daily life, just as they protect tender young growth from the harsh Canadian climate: "No chilling, biting, winds or searching frosts penetrate the woods, – to nip the early buds of leaf and flower as on the exposed clearings," she writes; "[w]ithin the forest all is quiet and warmth, when without, the air is cold and the wind blustering"; the forest is "[a] kindly nursing mother," gentle and nurturing, rather than harsh and indifferent.[38] Even its cedar swamps – which, as Moodie shows, could be unnavigable to settlers – are appreciated by Traill for the shelter that they provide to countless living things; there she seeks out the partridge, woodpecker, tree creeper, and chickadee, and delights in observing the fascinating multitudes of "insect life" that frequent its tangled branches and decaying deadfall.[39] Wherever a superficial look might reveal only impenetrable wilderness, natural history uncovered sources of interest. As she wrote of the remote Fairy Lake: "[t]o some ... it may appear rugged and savage in its wildness of rocks and trees, and tangling underwoods; but not so to the Botanist and Field-Naturalist."[40]

The richness of Traill's wilderness spaces elicits a Wordsworthian reverence for the natural world over the built landscape, and thus anticipates the feeling, expressed in the poetry of Archibald Lampman (who would have met Traill when she visited his family at Gore's Landing on Rice Lake between 1867 and 1874) as well as in later natural histories such as S.T. Wood's *Rambles of a Canadian Naturalist* (1916), that Canada's wild spaces held the possibility of therapeutic escape from the growing cities with their "hideous wires, glaring lights, and torturing noises."[41] Anticipating Wood, Traill's botanical writings resonate with the mind-cure movement that was gaining momentum in the United States and Canada in the second half of the nineteenth century, and that promoted the physical and mental health benefits of cultivating a close kinship with nature. Responding to the stresses of urbanization, the movement's Canadian proponents – among them Lampman and others from the Confederation Poets[42] – would continue to reimagine habitable natural spaces and the relationship between urban, rural, and wild landscapes.

Perhaps needless to say, Traill did not exclusively write about wilderness; she was also a champion of (and an active participant in) the very processes that threatened it. In *The Backwoods of Canada* she celebrates the progress of land-clearing and agriculture with idyllic images of established farmland, and eagerly anticipates the appearance of fertile, ploughed fields. The letters refer specifically to architectural and industrial landmarks such as stone buildings and mills that herald the replacement of wilderness with humanized – and even urbanized – landscapes.[43] Like Moodie, Traill despairs at the "badness of the roads" in the bush and laments a "want of picturesque beauty in the woods."[44] But her sensitivity to such spaces as not only beautiful but also threatened deepened over the course of a long life of bearing witness to the Canadian version of what the American environmental historian William Cronon describes as "the ecological consequences of European invasion."[45] Indeed, even in this early paean to development, natural history begins to complicate her vision of the land, with religion playing a definitive role in her ambivalence about the "progress" of civilization.

Throughout her botanical descriptions, Traill draws attention to aspects of wild nature that surpassed human ingenuity. While she acknowledges that some species of plants improve under cultivation, she also notes that many fare equally well, if not better, in their native habitat. The "glorious Lily," for example, "can hardly be seen to greater advantage" than in its original environment.[46] Traill's wilderness offers many such reminders that humans cannot match nature, let alone improve upon it. As she writes of the sundew: "the eye that sees the beauty set forth in the little dew-gemmed leaf of this lovely plant, may behold in it with reverent admiration a work of creative mind, surpassing all that man's ingenuity can produce. The jeweller may polish and set the ruby and the diamond in fretted gold, but he cannot make one ruby-tinted leaf of the little Sundew."[47] The "creative mind" at work in the recesses of Canada's backwoods belonged, of course, to God. The veneration that Traill conveys for creations "surpassing" human capability elevates the wilderness into a sacred space with an immense capacity to nurture the mind and spirit of those who look at it in the right way. Her attention to the elements she felt were "most pleasing to the eye" attempts to refocus the lens through which the settler saw only "weeds – weeds – weeds, nothing but weeds," and to reveal, instead, "the works of the Creator."[48] For, although she at one point hesitates to call Canada "a land of Canaan," criticizing those emigration writers who failed to recognize the "long years of unremitting and patient labour" that helped to foster this positive impression, her naturalist's eye nonetheless reveals a world dense with interesting and lovely features and articulate with the message of Christianity.[49] Plant by plant, what emerges in *Canadian Wild Flowers* and *Studies of Plant Life in Canada* is a garden sown and tended by God's hand – a landscape "where the flowers ... flourish, bloom and decay unseen but by the all-seeing eye of Him who adorns the lonely places of the earth, filling them with beauty and fragrance."[50]

Evidence of God's presence in the wilderness was the main source of its comfort for Traill; this is what inspires her to urge emigrant readers of *The Backwoods* struggling with isolation and privation to "discard all irrational and artificial wants and mere useless pursuits" and attend instead to "the natural history and botany of this new country, in which they will find a never-failing source of amusement and instruction, at once enlightening and elevating the mind. ... To the person who is capable of looking abroad into the beauties of nature, and adoring the Creator through his glorious works," she promised, "are opened stores of unmixed pleasure, which will not permit her to be dull or unhappy in the loneliest part of our Western Wilderness."[51] Traill sought to redefine lands that settlers most often perceived as in need of cultivation and refinement as lands that could themselves bring about cultivation and refinement in settlers. As she implies in *The Backwoods* when she is more moved by hearing the liturgy in "our lowly log-built church in the wilderness" than anywhere else, religious contemplation may be more easily accessed, and its significance more readily apparent, in the wilderness than in the civilized realm.[52]

Using the medium of botanical description as a vehicle for this message, Traill hearkens back to natural history's roots in natural theology.[53] If this aspect of her work is what makes her "a splendid anachronism" in the eyes of the historian Carl Berger, in the opinion of the young botanist, entomologist, and parliamentary librarian James Fletcher (who became a valued friend and edited her manuscript of *Studies*), it brought a depth of meaning to natural history that was missing from "the irreverent materialistic philosophy, falsely so-called, of too many of our contemporary naturalists."[54] Traill's approach to nature aligns her with a "reactionary" school of Victorian naturalists who "quaintly insisted on taking delight in nature" and for whom natural history was "a personal, evocative, aesthetic science," rather than the secular practice Fletcher alludes to here.[55] Fletcher perceived Traill's work not as an outmoded or reactionary approach, but as a "thoroughly and patently original" contribution to the field of botanical study. Although he characterizes the experience of reading her *Studies* as one of "communing with nature," he reassures her that her powers of observation and description carry the impact of her natural history beyond mere appreciation.[56] "With regard to your disclaiming the title of botanist," he gently chides, "I wish that a fraction of one percent of the students of plants who call themselves botanist, could use their eyes half as well as you have done. I think indeed your work of describing all the wild plants, in your book, so accurately that each could have the name applied to it without doubt, is one of the greatest botanical triumphs which anyone could achieve."[57]

Appreciation alone may well have been enough for Traill, however. Her expressed hope, as she states in the opening pages of *Canadian Wild Flowers*, was that her work would "foster a love for the native plants of Canada."[58] Her attention to accuracy serves this desire as much as it facilitates the identification of species. As the specificity of the above statement – with its references to "native" vegetation and to "Canada" – suggests, a religious appreciation for nature was to be complemented by a patriotic affection for the uniqueness of the Canadian environment. Setting out as she does in *The Backwoods of Canada* "to redeem this country from the censure cast on it by a very clever gentleman I once met in London, who said, 'the flowers were without perfume ... the birds without song,'" she emphasizes in her botanical guides the ways in which Canada's wildlife is, if not always superior, then at the very least equal to that of the old world.[59] She is quick to point out, for example, that though "[v]ery lovely are the Water Lilies of England, ... their fair sisters of the New World excel them in size and fragrance."[60] And in *Studies*, she proudly remarks that the Canadian wilderness contains in untended profusion species coveted by gardeners back in England: "Everyone is familiar with that pretty, ornamental garden shrub, the Snow-berry, so often seen in English shrubberies, as well as in our Canadian gardens; but every admirer of it does not know that it is a native of the Dominion and may be found growing in uncultivated luxuriance on the banks of streams and inland waters, on the rocky banks of rapid rivers and lonely lakes, whose surface has never been ruffled by the keel of the white man's boat, spots known only to the Indian hunter or the adventurous fur-trapper."[61] Statements such as these regard wild species as desirable for even the most discerning of English gardeners. The subtle message is that the products of this country are enough, and that there is little need to improve the landscape by introducing species from Europe. Traill did not always oppose importing plants and flowers – on the contrary, in *The Backwoods* she closes one of her letters with a request that "flower-seeds, and the stones of plums, damsons, bullace, pips of the best kinds of apples" be sent from England.[62] Yet by the time she compiled her *Studies*, her growing affection for native plants and flowers had surpassed her desire to recover the English flora she left behind. Her patriotic message surfaces more explicitly in a criticism levelled at "Canadian ladies of taste" so preoccupied with "collecting exotic specimens" of "rare and costly" ferns that they remain unaware "that our own woods, and swamps, and rocks, afford many beautiful species not less admirable than those that are sold by the nursery-man at high prices."[63] In Traill's view, the Canadian wilderness contained rich stores of readily accessible natural objects to entice local gardeners and collectors as well as devout ramblers in search of God.

Furthermore, Canada's wilderness held literary interest, as Traill's many references to poetry and writing show. She repeatedly describes nature as a great "book" in need of transcription.[64] To her, it amply compensated for the dearth of other forms of cultural meaning in the young colony. "Here," Traill admits, "there are no historical associations, no legendary tales of those that come before us. Fancy would starve for lack of marvellous food to keep her alive in the backwoods"; and yet, "[i]f its volume of history is yet a blank, that of Nature is open, and eloquently marked by the finger of God; and from its pages I can extract a thousand sources of amusement and interest."[65] Traill's famous remark encapsulates the way in which the "illustration of natural history, and by extension of habitat, provided Europeans with a new understanding of the meaning of place" in "a land devoid of cities, palaces, gardens, canals, and aqueducts."[66] One source of pleasure she "extracts" is poetic: to move through Traill's flora is to move through an inventory of poems, fragments of which float among her petals, berries, and trees. The words of William Shakespeare, Robert Herrick, John Milton, Felicia Hemans, Sir Walter Scott, and the American poet William Cullen Bryant, among others, adorn her descriptions, making her Canadian wilderness resonate with long-established literary tradition. Thus, the "Canadian production ... wholly Canadian in its execution" of which Traill boasts in the preface of *Canadian Wild Flowers* extends into an imaginative realm that pays no heed to borders.[67] If these associations further legitimate Canada's native productions, both floral and literary, they also comfort the emigrant who feels acutely the loss of her cultural heritage. Just as the sight of the buttercup becomes "precious to the heart of the lonely immigrant who hails it as a tiny link between himself and his early home life," the sounds of familiar verses bring the world left behind closer to the land adopted.[68]

In addition to revealing similarities between Canadian and English flora, colonial natural history introduced the pleasures of describing Indigenous species and landscapes on which the settler could focus her growing love for her adopted country and mark her place there. Bringing her into contact with pockets of land that remained largely untouched by settlers, Traill's explorations of the wilderness led her to conclude that "[m]any an un-named flower exists" that some "fortunate naturalist" might one day "have his name conferred upon."[69] She was one such "fortunate naturalist": not only did she "take the liberty of bestowing names upon [nameless plants] according to inclination or fancy," but "Mrs Traill's Shield Fern," which she was the first European to identify, was named for her.[70] Like Adam in Eden, she gave new shape and meaning to her surroundings. She cast herself as the "floral godmother" of her region and described herself as among the first to name and provide "written descriptions" of landscapes that had thus far been defined only by "unlettered Indians" and settlers of the older, "hardy" breed who had little time for more than haphazard attempts.[71]

Traill's interest in naming signals another literary, or at least linguistic, appropriation of the wilderness that served, among other purposes, to establish an original relation between writers and the land. For Traill, inventing names was a way to inscribe herself – and by association emigrant experiences, imaginative proclivities, and cultural associations – into the increasingly legible text of the natural world. In a century defined by the struggles of emigrant writers to adapt imported languages and forms to unfamiliar colonial landscapes, this was significant. For Ballstadt, Traill's natural history is the most elemental form of an emerging Canadian literary tradition. He suggests that "Traill was one of the first to fulfil the directive of the early critics that the first step in the creation of a Canadian literature ought to be to take inventory of the distinctive features of the new country before more sophisticated forms of literature are pursued."[72] Looking to nature as a starting point for a new national literature was, in fact, in keeping with a nineteenth-century trend, for in this century in particular natural history "molded vision and put its stamp on language" by "transmut[ing] natural objects into texts."[73] Foucault, too, posits a special connection between natural history and "the origin of language": in its "fundamental articulation of the visible," he writes, natural history provides "the first confrontation of language and things"; "to know nature," he proposes, "is, in fact, to build upon the basis of language a true language, one that will reveal the conditions in which all language is possible and the limits within which it can have a domain of validity."[74]

Indeed, natural history allows us to see the world impressing itself upon language and thus generating the most intimate kind of text-map. Traill's botanical descriptions not only invite readers to revise their impressions of the Canadian wilderness, but also challenge them to refresh the language they use to describe it. Her recurrent interest in what makes a good name and what does not reveals a writer highly attuned to the power of language and the role it plays in understanding and connecting with the world. She expresses a critical view of scientific nomenclature, which in her opinion yields only "harsh-sounding, unmeaning" names, and prefers instead the more "poetical" ones that provide either "a sort of biography of the plant" or "an insight into the history of the flower we study, beyond the mere structure and definition of its parts."[75] Here, she edges towards a transparent relation between words and things by which "[t]he plant" itself, as Foucault would later put it, could appear to be "engraved in the material of the language into which it has been transposed, and," in the process of being read, "recomposes its pure form before the reader's very eyes."[76]

In a call for fresh, living metaphors that would directly reveal the world she saw and felt, Traill equally disapproves of those "old Greek or Saxon names" that "had reference to heathen deities or some strange idea or fancied resemblance to things, the likeness to which we cannot now see."[77] Her concern with meaningful naming practices works its way into her descriptions of specific flowers: for instance, "Enchanter's Night-shade" causes her to muse:

> With so ominous a name we might naturally expect to find some sad, lurid-looking, poisonous weed or sombre-leaved climber, instead of a very delicate, innocent-looking, leafy plant, with thin, light-green foliage, and tiny white or pale pink blossoms, dotted with minute spots of pale yellow. ... One can hardly imagine so inoffensive a little flower being introduced by the ancient Sybils into connexion with their unholy rites, nor understand why its classical name, *Circaea*, after a horrible old enchantress, should have been retained by our modern botanists.[78]

Traill sought the same vividness, clarity, and authenticity in names, it seems, that she strove for in her botanical descriptions. These goals served a literary aim as well as a scientific one. Aesthetic sensibilities surface in Traill's praises of "prettily sounding" names invented by "florists and herbalists of former times," such as "'Ladies' Tresses,' 'Sweet Cicely,' ... 'Mary-gold,'" and "Ladies' Slipper."[79] As she suggests in the first description (of a violet) in *Studies*, "the very name" of a flower could contain and create "music and poetry" – these, and not the pragmatic order of scientific inventory, would invigorate the alliance between humankind and nature.[80]

An Indigenous Ecology

Traill felt that the emigrant's was neither the most authentic nor the most poetic voice for the Canadian wilderness. In her view, the land's Indigenous inhabitants were its true poets, in contrast with the "more prosaic" settlers.[81] It was not uncommon for imperial natural histories to represent Indigenous peoples as part of the landscape, describing their attributes and ways of life alongside those of flora and fauna – making them part of the inventory, so to speak. Traill does this very thing in her book *Lady Mary and Her Nurse*. In *Canadian Wild Flowers* and *Studies*, however, the Anishinaabeg are fellow inhabitants of the backwoods and naturalists in their own right, to whose "authority" she defers on several occasions.[82] In *Studies*, she briefly expounds on the relationship between Indigenous languages and the land, underscoring that "Indian names have always some foundation" that reflects their "peculiar circumstances" and therefore acquire "a sort of historical value among the people."[83] She gives the example of "The Lake of the

Burning Plains," a name that refers to the Anishinaabe practice of burning brush to encourage the growth of deer grass and thus their ability to hunt deer on what was now called the Rice Lake Plains.

Extensive reflections on the literary value of Indigenous names appear in *Pearls and Pebbles; or, Notes of an Old Naturalist* (1894), an eclectic collection of natural history essays, anecdotes, and personal reflections compiled late in her life. There, Traill urges readers to consider the poetry of Indigenous names such as "Miskodeed" and "Moccasin flower" that appear alongside English ones in her botanical texts: "Judging from the natural reticence of the dusky-skinned Indian, one would not suppose him capable of conceiving one poetical idea, yet under the stolid and apparently unimaginative exterior there lies a store of imagery, drawn from the natural objects around him, which he studies more carefully than we do our most interesting books ... [H]e seeks for no rhymes in which to clothe his simple thoughts, no flowery verse; but there is poetry in his speech, and a musical ring in the names he has given to the rivers, lakes and flowers that is absent in ours."[84] Traill did not escape from reiterating prevalent essentializing, paternalistic attitudes towards Indigenous peoples. Here, she echoes a principle of the four stages theory of social development that identified in peoples of the "savage" and "pastoral" stages a tendency towards poetic utterance.[85] Traill's simplistic defence of Indigenous languages nonetheless sharpens her desire for a more perfect union between the land and the words used to describe it. She envies Indigenous peoples' "expressive language" that either described nature directly and concretely – as does the name "Otonabee" (the river on the banks of which the Traills had settled), which means "flashing water running fast" – or mirrored its sounds, as does the lamentation "Wo-ho-ha-no-min," which seemed to her to be "an imitation of the mournful cry" of the long-eared owl. The unique poetics of Anishinaabemowin extended, as Traill saw it, to the names that the Anishinaabeg had bestowed on the geographical and botanical features of their country, which, she writes, "are both descriptive and characteristic, and in some instances contain the germ of local or distinctive history, which change or mispronunciation would obliterate for ever."[86]

The lament that follows for either the loss of the significance of certain names or the erasure of the names themselves is instructive for readers of her natural history, as well: "What a pity it is that the meanings of all the Indian names remaining to our lakes, rivers or cities are not understood and made familiar; and greater pity still, that in some cases they have been set aside to make room for European names that have no significance to Canadians."[87] Even as she seeks to define the same landscape afresh from her own perspective, Traill also attempts to preserve what threads of the Indigenous significance of the Canadian wilderness she can, albeit in an patchwork manner: only here and there does she include actual Anishinaabe names, although she offers descriptions of "Indian Turnip," "Indian Hemp," "Indian Bean," "Indian Tobacco," "Indian Pipe," and "Indian Grass," and frequently refers to Indigenous uses for various other plants. Her attention to their practice of harvesting the wild rice (for which Rice Lake was named), however, develops into the most sustained defence of their claim to the area. She moves from an aesthetic description of "the low Rice islands" on the lake that, "as they catch the rays of the sun take the form of sands glowing with yellow light," to an account of Indigenous women harvesting the ripened grains in their canoes "to give pleasant, nourishing and satisfying food to her hungry family," to pointed remarks about the rice's increasing scarcity.[88]

The wilderness Traill describes is not a pristine space unadulterated by human activity, but rather a place that had long sustained human life and been marked by it. If, to a certain extent, "[b]y naming and defining the Canadian terrain, Catharine banishes strangeness, exerts control, [and] imposes a masculine logos of rational order on the tangle of a new Eden" (as Fowler suggests), it is also the case that by gesturing to Indigneous people who defined the land in their own ways, she exposes the complexities of "making [the land] one's own" in a colonial context.[89] Like Moodie, she shares the wilderness, and the task of describing it, with people with prior claims who still hold the key to many of its secrets: they alone know where to find the "Indian Grass," she tells her readers, or how to extract the "virtues" of the poisonous "Blue Cohosh."[90] Traill's natural history models its desires for a closer connection between settler culture and the wilderness after this perceived sympathy between the land, its Indigenous inhabitants, and language. At the same time, Traill writes elegiacally about this "uncared-for race" that is, she believes, "fast fading away like many of the native plants," at one point noting that "[w]ere it not going beyond the bounds of my subject, I might plead earnestly in behalf of my destitute, and too much neglected, Indian sisters and dwell upon their wants and trials."[91] As she lays her own "grid" over the wilderness, however, she remarks on the impact that some of the ways in which settlers have reshaped the land – drawn borders, carved roads, and established villages, for instance – are having on its Indigenous peoples. She refers to the Mississauga of Rice Lake now "[c]onfined to their villages" and therefore cut off from "the resources that formerly helped to maintain them," and to the Mohawk hunting grounds on the south shore of the lake "now all under cultivation."[92] She also creates a haunting image of a village where "[t]he Indian treads the busy streets, where once the Deer stole forth from its leafy covert in the dense Cedar swamp, where now stands the lofty church or busy mart. That lofty tree alone," she writes, "remains a memorial of the Indian's hunting grounds, and he himself stalks along those crowded streets the shadow of a dying race."[93] In such moments, Traill emerges from the recesses of her wilderness to lament the changing contours of the land and its economies.

Challenging the Settler Map

Traill's interest in ecological transformation extended to Darwinian speculation about the "causes and effects as regards the physical geography of our land" on which, she imagines, "once a very different order of things existed"; ultimately, however, as Elizabeth Thompson stresses, "Darwin's ideas cannot explain or contain the abrupt changes of pioneering," the shock of which runs through Traill's natural history writings.[94] She was keenly aware of settlement's ecological impact. If, upon first entering the colony, she "watched the progress of cultivation" in regions that she initially describes as "rugged and inhospitable ... with positive pleasure," by the time she reached Peterborough, where "[t]he plains" were being "sold off in park lots," she had already begun to recognize the potential of settlement to mar the landscape as well as enhance it: "I much fear the natural beauties of this lovely spot will be soon spoiled."[95] This fear would remain with her – and be repeatedly confirmed – over the remainder of her life. From observations of her own family's land, she concludes that "[t]he same plants do not grow on cleared land that formerly occupied the same spot when it was covered with forest-trees" and speculates that "[s]ome years hence [even] the timbers that are now burned up will be regretted."[96]

A survey of the body of writing that Traill produced over her long career in Canada reveals a shift in her characterization of land-clearing activities. Although the struggle between settlers and the forest is a difficult one in *The Backwoods*, in *Studies* settler domination of nature is portrayed as swift and devastating. "To-day," she observes, "I go forth into the woods and discover some interesting plant, which I desire to see unfolded in perfection; a few weeks pass, and lo! the axe of the chopper has done its work, the trees are leveled to the earth, the fire has passed over the ground and the blackness of desolation has taken the place of verdure and living vegetation."[97] She describes the woodsmans' work with animated grief, the forest becoming, under her pen, a noble victim of a tragic end: "the lonely echoes of the forest are ringing with the blows of the sturdy axeman on the devoted trunk – and many a vigorous blow is struck before that forest giant inclines its dark-plumed head, and with a rending crash, measures its length upon the groaning and trembling earth."[98] The "devoted" tree, "giant" though it may be, is no match for the "sturdy axeman." In her objections to the fate of wild nature, Traill simultaneously mourns the loss of native wildlife and the displacement and perceived imminent disappearance of Indigenous peoples. With regards to both, however, she stanches her regret with the myth of progress and necessity, her rhetoric of inevitability foreclosing the possibility of any alternative to the takeover of land and resources by Europeans. She attributes the destruction of the wilderness to an unstoppable and necessary force of which she is a part: "such things," she grants, "are among the 'must be' of colonial life, and so it is useless to grumble."[99]

At the same time, her regret about the "disappearing Indian" as well as for the native plants she has grown to know and love has a role to play in a quiet but nonetheless powerful vision of wilderness conservation. In addition to the appreciation she solicits for the wilderness as a unique, complex, self-sustaining, intricate, and balanced natural landscape – or, in today's terms, ecosystem – its significance as the home of Canada's first peoples (and first poets) combines, in Traill's botanical texts, with its significance as a rich and vital source of aesthetic, intellectual, and spiritual inspiration for emigrants, to deepen her readers' interest in and affection for what she repeatedly reminds them is a vulnerable landscape. In *Canadian Wild Flowers* and *Studies*, botanical description becomes a medium for a broad appeal that anticipates enduring environmental concerns about the destruction of a range of complex habitats in order to support an agriculture- and resource-based economy. Traill's natural history, as Marianne Gosztonyi Ainley points out, "explored issues that concerned few Canadians in the late nineteenth century, such as the need to preserve fragile habitats and create national parks," ideas that placed her "in the forefront of natural history and conservation in Canada."[100] Traill's most explicit proto-environmental message is a call to create botanical gardens that would preserve "some record" of the "uses" and "beauties" of the "woods ... and the plants they nourished and shaded" before they "are utterly despoiled" by settlers.[101] This model, while innovative for its time and place, relegates the wilderness to a clearly demarcated space not unlike modern national parks in a manner that shifts but nonetheless maintains the rigid boundary that her botanical writing otherwise challenges. The botanical garden and its accompanying "record," it seems, would function not unlike a museum – a monument filled with relics of something no longer a living part of the present.

Traill's own "record," however, implicitly proposes another model of conservation that invokes neither the boundaries nor the museum-like quality of the botanical garden. Her natural history posits a more integrated relationship between humankind and nature that depends on mutual adaptation between two entities – wilderness and civilization – overlapping to share the same geographical space. In the close contact they both document and encourage, as well as in the respect they elicit for the wilderness as a unique and beautiful part of God's creation, her botanical texts convey a fluid, continuous interaction between humans and nature. Guiding readers into the dense and labyrinthine vegetation, her neatly ordered catalogues invite them to reimagine the wilderness landscape as a place of retreat, spiritual betterment, and leisure; as a vital and beautiful part of Canadian life, as well as an important resource. If in the process Traill brings cultural values such as religion and aesthetic and intellectual refinement to the wilderness, she equally brings those of the wilderness to civilization. The "wild garden" of which she boasts, with its "twenty-two different kinds of Ferns, brought from the woods and swampy ground about the neighbourhood," along with several other native varieties of flora, exemplifies the integration of wilderness into a domestic landscape that had been overwhelmingly defined in opposition to it.[102] Indeed, the way in which Fitzgibbon arranges the wild flower specimens not only to show their botanical features, but also to suggest their aesthetic beauty, complements this breaking down of the boundary between wild nature and settler culture. Advocating the appreciation and use of native species over imported ones, Traill works against the trend of "ecological imperialism" that was contributing to the destruction of wild landscapes in Canada and dissolves the distinction between "wilderness" and "garden" that formed a basis of colonial land appropriation.[103]

In the process, she replaces traditional images of human dominion over nature not with vulnerability, as Moodie does, but with balanced cohabitation.

Traill's wild garden is a microcosm of her vision of the wider settler landscape in which she also promotes the benefits of allowing the wild to shape the cultivated. Buried in her botanical studies is an implicit message that leaving room for wild nature and agricultural land to coexist would maintain not only an ecologically, aesthetically, and culturally rich topography to be enjoyed by the growing population, but also the delicate natural balance upon which farmers depended. Convinced of a direct connection between the native vegetation of the land, the richness of its soil, the purity of its water, and the quality of its climate, Traill worries that the destruction of wilderness was upsetting a balance in the natural world that was beneficial to agriculture – even if dense tracts of forest and bog were, at first glance, not. "Many of our inland creeks and springs," she writes, "take their rise from, and are cherished in the deep shade of the Cedar and Tamarac swamps. When these reservoirs are cut down and destroyed much of the fertility of the land will be lost. People are only now beginning to learn the uses and value of the trees that they destroy; looking only from one point of view they regard them as enemies."[104] Once again, readers are compelled to complicate their perspective of the wilderness, to see it from a "point of view" broader than that of nineteenth-century settlers eager to transform it as quickly as possible into farms, towns, and cities. In addition to "the drying up of ... inland streams and smaller tributary waters," the loss of native woodland, Traill warns, would also eventually cause the climate to change, which observers had noted in other countries and therefore would also be "an established fact" in Canada.[105] "If this be so," she argues, "then surely it behooves the legislators of this country to devise laws to protect future generations from similar evils, by preventing the entire destruction of the native trees. There are large tracts of Crown Lands yet in the power of the Government, and reserves might be made or laws enacted by which the valuable products of the soil might be in some measure protected. Let our wise, far-seeing statesmen see to it."[106] Traill's call for conservation is both bold and prescient. It reaches beyond a model that seeks merely to preserve some record of a long-lost original nature, as the national parks would seek to do. It asks, rather, that readers appreciate – and that "legislators" protect – the wilderness as an important and integrated part of the emerging settler landscape.

When Berger claims that "natural history was born of wonder and nurtured by greed," he identifies a paradox that, to varying degrees, inflects all expressions of natural history, both scientific and amateur.[107] While on the one hand natural history did indeed serve British and Canadian imperial and colonial interests by identifying wilderness areas suitable for development and therefore destruction, on the other hand it laid the foundation for wilderness conservation by revealing to settlers the native treasures that were increasingly threatened by the "march of civilization." In Traill's work, wonder rather than greed is the prevailing sentiment, and accordingly her natural history cannot be understood only as a method of appropriation or domestication; for, to quote Stephen Greenblatt, "wonder continually reminds us that our grasp of the world is incomplete."[108] Even as she labours to capture the Canadian wilderness in careful descriptions, to align it with the designs of poets, and to contain it in her tidy volumes, the sense that it nonetheless remains ultimately beyond her understanding and control is ever-present. It even surfaces in her description, early in *Studies*, of a "common little weed that is known by the familiar name of Carpetweed, a small Polygonum, that grows at our doors and often troubles us to root up, from its persevering habits and wiry roots. It is crushed by the foot and bruised, but springs again as if unharmed beneath our tread, and flourishes under all circumstances, however adverse."[109] This humble plant – like the unruly one she labels "mesembryanthum" in *The Backwoods of Canada* – offers "lessons" about maintaining "courage" in the face of enormous challenges, but only by exemplifying nature's persistent disregard for the settlers' attempts to subdue it.[110] Examples of wild nature's imperviousness to human control are not uncommon. To peruse Traill's botanical writings is to meander through vegetation that is forever spilling over the neat lines of her botanical "grid" – to witness not, ultimately, specimens singled out for human consumption, but rather an interconnected web of living things that have much to teach the emigrant naturalist.

In Traill's hands, natural history illuminated the topography that most distinguished Canada from England, but that was diminishing under the flags of first Britain and then the Dominion. Although she believed that the colony could not expand and develop into a nation without extensive human impact on the land, Traill also hoped this human intervention need not entail a wholesale eradication of wilderness, even in settled areas. Her inventory of its features is reverent and affectionate, as well as an attempt to persuade other "emigrants from the dear Old Country" to look at Canada's unique ecologies with fresh eyes.[111] She asked them to see, in the dense tangle of wild nature, neither a resource to thoughtlessly appropriate, nor a blank slate to shape into a man-made landscape reminiscent of agricultural Britain, nor a no-man's land to avoid altogether, but something worth knowing and ultimately preserving for its own sake.

In *Making Ontario*, a history of the impact of colonial settlement on the land in that province, J. David Wood remarks that in the process of transfiguring the land from wild to cultivated, "what was gained was the material progress of tens of thousands of settlers," but "what was lost was the awesome complex of eastern woodland plants and animals that stood in the way of agriculture."[112] Traill was not the first writer to observe first-hand the enormous destruction associated with colonization. In *Three Years in Canada*, MacTaggart laments:

> Our wish seems to be to despise the good things which the country naturally affords in abundance, and to introduce into it, with much care and labour, those things which we and our forefathers were accustomed to. We cut down the beautiful umbrellas that Nature has prepared to hinder the sun from glowing upon us; we frighten and extirpate the game which breed and thrive so plentifully in the woods. Where are the herds of deer, and flocks of turkeys now? – they are retired with their friend the Indian to remote territories. And where are the fish that gambolled in shady pools? – why, the pools are dried up in summer's drought, and the trout are no more.

"Where, then, are our boasted improvements?" he asks.[113] When Traill celebrates the spread of natural history across the Dominion, noting that the enthusiasm for collecting native plants was growing "even in remote inland villages," she looks not to those elements of natural history that facilitated the appropriation of wilderness resources, but rather to those that enhanced settlers' feeling for what they were losing in this process: "It is true a new race of vegetables takes possession of the ground," she writes, "but something has been lost."[114] Both appreciation and conservation depend at once on a respect for wilderness as other – which is to say, a biological community that humans could neither create nor improve upon – *and* on a respect for wilderness as nonetheless compatible with, and in fact necessary to, human civilization. Traill's natural history thus breaks down the boundary between

Canada's settler society and wild nature, and reveals a treasure trove of resources that could improve the lives of emigrants in countless ways, including by simply being allowed to exist. Modest as were its pleas, her natural history carved out a space for Traill at the forefront of the conservation movement that required, above all, such reimaginings of Canada's endangered wild spaces.

Chapter Four

Writing and Reading the Northwest: George Monro Grant and the Palimpsest of Settler Space

While Catharine Parr Traill was busy training her readers' eyes on the details of her local forests, meadows, and swamps, she only occasionally alluded to the emerging country's wider geography. Her son William had moved out to the "Wild North Land" of the "North-West Provinces," as Traill called them, in 1862 as an employee of the Hudson's Bay Company, and was likely among the "kind friends" who sent her plant specimens from the prairies.[1] In her books, however, "Canada" remains localized in the eastern forests and clearings. The dramatic transformation of the nineteenth-century settler spatial imaginary would eventually encompass this Wild North Land as well, as the Dominion expanded and Canada assumed something closer to its current shape. This chapter considers the imaginative metamorphosis of the northwest from a space marked by its distance from, and incongruity with, Canada in the east, into a habitable place continuous with it. It explores the expansionist spirit that motivated the reinscription of the northwest as Dominion territory, and the book that gave this spirit its first and fullest popular iteration: George Monro Grant's widely read narrative, *Ocean to Ocean: Sandford Fleming's Expedition through Canada in 1872* (1873).

Grant may be better known to historians than to literary scholars. An influential liberal-minded Presbyterian minister in Halifax, an ardent Tory supporter of Confederation and the Canadian Pacific Railway, and a professor of divinity and principal of Queen's University from 1877 until his death in 1902, Grant was an important figure in early Canadian intellectual life; his descendants include the philosopher George Parkin Grant and the historian and former federal Liberal Party leader Michael Ignatieff. In 1872, Grant took leave from his post at St Matthew's Presbyterian Church in Halifax to accompany Sanford

Fleming, the Canadian Pacific Railway's chief engineer and a member of Grant's congregation, as secretary as he travelled the proposed railway route. *Ocean to Ocean* recounts this journey in the form of a daily diary. The book has garnered less attention in recent literary studies than the popular two-volume *Picturesque Canada: The Country as It Was and Is*, a richly illustrated compendium of essays to which Grant contributed as both editor and writer between 1882 and 1884. Yet *Ocean to Ocean* is a powerful work of literary cartography, and as the author's son and biographer William Lawson Grant attests, it "made a sensation, and several editions were called for."[2] The book conforms to a number of genres and descriptions. According to Joseph Edmund Collins, a friend and mentor of the Confederation Poets, it is "a sort of pastoral poem, written in prose, containing a wholesome spice of the practical with the exuberant and the spiritual"; it has since been described as a "travel narrative" fuelled with "immense hope, far-reaching vision, and imaginative westward dreaming," an "adventure story," a "mythic chronicle," and "an important document in Canadian cultural history."[3]

Whatever else it might be, *Ocean to Ocean* is primarily a book about land. In the conclusion, Grant underscores the purpose of the journey and the changing sense of space that motivated it: "To find out something about the real extent and resources of our Dominion, to know whether we had room and verge for an Empire or were doomed to be merely a cluster of Atlantic Provinces, ending to the west in a fertile but comparatively insignificant peninsula in Lake Huron, was the object that attracted a busy man from his ordinary work, on what friends called an absurd and perilous enterprise."[4] Despite the potential in the expedition for heroic tales suited to nineteenth-century adventure stories and national myth-making, readers learn less about the men who made the expedition than they do about the ground over which they trod. The narrative includes detailed descriptions "so that others might see, as far as possible, a photograph of what we saw and thought from day to day," ultimately feeling as though they had "accompanied us on our long journey."[5] Grant thus carries his readers from the settled towns and farmlands of southern Ontario through the lake-strewn boreal shield until it softens into prairie, across the prairie until it wrinkles into foothills, and finally over the sharper, bolder contours of the Rocky Mountains to the Pacific Ocean. Weaving together topographical description and inventory, travelogue, political treatise, poetic and religious musings, photography, and cartography, he appeals to armchair travellers as well as prospective settlers, extending their range of vision across what was becoming a vastly different configuration of the emerging nation.

The Dominion's purchase of Rupert's Land in 1869 marked a monumental shift in the colonial Canadian spatial imaginary. In 1816, John Strachan, the influential Anglican clergyman from York (now Toronto), had declared that "'no British colony will ever approach nearer than twelve or thirteen hundred miles' to Red River," let alone cross the continent.[6] When the British adventurers Viscount Milton and W.B. Cheadle published their popular book *The North-West Passage by Land* almost fifty years later, their readers would encounter a terrain still dominated by wolverines, coyotes, and Indigenous and Metis hunters, with the odd European trapper, trader, missionary, or adventurer among them. *Ocean to Ocean* followed closely on the heels of the British army officer William F. Butler's *Great Lone Land* (1872), with its powerful images of a final frontier of "unknown savage tribes, long days of saddle-travel, long nights of chilling bivouac, silence, separation, and space!"[7] *Ocean to Ocean* brought into view places that, in 1873, few Canadians had laid eyes on – places that, to many easterners, remained "comparatively unknown, and therefore supposed to be dangerous."[8] Grant countered lingering impressions of the northwest as "a sub-arctic region" menaced by "hailstorms, hostile Indians, and grasshoppers," "British Columbia a sea of mountains," and "new Ontario a barren wilderness effectually separating Eastern from Western Canada."[9] Anticipating the nation that the CPR's iron path would soon reshape, *Ocean to Ocean* became the first book of its kind to envision the Dominion as a unified territory from sea to sea.

In both editions, cartographic illustrations complement the emerging view of the land: while a small-scale map of the route in its entirety folds out from the back of the revised and enlarged edition, the first edition (to which I refer throughout this chapter unless otherwise specified) is punctuated by a linked series of large-scale maps. Most of these were copied from maps supplied by Captain John Palliser, who made his own expedition to the eastern edge of the Rockies in 1857, and Joseph Trutch, the first lieutenant governor of the new province of British Columbia. Along with the other illustrations, which are mainly landscapes drawn "from photographs and on this account ... of special interest,"[10] these maps anchor Grant's lively anecdotes and topographical descriptions in an expansive yet detailed sense of space. They at once enhance the aura of accuracy that the author cultivates and significantly complicate this rhetoric by presenting the land as a text to be written on as well as read.

Assuring his readers that "the one merit this diary aspires to is to be a frank and truthful narrative," Grant characterizes *Ocean to Ocean* as the product of a direct encounter with the land, assembled from candid eyewitness observations during more than three months of travel through it.[11] Such disclaimers are numerous and, in the estimation of David Jackel, Grant protests too much. In his reading of *Ocean to Ocean*, Jackel emphasizes the extent to which this "round, unvarnish'd tale" is transformed by Grant's "artistry" into a carefully crafted expression of imperialist and expansionist propaganda that presents "not so much a vision of the west as it was in 1872 but of the west as Canada of the post-Confederation period wanted it to be."[12] Indeed, insofar as it is calculated to inspire patriotic confidence in the transformation of the northwest into an "earthly paradise" for emigrants, "a practical solution" to poverty and famine in Britain, and a new colonial and trade empire for Canada, *Ocean to Ocean* confirms that "the mode of eyewitness reportage is a rhetorical device" used to stamp fabulous chimeras with documentary truth.[13] Exuberantly optimistic and charged with national and imperial ambition, *Ocean to Ocean* presents the country as Grant claims to have seen it: "Looking back over the vast breadth of the Dominion when our journeyings were ended," he writes, "it rolled out before us like a panorama, varied and magnificent enough to stir the dullest spirit into patriotic emotion."[14]

While Grant's professed "authority of ... eyewitness" supports the creation of myth, however, his commitment to objectivity also hinders it, particularly when what he wants to see – an empty land whose story is waiting to be told – is at odds with what he does see – an inhabited place already inscribed with stories, European and, especially, Indigenous. Jackel unwittingly makes this point when he posits that "*nearly* everything [Grant] discovered on the prairies appeared to conform to the shape of that national policy formulated in eastern Canada" – the word "nearly" signalling a lacuna in Grant's attempt to present an uncomplicated vision of new Dominion territory.[15] As it maps and mythologizes the northwest as Dominion territory, *Ocean to Ocean* also foregrounds its textual and the heteroglossic character. The land comes into focus not just as a collection of topographical regions and natural resources, but also as an assemblage of signs that are read, interpreted, and written – or, as the book ultimately shows, *re*read, *re*interpreted, and *re*written – in and from the terrain and its inhabitants. Imbuing the land with layers of meaning potentially endless in number and scope, these signs reveal the fragile and contingent nature of any single colonial inscription of the space.

Inscribing the Northwest

Throughout *Ocean to Ocean*, the land itself becomes a kind of text, a space marked with signs of passage. Nowhere is this clearer than the moment, mid-way through the journey, when the survey party discovers the "testimony" of "the Canadians who proceeded [*sic*] Milton and Cheadle," in 1862, "chalked with red keil on a large spruce tree in the swamp, five or six miles to the east of the [McLeod] river" near the foothills of the Rocky Mountains. In the ten intervening years, much of the writing has faded, but the "words and half-words" that remain are traces of a narrative written about and recorded upon the land.[16] A passing moment in a travelogue that covers more than three months and four-thousand-odd miles, these traces are no sooner described than they are left behind. Nonetheless, the anecdote focuses on how the land has literally been inscribed by other explorers and travellers eager to mark their passage. The discovery connects Fleming's expedition with a long line of explorers and adventurers who marked the landscape with writing as well as other signs – with Henry Kelsey, for instance, who drove a wooden cross into the ground at "deerings point / ... In token," he writes, "of my being there"; with Sir Alexander Mackenzie, who wrote his name on a rock face; and with William Clark (of Lewis and Clark), who carved his into a pine tree.[17] As "accepted token[s] of imperial possession," such inscriptions, notes Bentley, "announce" the "appropriation" of the land as loudly as its legal purchase.[18]

Grant and his party, then, join the ranks of explorers who, by leaving their mark, have turned the land itself into a map that tells the story of its conquest. If he never writes his own name into the actual topography of the northwest, he participates in the process of marking it as Dominion territory in other ways – most obviously when he suggests that certain peaks of the Rocky Mountains ought to be named in honour of "the statesmen who have been most identified with the great project" of the CPR.[19] Grant's own lasting inscription is made, of course, in the narrative of *Ocean to Ocean* itself, which links the names and experiences of the men who participated in the trip, and the expansionist aims that guided them, to the route over which they travelled.

Following the proposed route of the railway, Grant's narrative mirrors Canada's geographical reorientation westward, with British Columbia serving as both the literal and symbolic terminus of the country. The opening sentence neatly sums up this reorientation, along with the mobility and unity that accompanied it: "Travel a thousand miles up a great river; more than another thousand along great lakes and a succession of smaller lakes; a thousand miles across rolling prairies; and another thousand through woods and over three great ranges of mountains, and you have travelled from Ocean to Ocean through Canada."[20] This sentence anticipates the panoramic view that unfurls in his imagination at the end of the book. Then in their heyday, panoramas were large, moving landscape paintings that gave viewers the illusion of travel that Grant's diary seeks to replicate. As Anne Baker notes, this medium "went hand in hand with the growing power of the British Empire and with American expansion," and, indeed, her description of the "vicarious visual experience" that panoramas offered Americans who "were dealing with dimensions ... that could not be grasped or conquered simply by climbing to an elevated point and surveying the horizon" resonates strongly with the experience of reading Grant's Canadian narrative, which seeks not only to display but also to possess a terrain that "seemed, like the panoramas themselves, to be continually unrolling to include more territory."[21]

This opening sentence also subjects a vast and varied geography to the synthesizing control of the survey, conveying in words the effect of the "Map of the Dominion of Canada between Lake Superior and the Pacific Ocean" that folds out from the back cover of the revised and enlarged edition. Recalling Adam Hood Burwell's desire, in *Talbot Road*, to "see, as on a single sheet" a land "unbroken and complete," the sentence's parallel structure at once divides the country into geographical regions and draws those regions together. It is into this still new political whole that the northwest becomes subsumed: "All this Country is a single Colony of the British Empire," Grant continues, "and this Colony is dreaming magnificent dreams of a future when it shall be the 'Greater Britain,' and the highway across which the fabrics and products of Asia shall be carried, to the Eastern as well as to the Western sides of the Atlantic."[22]

Fulfilment of this dream depended upon the completion of the CPR. While Fleming's party travelled across the country by "[c]anoe and barge, buck-board and cart, saddle and pack-horse, buggy and express wagon,"[23] in an important sense the book stands in for a journey that readers would one day be able to make themselves by rail. *Ocean to Ocean* continues a story already being told in the east – not by other writers, but by the railways that traversed the country between Halifax and Moncton and that, "in a year or two," would run as far west as Toronto. Accordingly, despite the book's titular commitment to showcasing the entire sweep of the continent, Grant glosses over in a few pages the terrain of the eastern provinces, which, he stresses, "may at any time be seen" from the window of a Pullman car. Charting instead those "out-of-the-way places" that remained beyond the reach of most of his readers, Grant's cartographic story might be said properly to begin in the lesser-known landscapes that skirted Lakes Huron and Superior.[24] Similarly, the return trip east through the United States is covered in a hasty two-and-a-quarter pages of text. British Columbia, then, and the Pacific Ocean lapping at its shores, serves for all intents and purposes as the book's monumental end.

Both the linear form of the book and its dominant metaphors further this vision of sweeping unity. Without the railway, Grant warns, the new province of British Columbia would be "a mere finger-joint separated from its own body."[25] The corporeal metaphor – reminiscent of John Dunbar Moodie's description of roads as arteries in *Roughing It in the Bush* – suggests the organic necessity and the urgency of the project. With the railway imminent, Grant reassures readers that British Columbia "has now the prospect of being no longer a dissevered limb, but of being connected by iron, as well as sympathetic, bands with its trunk; and it is already receiving the pulses of the larger life," and that "larger life" will one day enable the northwest to "be the very backbone of the Dominion."[26]

Although at the end of the journey he feels the proximity of "Japan and China, sleeping peacefully" just across the Pacific, the northwest represents much more than simply a link in a chain of imperial trade that would make up for failed attempts to find a northwest passage; it becomes a crucial part of the Dominion's geopolitical space, a valuable possession in its own right.[27] To this end, Grant enriches his expansive panoramic and cartographic views with topographical details of each region he passes through, accumulating an inventory of signs of the land's abundant fertility and resources. John Macoun, the botanist who joined the party and would go on to become the Dominion botanist for the Geological and Natural History Survey of Canada in 1881 (from which position he supported the publication of Traill's *Studies of Plant Life in Canada*), plays a significant role in Grant's representation of the northwest as suitable for settlement. Macoun's prominence in *Ocean to Ocean* conveys the extent to which "[t]he tasks of identification, inventory, and mapmaking gave form to the idea of a transcontinental national existence" as well as to more localized imaginaries.[28] A self-taught "enthusiast to the point of self-caricature,"[29] Macoun is frequently a source of comic relief in the narrative. Yet the botanist's eccentric but infectious passion for collecting specimens of local – and, to Europeans, often new – species of vegetation along the route transforms the unknown into a realm of infinite potential. From the "abundant" reserves of "wild fruits" such as "raspberries, currants, gooseberries, and tomatoes; flowers like the convolvulus, roses, a great profusion of asters, wild kallas, water-lilies on the ponds, wild chives on the rocks in the streams" with which he fills in the terrain around Lake Superior to the "great masses of natural hay" and "vetches ... from four to six feet high" that he finds in the parkland, he relishes everywhere signs of the land's fecundity.[30] This botanical inventory is enriched by minerals along Lake Superior, coal on the prairies, and salmon in British Columbia, which among other potential commodities combine to excite new interest in places long deemed undesirable for settlement, but which, Grant writes, now invitingly call, "come, plough, sow, and reap us."[31]

Macoun's inventories generate mental images of the kinds of vast collections that could be found at the international exhibitions that, by the mid-nineteenth century, had already begun to awaken interest and pride in Canada's resources.[32] They also at once register and feed a desire for habitable land that had been growing in Canada for some time. Behind these descriptions lie the anxieties of a Dominion that had recognized shrinking reserves in the east: when Canada purchased Rupert's Land, all the arable land in Ontario was already under cultivation and the Geological Survey had revealed a dearth of coal reserves throughout the eastern colonies. As Grant underscores, many feared that, if Canada did not acquire it first, the northwest with its potential reserves of agricultural land and sources of coal and other minerals would simply "drop like a ripe pear into the lap of the Republic" of the United States.[33] More pointed in its expansionist aims than Traill's natural history – and, perhaps unsurprisingly given the sheer size of the country in question, apparently unburdened by her concerns for conservation – *Ocean to Ocean* lays symbolic claim to each feature that it catalogues.

Every reference to the richness and variety of vegetation and potential resources builds towards Grant's resounding conclusion: "Thank God, we have a country." "Over all this we had travelled, and it was all our own," he writes; "given" by "God ... into our possession," each of region's attributes will benefit Canada once the country has been opened up (to borrow one of Grant's favourite tropes) for settlers.[34] In anticipation of the transformation of land into private property, Grant superimposes an imagined landscape of farms and homesteads onto the topography. En route to Fort Carlton, for instance, he describes "a country of unequalled beauty and fertility; of swelling uplands enclosing in their hollows lakelets, the homes of snipe, plover and duck, fringed with tall reeds, and surrounded by a belt of soft woods; long reaches of rich lowlands, with hillsides spreading gently away from them, on which we were always imagining the houses of the owners; avenues of whispering trees through which we rode on, without ever coming to lodge or gate."[35] The proliferation of such seductive descriptors as "unequalled," "swelling," "tall," "soft," "long," "rich," and "spreading" in this passage both recalls Cary and Burwell's effusive topographical descriptions and anticipates Annette Kolodny's comparison, in *The Lay of the Land*, of the male colonial enterprise with the possession of a feminized, virgin continent. This is no hostile frontier; on the contrary, it is an inviting landscape that exudes gentle fecundity and pastoral restfulness. Over this, Grant imagines a future prospect of houses, lodges, avenues, and gates – distinct markers of landed country gentility, embedded in an order that the Dominion Lands Survey, established in 1869 and destined to become one of the largest survey projects in the world, had already begun to impose on the grasslands, which would be carved up into townships and farm sections over the following decades. Grant's vision amounts to a complete reorganization of space, a map that precedes a territory that he prophesies will emerge with the construction of the railroad.

His inscription of the land also draws out its aesthetic value that both emphasizes the picturesque qualities of each region and conveys the sublime grandeur of its scenery with metaphors and similes that link it with Europe. The great rocks known as "the portals of Lake Superior" become "bold warders" that usher the travellers into a body of water as "wild, masterful, and dreaded as the Black Sea." The wide prairie sky is "like a great shield of which only the rim is embossed" with clouds. An approaching evening storm turns the sky "such blue as Titian loved to paint: blue, that those who have seen only dull English skies say is nowhere to be seen but on canvas or in heaven"; then transforms the scene into "a picture for Rosa Bonheur; the storm driving across the vast treeless prairie, and the men and horses yielding to or fighting against it." Entering the Rocky Mountains, the dramatic form of Roche Miette – one of the most imposing mountain peaks in the Athabasca River Valley – shows its "sphinx-like head with [a] swelling Elizabethan ruff of sandstone and shales all around the neck, save on one side where a corrugated mass of party coloured strata twisted like a coil of serpents."[36]

As I.S. MacLaren remarks, such fanciful descriptions elide the difficulties that mountains posed for CPR surveyors such as Walter Moberly, whose unpublished account "disabuses one of any romantic illusions of the beauty of mountainous terrain to a surveyor."[37] Yet the tropes with which Grant transforms an imposing mountain into a natural sculpture reminiscent of both Elizabethan England and classical antiquity, like those that invite readers to imagine wide prairie skies as shields and Titian paintings, provide orientation of another sort. Reinforcing the northwest's continuity with Europe and marking it as a space of cultural, as well as agricultural, fertility (as Thomas Cary and Adam Hood Burwell also did), they introduce meanings that begin to transform the northwest into a new kind of place.

Reconceiving the emerging Dominion as a panoramic spectacle, an east-to-west route, a living body, and an Edenic and almost limitless expanse of fertile land and sublime scenery, these tropes do much to solidify the reader's sense of the land as a blank slate that facilitates the displacement and dispossession of Indigenous nations. Grant's only explicit reference to Indigenous mapping is dismissive. In the introductory chapter, where he observes that "[n]o white man is known to have crossed from the Upper Ottawa to Lake Superior or Lake Winnipeg," he writes:

> There were maps of the country, dotted with lakes and lacustrine rivers here and there; but these had been made up largely from sketches, on bits of birch-bark or paper, and the verbal descriptions of Indians; and, as the Indian has little or no conception of scale or bearings; as in drawing the picture of a lake, for instance, when his sheet of paper was too narrow, he would, without warning, continue the lake up or down the side; an utterly erroneous idea of the surface of the country was given.[38]

In addition to appearing unmapped, much of the land, according to Grant's descriptions, is also underused – as he observes of the Ojibway, for example: "Poor creatures! not much use have they ever made of the land." Finally, the land is unwritten, for "here," he writes, "there never had been bold moss troopers, and there were no 'Tales of the Borders.' Crees, and Sioux and Ojibbeways may have gone in the war path against each other, and have hunted the buffalo over the plains to the west, but there has been no Walter Scott or even Wilson to gather up and record their legends, and hand down the fame of the braves."[39] Steeped in the literary heritage of his Scottish ancestry, Grant seizes on the lack of a similar written legacy in the northwest. In this moment, he recalls Butler who, looking out over the prairie for the first time two years earlier, saw only an "ocean" of grass on which "men have come and gone, leaving behind them no track, no vestige, of their presence."[40] Similarly, Grant mythologizes a land in which "[s]ilence reigned everywhere, broken only by the harsh cry of wild fowl rising from lakelets, or the grouse-like whirr of the prairie hen on its short flight."[41] From the thousands of miles of apparently uninhabited land that echo through his opening sentence, to the unified vision that stirs his patriotic emotion in the conculsion, the panoramic lines of *Ocean to Ocean* foreground this sense of silent space that is waiting for settlers to write their own stories into it.

The Northwest as Deep Map

The specificity of the diary form introduces into Grant's sweeping vision the richer and more complex textures of a land encountered not just as a blank slate, but also as a repository of pre-existing meaning. In the course of their day-to-day travel through it, his guides frequently break the "silence" that Grant observes: the "Iroquois canoe songs" that Baptiste (a guide from Caughnawaga) sings as he paddles Grant and his party across Lake Nameukan and the voices of the Blackfoot, who gather around their campfires to tell "[m]any a stirring tale of headlong valour ... as, long ago in moated castles, bards sang the deeds of knights-errant, and fired the blood of the rising generation," are just two examples of songs and stories that Grant hears.[42] If he denies them their full significance because they are unwritten, he nonetheless points to a parallel literary legacy of oral traditions that imbue the land with culture and history. Written, albeit in a fleeting and fragmentary way, into his own narrative, these songs and stories begin to define, and even to create, Indigenous territory that will help to shape his conception of Canada.

The Indigenous maps to which Grant alludes in the aforementioned passage, although untranslatable to those who rely on the European system of "scale" and "bearings," also remind the reader of the gap between Indigenous knowledge and white inexperience in the geography through which Grant travelled. Western exploration exposed many clashes between European and Indigenous cartographic techniques. A notable western example is Ac ko mok ki's Map, originally drawn in the snow by Ac ko mok ki (translated as Old Swan), a Siksika headman, for the explorer and fur trader Peter Fidler in 1801. Sent to London in 1802, Old Swan's map was incorporated into one of Aaron Arrowsmith's maps that would later befuddle Lewis and Clark on their expedition up the Missouri River in 1805. As Theodore Binnema argues, "[w]e *must* assume that other societies devised sophisticated cartographic styles that members of the community readily understood even if modern Western readers find them baffling" – in his reading of the map, he points to its complex inscription of Blackfoot culture on the plains between the North Saskatchewan and Yellowstone Rivers. In other cases, translation was easier: Henry Youle Hind told of meeting "an old Indian seventy years of age" who, "[w]ith a peace of charred wood ... drew on the floor a map of the Qu'Appelle Valley from the Fishing Lakes to the Assiniboine, showing every little creek so accurately that I easily recognised them." Such maps attest to the wide-ranging geographical and territorial knowledge that already marked the land. Fleming's survey party depended on this kind of knowledge from their Indigenous and Metis guides, knowledge to which Grant would draw specific attention in the enlarged and revised edition of *Ocean to Ocean* when he remarks that "[a]n Indian on his own ground or water is never mistaken."[43]

While he notes the dearth of written texts, Grant reads signs of Indigenous economic and cultural practices on the surface of the land. Against his imaginary vision of "avenues," "lodge[s]," and "gate[s]" on the prairies, for example, the discovery of bison bones calls to mind another scene, this time of the land's recent past, "[w]hen the buffalo ranged through this country." Traversing "a vast plain" that "had once been a favourite resort of the buffalo," Grant recalls passing "in the course of the day more than a score of skulls that were bleaching on the prairie."[44] The buffalo skulls might easily be read as traces of the receding presence of both the bison and Indigenous peoples in this region. A mere six years later, the bison would be virtually nonexistent on the Canadian Prairies, the nations that depended on them devastated with starvation. Grant's image, however, bears scant resemblance to Butler's elegiac portrait, in *Great Lone Land*, of the prairies as a vast bison graveyard. Everywhere Butler turned, he writes, "the same wrecks of the monarch of the prairie lie thickly strewn over the surface ... the relics of the great fight waged by man against the brute creation"; he describes an "unspeakable melancholy" hanging over the land, "silent and deserted – the Indian and the buffalo gone, the settler not yet come."[45]

In a sense, Butler was clearing the way for writers like Grant, who has an obvious interest in "the settler not yet come" and who alludes several times to *Great Lone Land* as an influential precursor to *Ocean to Ocean*. In Grant's account, however, bison bones are read as signs not of vanishing Indians, but of their presence. His observation that "the other bones had been of course chopped and boiled by the Indian women for the oil in them" underlines the centrality of the bison in the Indigenous hunting economy – his "of course" subtly countering stereotypes of Indigenous people as indiscriminate and wasteful hunters. Moreover, the bones occasion a humorous exchange between Fleming and the Cree servant, Souzie, that exposes the clash of European and Indigenous perceptions. Souzie cannot fathom the white man's interest in the skulls as "specimens": "the idea of the great O-ghe-ma coming hundreds of miles, to carry home bones with no marrow in them, was inexplicable" to Souzie, who descends "into fits of laughing" whenever he thinks of this practice.[46] Like the encounter that Susanna Moodie describes between her "Indian friends" and the map of Canada, this exchange brings to the fore two contesting realities, two ways of being, two diverging sets of knowledge in competition to define this place. As legible signs of Indigenous land use on what was, in European terms, still largely unmapped terrain, the bones here serve not to expand so much as to delimit the "great breadths of unoccupied land" that Grant also describes.[47]

Ocean to Ocean is full of such signs. In addition to bones and graves that point to the past, footpaths, place names, villages and encampments, and monuments define the landscape over which he travels, reminding readers of the land's rich Indigenous history and present use and occupancy. Fragments of larger narratives combine with encounters with individuals who communicate a profound sense of belonging to the land to remind readers that this colonized space is neither *terra nullius* nor vacant land, but a palimpsest of competing meanings. This palimpsest is part of Grant's literary cartography. Indeed, the maps that illustrate the first edition reveal rather than conceal the intersecting stories that make up the northwest's complex textuality. Unlike the single map that unfolds from the cover of the second edition, which shows only the bold outlines of the land as seen from a distance, these maps are close and detailed enough to expose other layers in a multifaceted geographical story to which the cartographer contributes his own narrative. In the map depicting the terrain from Fort Pitt to Edmonton, for example, writing almost overwhelms the map's contour lines (figure 7). One region, for instance, is "hilly country" with "good pasture," but "no wood" – for agricultural settlement, an inferior tract, it would seem, to the "open poplar woods, rich in soil and Fine pasture" that is found closer to Fort Edmonton. Just as its longer descriptions reveal the land from the point of view of the prospective settler who requires shelter, good soil, and fuel, many names of locales and landmarks tell the story of exploration and emigration and (most evidently, perhaps, in a name like "Victoria") betray the colonist's desire for a direct and unproblematic transplantation of European associations – and hence customs, values, and history – into the "New World" landscape.

These inscriptions reveal little about the land's present or past (at least beyond what serves its imagined colonial future). Others, however, reveal more: "Lac la Biche" (a trace of French habitation) and "White Fish Lake," we read, are "favourite wintering places for free trading trappers from Red River," while the areas near "Vermillion River," the "Beaver Lakes," and "Battle River" remain the domain of the "Cree Ind[ians]." What emerges from the written elements of this map is not a clean, unambiguous narrative of colonial appropriation, but a tangled and at times competing set of stories. "Manito L[ake]," "Eyebrow Hill," "Fishing L[ake]," "North Saskatchewan Riv[er]," "Beaver," "Horse," "Moose," "Dried Meat," "Four Blackfoot," and "Masquachis Bear's Hills" point to a set of histories that intersects and in some ways conflicts with those of "Victoria" and "Fort Pitt." The map as a whole thus presents not a "socially empty space"[48] of the kind of which geographers such as Harley are rightly suspicious but, rather, a complex human territory thick with social meaning encoded by Indigenous as well as colonial logics.

Like the maps that illustrate his narrative, Grant also frames the land as a text that is both written on and read. At one point he remarks that "[i]t is interesting as one travels in the great North-west to note, how the two old allies of the middle ages have left their marks on the whole of this great country. The name of almost every river, creek, mountain or district is either French or Scotch."[49] Many of the names that Grant includes in his own text-map, however, are neither French nor Scotch, but Cree or Anishinaabe. Untranslated, these names elude the English-speaking reader, becoming in effect what de Certeau would call "verbal relics" of "lost stories and opaque acts"[50] rather than legible signs of meaning. But meaning of another kind emerges from the unfamiliar sounds of "Windegoostigwan" and "Kaogassikok," "Shebandowan," "Assiniboine," and "Saskatchewan" – among the many others that have been spared what Grant refers to as "our absurd custom of discarding the muscial, expressive, Indian names for ridiculously inappropriate,

European ones."[51] Merely pronouncing these words reminds readers that English is not the only language spoken here, and the settler is not the first to inscribe the meanings of this place and call it home.

Place names such as "Horse Hill" and "Lobstick Creek," for their part, enhance the region's cultural significance when they prompt Grant to tell the stories that lie behind them: "Horse Hill, so called from a fight between the Crees and Blackfeet, forty years ago," and "Lobstick Creek," named for "the Indian or half-breed monument to a friend or to a man he delights to honour," inscribe a shorthand record of First Nations and Metis history and relationships with each other and with the geography.[52] Grant's ability to read and interpret this shorthand is limited, and yet every time he pauses to do so he shows that the land is not just soil and rock, water and wood, but a cultural landscape that is tied to the histories and identities of particular communities.

To the extent that it incorporates paths, traces, and glimpses of other stories into his narrative, *Ocean to Ocean* foreshadows another genre of literary cartography that would later develop on this very same landscape: the deep map. Countering the flatness both of the plains and of "the pull of grandiose myth" with a narrative form "in which many voices speak, many, often contradictory, histories are told, and many ideologies cross, coexist, and collide," deep map writers "survey both the widest and smallest of spaces to elicit the most subtle and profound forms of knowledge"; but, like the rhizomatic map that recognizes the infinite mappable objects and perspectives in any given place, the deep map conveys the "indeterminate complexity" of a place, while "the place itself remains elusive and incompletely limned."[53] Attached as it is to the metanarrative of expansionism, *Ocean to Ocean* can do little more than loosely anticipate the deep mapping of the prairies by writers such as Wallace Stegner, who would develop the literary deep map as a form that weaves fiction, memoir, and history of the prairie grasslands south of where Grant travelled.[54] But the palimpsestic qualities of his spatial narrative prompt consideration of "the heteroglossic nature of all mapping"; as John Pickles, following Derrida, argues: "Language – even imperial language – is never univocal, but always a dialogue of histories, cultures and places shaped by those it possesses as well as those that seek to control it."[55] To regard Grant's northwest as a palimpsest is to understand the nineteenth-century project of Canada's expansion into those territories as only a partial and incomplete process of overwriting in an already occupied space, not a vacant one. The traces that mark the northwest in *Ocean to Ocean* complicate its sense of

Dominion territory with a fragmentary yet enduring counter-map that has the potential to destablize Grant's territorializing inscription. This is, and always was, contested space.

Indeed, throughout the book, Indigenous habitation is clearly expressed as ownership. On the banks of Rainy River at the south end of Lake of the Woods, for instance, Fleming's party is approached by "an old stately looking Indian, a chief, we were informed, and the father of Blackstone ... Pointing, with outstretched arms, north, south, east and west, he told us that all the land had been his people's, and that he now, in their name, asked for some return for our passage through it."[56] The chief's words recall Grant's earlier reference to "the great Ojibbeway ... nation that extends from the St Lawrence to the Red River" – a reference that reinscribes "[t]he extent of territory occupied by the Ojibway" that George Copway (Kagegahgahbowh) had described some years before in his bestselling *Traditional History and Characteristic Sketches of the Ojibway Nation* (1850): "When the Champlain traders met them in 1610, its eastern boundary was marked by the waters of Lakes Huron and Michigan. The mountain ridge, lying between Lake Superior and the frozen Bay, was its northern barrier. On the west, a forest, beyond which an almost boundless prairie. On the south, a valley, by Lake Superior, thence to the southern part of Michigan. The land within these boundaries has always been known as the country of the Ojibways."[57] The chief's outstretched arms confirm his historic relationship to the territory that Copway more sharply defines. The differences between Copway and Grant's spatializing gestures, however, are not insignificant. Despite Copway's account of wars with the Iroquois and the Sioux, which suggests the precariousness of these fiercely defended and shifting boundaries, there is a feeling of stability and permanence in his present perfect "has always been" – a feeling that arguably begins to break down with Grant's past perfect "had been." While Copway underscores the ongoing significance of this ancestral homeland, Grant, perhaps in anticipation of the treaty to which he points in the same chapter, implies the immanent extinguishment of Indigenous title. And yet, if "had been" can also be interpreted as past perfect continuous, it may well persist as an expression of historic title in which Copway's text-map resurfaces in the chief's gesture. Like the treaties that negotiated the transfer and sharing of land, the apparently simple exchange signifies a complicated negotiation of territory, rife with all the contradictions of colonial overwriting and Indigenous habitation.

A parallel incident, if slightly different in tone, occurs much later as the survey party is crossing the prairies. "At one point," Grant writes, "the road ran within two or three miles of the Saskatchewan, and a prominent hill on the other side was recognized by *Souzie*. 'Ah!' said he to his master, 'I know now where I am'; and, on arriving at the camp, he went up to Frank and formally shook hands with him, to indicate that he welcomed him to his country."[58] Both of these exchanges, as Grant represents them, are friendly. The chief, we are told, only desires "breakfast" in return for passage through his people's land; and Souzie communicates nothing if not warm hospitality to the party for which he has served as guide. Although laconic by comparison, however, Souzie's words are no less eloquent than the chief's. In the middle of the prairies, where Grant has been waxing poetic about the prospect of colonial settlement on a land of great natural beauty, his gesture occasions a meaningful pause that, read as literary cartography, marks the territorial boundary of his Cree nation. Gentle though they are, these encounters interrupt the easy narrative of territorial appropriation to emphasize the relationships between Indigenous peoples, their lands, and the newcomers, who are in these moments positioned as guests. Both the chief, who signals the debt that newcomers owe, and Souzie, who embodies the benevolence upon which they rely, are individuals who speak with authority for territories that are neither silent nor unmapped.

These encounters mitigate the extent to which Indigenous peoples can be pushed off the land by being relegated to either history or stereotype. Of the chief on the bank of Rainy River, Grant writes: "[i]t was astonishing with what dignity and force, long, rolling, musical sentences poured from the lips of one who would be carelessly classed by most people as a Savage, to whose views no regard should be paid."[59] In his indictment of the newcomers' prevailing attitudes towards Indigenous peoples, Grant might have had in mind the kinds of remarks that had prompted Catherine Suneegoh Sutton, an Ojibway missionary living near Sault Ste Marie (whose Anishinaabe name was Nah-nee-bah-wee-quay, or Upright Woman), to defend Indigenous land rights just a few years earlier. A vicious editorial in the *Leader* had compared the people of Goulais Bay and Batchawana to "monkeys" and called their reserves "publick nusiances." Sutton sardonically retorted that she "did not think monkeys lived so far north," and questioned the implied argument that "every band of indians" should be "drove on to the baran waste of granite rocks north of Lakes huron and superior [*sic*]"; moreover, she went on to ask, "why are indian reservations aney more a publick nusiance then large blocks of land bought and held by speculators [*sic*]"?[60] Whether or not Grant followed this exchange, he weaves his own defence of Indigenous humanity and land rights into the territorial vision of *Ocean to Ocean*, engaging in what could become heated debates.

Rather than interpreting the friendly encounters that he describes as simply propping up Grant's assertion that "there are no Indian difficulties in our North-west,"[61] we might read them as affirmations of important relationships between Indigenous peoples and newcomers that negotiate the meaning of the land as treaty territory. As the reader also learns, Souzie "had established confidential relations with Frank [Fleming's son] from the first, taught him Cree words, and told him long stories."[62] This friendship, rooted in the teaching of local language and literature, models the relationships that Grant celebrates throughout the book: relationships based on mutual goodwill, trust, and shared humanity, and on newcomers recognizing their role as guests on the land and listening and learning from its inhabitants.

From the very beginning of the book, Grant also makes clear that these relationships are nation to nation. In the context of broken treaty promises and ongoing Indigenous land claims in Canada, these relationships are not insignificant: as the Northwest Resistance of 1885 later demonstrated, things could go very wrong when they are not honoured. Grant has surprisingly little to say about the Metis. They were not included in the treaties, and Grant does not anticipate the complex iteration of sovereignty, land sharing, and nation building that, as Margery Fee demonstrates, emanated from Louis Riel's *Address to the Jury* that year.[63]

Grant's anxiety regarding the legitimacy of Canada's claim to the northwest, however, when it rises to the surface of his narrative, is unmistakable. Its most explicit expression occurs at Fort Frances, where "[a] thousand or twelve hundred Ojibbeways had assembled to confer with Mr Simpson, the Dominion Indian Commissioner, as to the terms on which they would allow free passage through, and settlement in, the country."[64] Even as he concludes that "some of them are vain, lazy, dirty, and improvident," Grant argues that

> whatever their natural defects, they surely have rights to this country, though they have never divided it up into separate personal holdings. They did not do so, simply because their idea was that the land was free

to all. Each tribe had its own ground, which extended over hundreds of miles, and every man had a full right to all of that as far as he could occupy it. Wherever he could walk, ride, or canoe, there the land and the water were his. ...

And now a foreign race is swarming over the country, to mark out lines, to erect fences, and to say "this is mine and not yours," till not an inch shall be left the original owner.[65]

This passage merges racist, Eurocentric opinions with a nonetheless forceful and convincing defence of Indigenous land rights. It tells a different story from the one first told by Locke and then promulgated by many early colonists, who denied Indigenous nations their rights to the land on the basis of their migratory hunter-gatherer cultures.[66] Instead, it detaches property from conventional British signs of individual ownership such as fences and settled labour. This model of territorial rights is thus more flexible and sympathetic to the Indigenous peoples of this country. The image of Grant's "swarming" settlers both recalls Burwell's image and makes it far more menacing, recasting the settler as a foreign invader coming to dispossess "the original owner" of what is rightfully his in terms that Euro-Canadian readers could readily appreciate. The question that follows is telling: "if 'a man may do what he likes with his own,'" Grant asks, "would they not be justified in refusing to admit one of us to their lakes and woods, and fighting us to the death on that issue?"[67]

His answer to this question is only implied; at this particular moment in the text, he dismisses it, resignedly making the case that "it is too late to argue the question" and that "[a]ll this may be inevitable."[68] In part, such statements defuse the tensions that Grant's counter-map introduces into the text. The rhetoric of inevitability subsumes Indigenous peoples' claims in an unstoppable future of colonial appropriation, appearing to relegate their rights to a past that it is already "too late" to recapture. Like the buffalo bones (which, as the remains of the dead, relegate the story of the plains bison and the communities that depended on them to the past), other traces of Indigenous land use perhaps fit all too easily into Grant's vision of a territory in the process of being irreversibly redefined by colonists. Indeed, he participates in this erasure when he elegiacally compares, for example, "the great number of cellar-like depressions along the banks of the [North Thompson] river [that mark] the sites of former dwellings" to "the sad mementoes of old clans to be seen in many a glen in the Highlands of

Scotlands [*sic*]."[69] Other signs, such as the bison skulls that are sent "as specimens to Ottawa," also become "mementoes," appropriated as relics of the receding history of a vanishing race.[70] Banished to an obsolete, almost mythic past, these signs become traces subsumed by a narrative of colonial domination that undermines their potential to subvert the key tropes of that narrative, tropes that work continually to imaginatively entrench the basis of what Daniel Coleman describes as "white civility" in Canadian culture: "[t]he denial of Indigenous presence in these lands, the disregard of pre-contact history, and the continuing suppression of First Peoples' claims to lands and sovereignty."[71]

It may be the case that all traces of an alternative, Indigenous mapping of the northwest that Grant admits into his narrative suffer the same fate as the "skull of the headless Indian" – a Shuswap presumed to have been killed and buried in two places by an Assiniboine "on his unsuccessful hunt for game" – that the party unearths en route to Kamloops.[72] That is, they are assimilated into a narrative that restricts their power to meaningfully disturb the book's colonial metanarrative. Both Grant's written account of the discovery of the Shuswap's skull and its accompanying illustration reveal an attitude of unquestioning conquest and appropriation among members of the survey party. Alongside the maps and photographically accurate illustrations that otherwise complement *Ocean to Ocean*, the drawing entitled "Skull of the Headless Indian" (figure 8) stands out as an anomaly. Unlike the book's otherwise naturalistic landscapes, there is nothing of the snapshot about this carefully staged still life. The Shuswap's skull rests like a memento mori on a closed copy of Milton and Cheadle's *North-West Passage by Land*, his spoon and scalping knife at intersecting angles below so that the overall effect resembles a skull and crossbones. The centrality of Milton and Cheadle's book in the composition pays homage to the earlier adventurers and implicitly grants them a kind of proprietorship over the Shuswap's story, which Grant's framing of it confirms when he refers to him as "Milton and Cheadle's 'Headless Indian.'"[73] Removed from their geographical context and artfully arranged on an artificial background, the Shuswap's remains are transformed into artefacts on display for the consumption of a readership in search of exotic curiosities. This illustration is a revealing sign of the book's artistry – a key, perhaps, to the ideological agenda behind its objective facade. Its effect is not unlike that of a conventionally emblematic cartouche in which the cartographer's political biases can be read more easily than in the more abstract and apparently (though never truly) neutral lines of the map itself.

The illustration of the Shuswap's remains epitomizes a practice of colonial appropriation that construes the Indigenous subject as an exotic other, his remains mere curiosities to which the colonial explorer is entitled. Grant's narrative of the party's discovery of the gravesite reflects a similar attitude: "Scratching the ground with his wooden spade the Dr was soon in possession of the skull and the rusty scalping knife, that had been thrown in beside it, and finding the old kettle near, he appropriated it too, and deposited all three with his baggage, as triumphantly as if he had rifled an Egyptian tomb."[74] Like the skulls of the bison on the prairies, the Shuswap's remains are displaced and reconstituted as part of an imperial inventory, rather than respected as human remains that are part of the land's living story. Thus relegated to the party's "baggage," such traces pose no apparent threat to Grant's colonial reinscription of the northwest. While these remains are different from the signs of ongoing Indigenous land use and occupation that he also notes, Grant's rhetoric of inevitability removes these, too, from their active present, and the sense of Indigenous territory as a whole threatens to disintegrate under the pressure of Canadian expansion. In this, Grant was no different from the majority of his contemporaries who represented Indigenous peoples as victims of the inevitable westward course of empire. At several points, he downplays the seriousness and relevance of active challenges to colonial expansion. With little inkling, for instance, that it would culminate in what at least one historian has since called a "civil war" in 1885, he dismisses the Metis resistance at Red River in 1869–70 as Riel's "little rebellion."[75] He goes so far as to concur that the eventual disappearance of Indigenous peoples "as a race ... is not unlikely. Almost all the Indians in the North-west are scrofulous."[76]

Powerful as it is, his belief in the vanishing race theory fails to hold up against what he sees, which includes not only those "christianized self-supporting communities" that "have multiplied and prospered" and "are beginning to ask for full freedom," but also the large numbers of "heathen Crees and Salteaux" who continue to hold their "great annual 'pow-wow'" at Jackfish-Lake River under the direction of "'medicine men' who have still much influence among them" – along with many other individuals and communities exhibiting their enduring cultural independence.[77] The limits of Grant's imagination are clear: he hopes for the imminent end of what he regards as "heathen" practices along with the "wild, wandering life" that is "inconsistent with modern requirements"[78] – that is, the emergent structures of agricultural and industrial capitalism. But as he also shows, that end has not arrived. The encounters that expose this fact reveal the posturing by which Grant relegates so many traces of Indigenous life in the northwest to a vanishing past as a fantasy of settler space.

Ultimately, Grant's vision of Canada incorporates a multiplicity of races and cultures. Describing "[a] walk through the streets of Victoria," for instance, he is delighted to find in "the little capital ... a small polyglot copy of the world":

> Its population is less than 5,000; but almost every nationality is represented. Greek fishermen, Kanaka sailors, Jewish and Scotch merchants, Chinese washerwomen or rather washermen, French, German and Yankee restaurant-keepers, English and Canadian officeholders and butchers, negro waiters and sweeps, Australian farmers and other varieties of the race, rub against each other, and apparently in the most friendly way. The sign-boards tell their own tale: "Own Shing, washing and ironing"; "Sam Hang," ditto; "Kwong Tai & Co., cigar store"; "Magasin Francais"; "Teutonic Hall, lager beer"; "Scotch House"; "Adelphic" and "San Francisco" saloons; "Oriental" and "New England" restaurants; "What Cheer Market," and "Play me off at ten pins," are all found within gunshot, interspersed with more common-place signs.[79]

This catalogue of ethnically defined civic spaces prefigures images of Canada as a mosaic of happily coexisting cultures. Grant adds: "[v]arious as are the nationalities and religions represented in Victoria; the people are wonderfully fused in one, and there is a general spirit of mutual toleration, kindness, and active good will that makes it a pleasant town to live in."[80] Ironically, as the historian Penelope Edmonds shows, during this period Victoria was becoming less, not more, ethnically diverse, and its society was considerably more frayed and ragged at its edges than Grant would have his readers believe; moreover, the conspicuous absence of First Nations signs in this urban landscape reflects concerted efforts to erase these members of Victoria society from its visible civic identity.[81] The spatial fiction that Grant upholds here, however, is an index of his faith that Canada could be an inclusive place. As he observes of the contested Red River territory, "after doing the fullest justice to the old settlers ... [t]here is room and to spare for all," and across the northwest "[w]e still have more good land than we know what to do with." Over this land he anticipates diverse peoples and communities bound by "[t]he tie of a common nationality."[82]

Drawing upon a sense of almost limitless geographical resources, *Ocean to Ocean* symbolically absorbs the land rights of Indigenous peoples into its national vision through an endorsement of treaties. Presented as a happy medium between the preservation and alienation of Indigenous title, treaties form an important component of Grant's paternal model of colonial-Indigenous relations.[83] As documents that delineate territories with words and signatures, treaties represent another way that Grant reinscribed the significance of the northwest. Arguing that they are the only means of providing "substantial justice and ... satisfaction to the Indians," Grant appeals to the idea of "the treaty commonwealth": the idea with which Locke qualified his theory of annexation through labour, and that, James (Sákéj) Youngblood Henderson argues, "respected Indigenous autonomy, ... accepted Indigenous land tenure and started the policy of fair and honest purchases from Indian tribes under British law."[84]

A treaty, writes Grant, "extinguishes their claims to the land" while also securing for each Indigenous community a territory that "no one can invade."[85] Construing the settler as an invader, this definition registers the impact of colonial expansion with sobering, if unintentional, ambivalence. As Irene Spry remarks, the reserve system that developed through the signing of Treaties 3 to 7 in the four years following the publication of *Ocean to Ocean* was "neither fully a matter of common property nor fully a matter of individual private property"; rather, it created spaces of "uneasy limbo" between the two.[86] This assessment throws into relief the idealism and naivety that underwrites Grant's panoramic vision of a great northwest in which Indigenous peoples figure prominently, where "the Ojibbeway is at home in his canoe" and "the Cree is equally at home on his horse" while the whole is yet "all our own."[87]

Grant's awareness of "the difficulties of drawing up a treaty that shall express the same thing to both parties" illuminates the tensions and contradictions in the negotiation of settler space.[88] Moreover, with a growing sense of urgency, in the enlarged and revised edition that first appeared in 1877 he would draw attention to the enduring stereotypes that had to be broken down in order for treaties to do the kind of "justice" of which he writes:

> Some people smile at the notion of treaties with a few thousand half-naked, painted savages. And to him who sees only the ludicrous in anything dif-

> ferent from his own use and wont, the scene may appear a travesty of treaty-making. ... [T]he Indian is a man, and God has implanted the sense of justice in the breast of all men. To the Indian his land or fishing ground is as important as it would be to you, and the memory of his fathers may be as sacred. Said the Lac Seul Chief at North-west Angle: "We do not wish that anyone should smile at our affairs, as we think our country is a large matter to us."[89]

Here Grant once again echoes the voices of Indigenous people that had risen across the country in defence of their lands. Mississauga Chief Peter Jones had also strategically appealed to British conceptions of property in his defence of Anishinaabe land: "Each tribe or body of Indians has its own range of country," he wrote, "and sometimes each family has its own hunting grounds, marked out by certain natural divisions, such as rivers, lakes, mountains, or ridges; and all the game within these bounds is considered their property as much as the cattle and fowl owned by a farmer on his own land."[90] Farther west, Chief Peguis had addressed the Aboriginal Protection Society at Red River in 1857 with a strong plea for treaties that would ensure the kind of justice that Grant describes: "[B]efore whites will again be permitted to take possession of our lands we wish that a fair and mutually advantageous treaty be entered into with my tribe ... and we ask ... a wise, discrete, and honourable man, who is known to have the interests of the Indian at heart, may be selected ... to see that he is fairly and justly dealt with for his land."[91] Grant added his voice to these pleas, impressing upon his readers that treaties must be fairly negotiated and honoured "to the letter and in the spirit" – that is, as both parties understood them through text and oral agreement alike. The northwest was, indeed, "a large matter" to which the treaties, along with the other possible mappings of the land from which they stem, collectively point.

Of all the texts on which I focus, *Ocean to Ocean* may be the clearest and most sustained celebration of Canada's imperial and colonizing imperatives. At the same time, there is much in the book that might have anticipated the critique of Canada's duplicitous myopia leading up to the Northwest Resistance that the Mohawk-English writer Tekahionwake (E. Pauline Johnson) would offer in her poem "A Cry from an Indian Wife" (which she performed on tour before publishing it in her 1895 collection *The White Wampum*). In Johnson's dramatic monologue, an "Indian wife" voices her conflicted feelings about sending her husband to join the resistance. At one point, she attempts to understand the government's actions: "They but forget we Indians owned the land / From ocean unto ocean; that they stand / Upon a soil that centuries agone / Was our sole kingdom and our right alone."[92] These lines address colonial forgetting, reinscribing not only the northwest but all of Canada as "Indian ... land." Reclaiming the overarching spatial image of *Ocean to Ocean* (which in turn derived from the Biblical image that John A. Macdonald had turned into an expansionist motto), these lines also remind us to read Grant's narrative, and other colonial texts like it, for their own mnemonic landscapes of Indigenous habitation, knowledge, and rights. The gestures that mark these things are significant. Neither Grant nor his readers should have forgotten what they meant.

Plotted along the route of the transcontinental railway, *Ocean to Ocean* transforms Canada's geographical space in a manner that, in some senses at least, encourages such forgetting. As Wolfgang Schivelbusch writes, "[t]he speed and mathematical directness with which the railroad proceeds through the terrain destroy the close relationship between the traveller and the travelled space. The space of landscape becomes, to apply Erwin Straus' concept, geographical space."[93] Recalling Cary and Burwell's poetics of the survey and the route, Grant showcases the power of literary cartography as a means of envisioning new colonial territories unfurling through the spatial rubrics of accessibility, mobility, and unity. Instead of the "infant" colony of *Abram's Plains* and *Talbot Road*, Grant describes a more mature Dominion that, in the face of diminishing exploitable land within its own borders, was "looking about for new worlds to conquer," as the *Globe* put it in 1856.[94] While there is much in *Ocean to Ocean* that "conquers" the land discursively, Grant nonetheless reminds us that to map the land is not just to mark it with one's own story; it is also to read prior inscriptions and to record the multiple and sometimes contradictory meanings of a place. Drawing attention to the textuality of the land, *Ocean to Ocean* reveals the layers of inscription and reinscription that attest to its complex possession. Canada, Grant suggests, did not assume its transcontinental shape by virtue only of metanarratives of empty land that allowed the Dominion to expand unimpeded. This shape was also premised on negotiations and good relations that inform current understandings of the treaties as the combination of oral and written agreements to share the land. Despite Grant's attempts to absorb signs of Indigenous habitation (and the negotiation, potential conflict, and shared space that it implies) into the myth of a budding transcontinental nation, the tensions persist between these signs and the expansionist story that he was charged with writing. These tensions leave their own imprint on the textual record, unsettling Grant's transformation of the northwest into an extension of the empire, and inviting us to read between the smooth lines of his text-map to a more tangled history of colonial appropriation.

Chapter Five

The Poet in Treaty Territory: The Literary Cartography of "The Height of Land"

This chapter returns to poetry, where this study began. Taking up Duncan Campbell Scott's "The Height of Land," it explores the relationship between negotiations of poetic and treaty territory. "The Height of Land" is a lyric poem that meditates on metaphysical concerns – concerns that transcend, and thus obscure, the poem's territorial underpinnings. Yet, not unlike the topographical poems discussed in chapter 1, "The Height of Land" is a poetic negotiation of both landscape and territory. The poem's metaphysical impetus cannot be entirely disentangled from the politics of its setting on the boundary of Treaty 9.

Scott is a significant and controversial figure in the literary cartography of Canada. As a member of the Confederation Poets and as a federal civil servant, he actively reimagined the contours of Canada's landscape both culturally and geographically. His contributions to literary culture are many and varied, but much recent scholarship centres around his role in the Department of Indian Affairs, where, seventeen years old and unable to afford the tuition for medical school, he began working as an accounts branch clerk in 1879. He remained in the department until 1932, serving as its deputy superintendent general for the last nineteen of those years. In 1885 – the year that the Canadian Pacific Railway was completed and Louis Riel hanged – Scott was still a relative newcomer. Nevertheless, as Brian Titley points out, he was an "ambitious young man who had recently been promoted to chief clerk and accountant," and on 27 July of that year, at not yet twenty-three years of age, he was asked to temporarily replace Lawrence Vankoughnet as acting deputy superintendent – a sign of the department's confidence in his abilities.[1] The seeds of many assimilationist policies for which Scott has come to stand, such as the prohibition of Potlatches, had been introduced the year before, yet he would make a lasting mark on Canadian history by expanding and articulating them.

Much of Scott's poetry has been read in the light (or shadow) of this career. While the majority of his lyric poems have nothing to do with his work as a civil servant and the specific sense of place and people that it fostered, several of his most enduring poetic works are rooted in a geographical sensibility drawn to the northern and boreal regions of Canada that fanned outward from the "crowded south" (to quote his own epithet) that was his home. These frequently anthologized poems invoke the remote rivers and lakes through which he travelled as an administrator and on recreational canoe trips with his friend and fellow poet Archibald Lampman. The toponyms that anchor titles such as "Night Hymns on Lake Nipigon" (or "Nepigon" in the 1905 version), "Spring on Mattagami" (1906), and "A Scene at Lake Manitou" (1935) bring into literary focus a geography that, like "the land" in his poem "Indian Place-Names" (1905), remains "murmurous" with an Indigenous history and spirit, at once real and imagined, of place.[2] In particular, his "Indian poems" have been read as imaginative offshoots of encounters with Indigenous peoples and their lands during the inspection and treaty-making trips that he made for the federal department, his poetic depictions of a "waning race" emblematic of the assimilationist attitudes and policies that the department espoused.[3]

From the perspective of a literary geographer, "The Height of Land" is a compelling example of literary cartography. An intensely lyrical engagement with the elusive meaning of life and artistic feeling, it is also a powerful poetic reinscription of Indigenous space: it is about land and a way of imaginatively inhabiting it. Not widely regarded as one of Scott's Indian poems (although Stan Dragland's hesitation on this point is a particularly fertile moment in his reading[4]), its topographical descriptions reverberate with the colonizing imperatives of Treaty 9, which Scott helped to negotiate with the Ojibway and Cree of northern Ontario during the summers of 1905 and 1906. Scott did not compose the poem until 1915,[5] yet its setting on the treaty's southern boundary subtly embeds it in the political space that the treaty embodied. Scott's encounter with the height of land was fraught with the task of transferring control of the territories of the Cree, Ojibway, and Oji-Cree (the Mushkegowuk and Anishinaabe peoples) to the Canadian government, whose primary interest was "to facilitate economic development and railway construction" in the region.[6] Like the treaty, the poem subjects the land to new forms of dreaming. It redefines this space as desired poetic territory: a spiritual resource to be occupied and ordered imaginatively.

The Territorial Underpinnings of Scott's Poem

A number of aspects of "The Height of Land" resist a literary-cartographic reading. Unlike the two topographical poems considered in chapter 1, this one does not anchor itself in a precise cartographic location. Beyond Lake Superior and Hudson Bay, it names no particular river, lake, or post, and therefore lacks the geographical specificity of an identified place. Moreover, its position in *Lundy's Lane and Other Poems* (1916), where it appears between "The November Pansy" and "New Year's Night, 1916" in the section "Lyrics, Songs and Sonnets," downplays its connection to geography, the treaty trips, and the Northern and "Indian" poems they generated. In keeping with the tradition of the greater romantic lyric and its emphasis on the workings of the mind, Scott's poet frequently leaves his physical surroundings behind to "deeply brood" – not on the topography that he so carefully describes, but on "the incomprehensibility of life" in the most metaphysical of senses.[7] As Tracy Ware notes, "The Height of Land" addresses such far-reaching themes as the "impermanence" of the universe, "the limitations of language," "the disjunction between man and nature," and the simultaneous allure and inadequacy of both "progressivist optimism" and "primitivist nostalgia," without appearing to be overly concerned with the material contexts of land and geography, place and space.[8]

Recently, however, critics have come to regard the geographical setting of "The Height of Land" as something more than incidental to the spiritual meditation that takes place therein. The poem's imaginative assimilation of baseland and hinterland visions into "one large geographical possibility," for instance, provides D.M.R. Bentley with his "phenomenological ground for Canadian poetry" in *The Gay]Grey Moose*. And Don McKay features the poem in his introduction to *Open Wide a Wilderness*, offering "the image of Duncan Campbell Scott at a portage on the height of land between the Lake Superior and Hudson Bay watersheds" as an icon of Canadian nature poetry and an emblematic expression of a modern and distinctively Canadian engagement with wilderness.[9] Behind McKay's reading of the poem lies Dragland's important study of Scott and Treaty 9, which roots "The Height of Land" "in the actual geography of the last phase of the 1906 [treaty] trip – the journey up the Pic River from Heron Bay, over the height of land, to Long Lake Post"; although, he suggests, "The Height of Land" likely combines memories of several places through which he passed on his treaty trips, including the Mattagami River.[10] These interventions have helped to connect this poem more clearly to its geographical context, yet they have not done enough to emphasize its subtle participation in the struggle over land that lies at the heart of colonial culture. Bentley's "geographical possibility" is ecological rather than political, and McKay, while registering both the treaty context and the unnerving presence of Indigenous figures and spirits in the poem, stops short of suggesting that it participates in the treaty's territorial impetus. Even Dragland has surprisingly little to say about the role that the treaty might play in the poem's imagined landscapes. After locating its setting on the boundary of Treaty 9, he goes on to read "The Height of Land" much as Ware, Kathy Mezei, and so many others have done – that is, as "a journey" not through treaty territory but rather "through the mind of the poet."[11]

Yet "The Height of Land" surveys and orders the northern landscape in ways that recall the appropriation and governance of land that Scott's work as a treaty commissioner epitomized. Its setting holds more than a canoe route, intricately described; more, too, than a northern aesthetic that anticipates the theosophical landscapes of Lawren Harris. It is also a contact zone across which colonial and Indigenous world views quietly but significantly shift and collide, the poet a stranger precariously poised in a landscape not fully his own. From the poet's cartographic sense of north and south, to the intimations of beginnings and endings that run through its imagery, to the unsettling Indigenous spirit of place that haunts its setting, "The Height of Land" is shaped by a colonial desire to reinscribe Mushkegowuk Territory as a place of spiritual homecoming for the non-Indigenous Canadian poet.

Scott recorded his impressions of the negotiations of Treaty 9 (also referred to as the James Bay Treaty) as well as of the geopolitical landscape that forms the fraught backdrop of "The Height of Land" in the 1906 essay that he (misleadingly) titled "The Last of the Indian Treaties." Anticipating the map showing the Indian treaties in Ontario that James L. Morris would hand-draw in 1931 (figure 9), Scott describes Canada as virtually covered by "a patch-work blanket" of treaties and surrenders. "A map colored to define their boundaries," he writes, "would show the province of Ontario clouted with them," and "as far north as the confines of the new provinces of Saskatchewan and Alberta the patches lie edge to edge." As the official means by which the Crown secured rights to Indigenous lands, these agreements were integral to the creation of "civilized Canada" as Scott understood it. He continues: "Until lately, however, the map would have shown a large portion of the province of Ontario uncovered by the treaty blanket. Extending north of the watershed that divides the streams flowing into Lakes Huron and Superior from those flowing into Hudson Bay, it reached James Bay on the north and the long curled ribbon of the Albany River, and comprised an area of 90,000 square miles, nearly twice as large as the State of New York."[12] Weaving together the concerns of the poet and the map-maker, the patchwork blanket metaphor (not unlike Adam Hood Burwell's conception of land-clearing as "re-clothing" in *Talbot Road*) represents the negotiation of treaties as a constitutive activity. Something is being added to the land rather than taken away from it, and a palpable uneasiness surrounds what has been left "uncovered" and thus subject to what Scott would refer to in 1914 as "overshadowing Indian title."[13]

A literary-geographic reading of "The Height of Land" reveals the extent to which the desires and fears that accompanied Canada's political and poetic reinscription of northwestern Ontario reverberate through the poem. Such a reading foregrounds the setting of the poem and its connection to a territorial vision that undergirds the poet's metaphysical flights from the land itself, giving the poem a deeper involvement with the question "Where" – and what – "Is Here?" Indeed, the poem's first line anticipates Frye's question with concrete directness: "Here," the poet declares, "is the height of land." Marking his confident arrival in a location that is significant at once as the destination of a day's travel and as the site of the powerful poetic mediation that follows, the adverb "here" focuses the reader immediately on geography. While not quite the picturesque promontory of the topographical poet, the height of land offers a point of elevation from which the landscape quickly comes into focus as the Precambrian shield, where "The watershed on either hand / Goes down to Hudson Bay / Or Lake Superior"; the poet and his crew, the reader learns,

> have come up through the spreading lakes
> From level to level, –
> Pitching our tents sometimes over a revel
> Of roses that nodded all night,
> Dreaming within our dreams,
> To wake at dawn and find that they were captured
> With no dew on their leaves;

Sometimes mid sheaves
Of bracken and dwarf-cornel, and again
On a wide blue-berry plain
Brushed with the shimmer of a bluebird's wing;
A rocky islet followed
With one lone poplar and a single nest
Of white-throat-sparrows that took no rest
But sang in dreams or woke to sing, –
To the last portage and the height of land.[14]

The hydrographic landscape of the canoe trip emerges both through Scott's descriptions of its flora and fauna and through the free verse form in which many of these descriptions unfold. Here, the irregular alternation of long and short lines evokes the "level[s]" of spreading lakes, the uneven rhyme pattern catching something of the rugged, asymmetrical beauty of the Precambrian shield. As literary cartography, Scott's poetic form evokes the canoeist's intimate view of the topography (rather than symmetrically framing or cutting across the land, as Cary and Burwell's regular couplets do). As he tends to be in the journal entries that he made during the treaty trips, he is also attentive to the natural history of the boreal landscape.[15] Spruce, poplar, and cedar make up its woods. Roses, bracken, dwarf cornel, blueberries, ferns, and mosses blanket the forest floor.[16] From the "rocky islet ... / With one lone poplar and a single nest / Of white-throat-sparrows that took no rest / But sang in dreams or woke to sing," to the smouldering bush fire and "lakelet foul with weedy growths / ... Where the paddle stirred unutterable stenches," Scott registers the complex beauty and texture of a boreal wilderness alive with colours, sounds, and smells.[17]

These intimate details of the region's topography and natural history give a concrete image of the poet's place in a geography that is sensed rather than directly observed:

Upon one hand
The lonely north enlaced with lakes and streams,
And the enormous targe of Hudson Bay,
Glimmering all night
In the cold arctic light;
On the other hand
The crowded southern land
With all the welter of the lives of men.[18]

Beyond the immediate scene of the camp, with its low-burning fires and encircling spruces, the poem conjures Hudson Bay looming, austere and cold, at the upper edge of the country, while crowds bustle in the cities and towns clustered along its southern border. The sense of place that Scott creates in this passage is cartographic rather than experiential: it is the product of an omniscient bird's-eye view that stretches the imagination beyond the immediate scene of the camp to encompass a far vaster geography. Like the speakers of *Abram's Plains* and *Talbot Road*, Scott's poet describes what he cannot possibly see, even from the highest point on the watershed. This felt space nonetheless etches itself into the poem with concrete immediacy, as if it were there before his very eyes.

Far from providing "only the background" for the poet's "sustained meditation,"[19] this geographical setting attaches the lyric to a politically significant cartographic sense of space, a territorial order that recalls the treaty's goals of appropriation and unification. Gordon Johnston, in his reading of the poem, points to the artificial polarity that underpins Scott's attention to the height of land: "The stunning fact about a watershed, as anyone knows who has stood on one," he writes, "is that things look very much the same on either side."[20] That Scott's height of land separates not only watersheds but also peoples and qualities of experience, however, subtly invokes its role as treaty boundary. Nevertheless, at the same time that it "partitions Canadian space into two antithetical zones,"[21] it gives the poet the 360-degree view that links the "lonely" north and "crowded" south in a single cartographic vision, echoing the unity that the treaty created as it allowed political and economic powers of the south to extend their reach into northern Ontario. The poet's easy survey of the province from its southernmost reaches to what in 1915, when Scott was writing the poem, had served as its northern boundary for only three years[22] – with the height of land stretching like a seam between them – recalls the image of Canada as a patchwork blanket in "The Last of the Indian Treaties."

Scott's Poetic Appropriation of the North

At first glance, Scott's "lonely north" in "The Height of Land" admits few vestiges of "overshadowing Indian title." Without going so far as to use the word "vacant" (the epithet that characterizes the North in his 1889 poem "Ottawa: Before Dawn"), Scott's stark and sweeping view of this apparently unoccupied region contrasts sharply with the concentration of people that distinguishes the south. The trope of vacancy or loneliness that characterizes his "lonely north" was only partly an illusion: in contrast with the southern parts of the province, the wilderness that extends north of Lake Superior is, even now, sparsely populated. A canoeist can still follow many of its intricate networks of rivers and lakes for days in succession "without seeing a living [human] thing," as Scott did in the summers of 1905 and 1906, and relatively little modern resource development extends "beyond its southern fringes."[23] By downplaying the people who nevertheless lived throughout the region, however, "The Height of Land" makes this terrain into one of those "socially empty" spaces that are among the cartographer's most harmful fictions.[24] As it does for Burwell and, at key moments, for Grant, the dearth of human habitation lends an aura of legitimacy to the poet's presence there. Anticipating Harris's empty northern spaces, the epithet clears the way for Scott's poetic and spiritual appropriation of the landscape. His poet assumes visual and poetic command over the area with such apparent ease that, even if his tent temporarily "capture[s]" a revel of unsuspecting roses,[25] he appears to be no more of an invader than the blue-bird or the sparrow that inhabit its woods.

"The Height of Land" thus joins poems such as "Night Hymns on Lake Nipigon" in portraying northern Ontario as a quiet and undisturbed wilderness into which human civilization (whether Indigenous or European) extends only a frail, almost inconsequential tendril. Yet this "lonely north" was not vacant; moreover, it had already been the arena of clashes between people and jurisdictions with divergent territorial interests. Scott became aware of the need for a treaty in 1899 when, on an inspection trip to New Brunswick House, he encountered people from farther north who were concerned about the increasing numbers of prospectors and developers on their lands.[26] Since before the turn of the century, mining and logging companies, eager to capitalize on the area's resources, had been eyeing this expanse of shield and forest, and the provincial and Dominion governments were keen to open it to developers and the settlers that would inevitably follow them. The Ojibway and Cree asked for the Crown's protection, which the treaty pledged to deliver by safeguarding Indigenous hunting, fishing, and trapping throughout the region and allocating reserves that would give Indigenous peoples "a secure and permanent interest in the land."[27] At the same time, by stating that these same peoples would "cede, release, surrender and yield up ... for ever, all their rights, titles and privileges whatsoever, to the lands" outside their reserves, the treaty also registered the government's interest in the resource potential of a "territory [that] contains much arable land, many million feet of pulpwood, untold wealth of minerals, and unharnessed water-powers sufficient to do the work of half the continent."[28] Defining Indigenous title as "indeterminate possession" and the wilderness as "waste" and "unproductive," the treaty text perpetuates the trope of hunter-gatherers as wanderers or nomads, their dwelling in this place only a vague occupation of inefficiently used land.[29] It then circumscribes these lands in accordance with colonial ideals about how they ought to be worked and owned, securing Indigenous property only by radically delimiting it. Reducing the legal territorial possessions of the Mushkegowuk and Anishinaabeg from a continuous area of 90,000 square miles to a series of scattered reserves amounting to 524 square miles of land not likely to "interfere" with commercial development, Treaty 9 created the kinds of "uninhabited" spaces that, like the map's *terra nullius*, provided colonial developers, settlers, and poets with "scope for dreams."[30] The lonely north that Scott's poet accesses on the height of land was in a significant sense, then, the product of Treaty 9.

Not only was the treaty responsible for bringing Scott to the setting of this poem in the first place, but it also made it possible for the poet, in keeping with the tradition of the greater Romantic lyric, to enter this place imaginatively as a solitary figure seeking access to the "[s]omething ... / Deeper than peace" that would inspire calm, clarity, and transcendence.[31] The height of land lends itself topographically to this symbolic signification as well. A hydrological point of origins, the height of land is the birthplace of the dramatic river- and lake-strewn landscape that the poem surveys, where "the soul seems to hear / The gathering of the waters at their sources."[32] The poet's imaginative appropriation of this place is predicated on this perceived connection between the landscape and primeval beginnings. Here, on the height of land, the poet can sense the "spell / Golden and inappellable / That gives the inarticulate part / Of our strange being one moment of release / That seems more native than the touch of time."[33] Scott's choice of the word "native" prompts Dragland's speculation that this "release" entails a kind of spiritual "homecoming, a momentary return to origins."[34] On the one hand, these "origins" are universal: Scott appeals to a core essence of the human spirit that has no bearings in the mapped world. On the other hand – when considered alongside his articulation of a "lonely north" – the speaker's discovery of a primitive spiritual "home" verges on a mythopoeic appropriation of a pre-colonial past[35] through which he can identify more closely with the land.

It is worth underscoring that Scott's original poetic "homecoming" in this region took place not in solitude, but in the company of the treaty party, their guides, and two influential friends who joined the 1906 trip: the literary critic Pelham Edgar and the painter Edmund Morris. Both artists in their own right, they helped to inspire the "poetic explosion" of 1906 that signalled Scott's renewed creative interest in a landscape that, in their absence the summer before, he had described as "desolate beyond compare, loneliness seven times distilled – a country never to be the glad home of any happy people."[36] If "The Height of Land" recasts the "desolate" wilderness as a place conducive to deep poetic insight, where the speaker can "hear / The thrill of life beat up the planet's margin / And break in the clear susurrus of deep joy / That echoes and reechoes in [his] being,"[37] it does so in part by transplanting the conventions of English poetry into Canada's "lonely north." Scott's "[s]omething" that comes "by flashes / Deeper than peace" resembles the "sense sublime / Of something far more deeply interfused" that "rolls through all things" in William Wordsworth's "Lines Composed a Few Miles above Tintern Abbey," his "ancient disturber of solitude" recalling the "presence that disturbs" Wordsworth's speaker "with the joy / Of elevated thoughts."[38] These echoes, among others, extend another "patchwork blanket" over the "uncovered" poetic terrain of northern Ontario.

The aesthetic relationship between Scott's poem and Mushkegowuk Territory is dramatized by the image of Scott reading aloud with Edgar from *The Oxford Book of English Verse* while Morris sketched his portraits of the Indians on the second treaty trip.[39] Such scenes point not just to the colonial encounters of which Scott's new world culture was a product (as his 1905 volume of poems, *New World Lyrics and Ballads*, suggests), but also to the flesh-and-blood figure of Scott that has resurfaced in contemporary culture – for instance, as Armand Garnet Ruffo's quietly antagonistic "black coat and tie" who came "from Ottawa way, Odawa country, / ... to talk treaty and annuity and destiny, / to make the inevitable less painful"[40] – a figure for whom the meeting of cultures signalled the end of one order and the beginning of another. As the Anishinaabe poet puts it in his "Poem for Duncan Campbell Scott," "he's always busy writing / stuff in the notebook he carries. Him, / he calls it poetry / and says it will make us who are doomed / live forever."[41] For Scott, as for many of his generation, Treaty 9's articulation of new ways to govern and inhabit northwestern Ontario heralded the end not just of Anishinaabe and Cree dominion in the vast region but of their existence as distinct nations and cultures. During Scott's tenure in the Department of Indian Affairs, the goal of Indian policy was the complete "absorption" of Indigenous peoples "into the general population" and the erasure of any "lingering traces of native custom and tradition." Along with "teachers, missionaries, and traders," Scott considered "treaties" to be among the main influences that would eventually bring about "the merging of the Indian race with the whites."[42]

In keeping with this purpose, while in "The Height of Land" the poet's "homecoming" is associated with beginnings, a palpable sense of endings hangs over the poem's Indigenous figures. The poem opens at the close of the day, and the Ojibway guides are weary. Their voices are "long" and "mournful" as Potàn "declares the ills of life" and Chees-que-ne-ne "makes a ... sound / Of acquiescence."[43] Cloaked in tones of melancholy and resignation, their conversation anticipates the images of impermanence that follow it:

> The fires burn low
> With just sufficient glow
> To light the flakes of ash that play
> At being moths, and flutter away
> To fall in the dark and die as ashes.[44]

Although the "Indian guides" are not directly associated with the dying fires, here, a reader familiar with "The Last of the Indian Treaties" will recall its infamous simile: "[t]he Indian nature now seems like a fire that is waning, that is smouldering and dying away in ashes."[45] The echo is eerie, and while in the poem the link is only suggestive, the proximity of the guides to the waning fire involves each in the other's atmosphere of decline. The poem operates on two levels: one that transcends the immediate scene, catching Scott's sense of a fin-de-siècle moment in Western culture, and another that resonates with his perceptions of the diminishing influence of Indigenous peoples in a territory that Canada was in the process of claiming.

The connection that Scott draws between the "Indian guides" and the surrounding environment reinforces the territorial nature of this transition. The nocturnal landscape, moving towards a new day, is heavy with signs of change. If the Ojibway are weary, the wind is "wearier" still; the onset of night is conveyed by a collective fatigue that is deepened by the blending of Ojibway voices with the landscape (and by the rhyme that links "wearier" with "Lake Superior").[46] Even the spruces "have retired a little space," and eventually the reader finds that "the

Indian guides are dead asleep" and silence descends on the scene.[47] The metaphorical equation of sleep and death in these lines has a sinister effect: it is, writes Dragland, an "ominous ... way of sweeping the Indians off the stage of the poem, a way that resonates uncomfortably with the cultural pattern of, in Leslie Monkman's phrase, 'Death of the Indian.'"[48] Although, as I will presently elaborate, this death-like sleep does not entirely deprive the setting of its Indigenous significance, the fact that it occurs before the poet begins his meditation suggests that their removal from the scene is necessary if he is to experience his own spiritual "homecoming" in their territory. If "The Height of Land" does not relegate Indigenous peoples entirely to the past, as did "Indian Place Names" in 1905, it does recall Scott's elegiac representations of Indigenous peoples as a "waning race."[49]

Scott's administrative work was motivated by the hope that, eventually, territorial and racial boundaries would be dissolved between Indigenous and non-Indigenous people in Canada. His poetry conveys a similar desire. "Night Hymns on Lake Nipigon" is a case in point, as are the many mixed-race individuals that function in Scott's Indian poems as symbolic sites of the cultural dissolution that he anticipated. "The Height of Land" is another of these sites, although inscribed on the land rather than on the body. Like the Indian poems, it blends the realities with the fictions of contact. "Here on the uplands where the air is clear," the poet can "deeply brood on life," moving through spatialized patterns of order and chaos – or "peace" and "welter" – upon which the binary of north and south is based, until life's "stormy scene" yields to the unity that is symbolized by the rainbow.[50] The metaphysical impetus of "The Height of Land" is towards a condition in which "oppositions" can be at least "temporarily" stilled.[51] The "ideals" that the poet seeks are premised upon a sense of things "interpenetrat[ing]," "mingl[ing]," and "merg[ing]." When he wonders whether the poet of the future will stand "with the deep fathomed, with the firmament charted," and "with life as simple as a sheep-boy's song," these ideals assume the form of a knowable, mappable space – a space as easily apprehended as his earlier, schematic vision of north and south.[52]

Shadows of Indian Title

Ultimately there is nothing "simple," however, about either the poet's state of mind or the setting that alternately inspires and stifles his ideals. In contrast with Wordsworth's retreat from the "fretful stir" and "fever of the world"[53] into the familiar landscape above Tintern Abbey, Scott's longing for restorative peace cannot be fulfilled by a setting that remains haunted by its Indigenous significance. As Bentley observes of the Indian poems, although Scott strives for "a harmonious union of alterities," frequently, "what he terms the 'Uncouth,' the 'pagan,' and the 'savage' are not conducive or amenable to harmony but, rather, haunting spectres that manifest themselves in alarming, threatening, and even deadly ways."[54] If "The Height of Land" is not one of Scott's Indian poems, it has much to reveal about the colonized spaces that produced them. Bentley does not address the Indigenous "spectres" of this poem, but they are there, muddying the clarity of its beauty.

Indeed, the setting and tone of "The Height of Land" is more intimately bound up with Indigenous subjects than might at first be supposed. As has been suggested, the moment when the "Indian guides" fall asleep helps the poet to establish a division between the physical circumstances of the poem – its wilderness setting, the canoe trip, and whatever practical purposes have brought him here – and the philosophical meditation that follows. It has been remarked that "[t]hat the Indians ... fall asleep and disappear from the poem implies that the guidance Scott sought from them was of a geographical rather than a philosophical nature."[55] But to characterize their slumber as a disappearance "from the poem" is to obscure the extent to which these figures remain associated with the land even after they fall asleep. At the very least, they imbue the poem's setting with a colonial significance marked by the relationship between white traveller and Indigenous guide. Included in the collective pronoun "we" that anchors the speaker's recollections of the journey "up through the spreading lakes" to the height of land,[56] the guides establish the poet as a foreigner unfamiliar with the route he is travelling and dependent upon the knowledge of people with a deeper connection to the land than he possesses. As Scott recalled, during the treaty trips, "[o]ur crew of half-breeds and Indians numbered not less than twelve and sometimes seventeen."[57] The quiet, retiring presence of the guides in this poem may not do documentary justice to their actual role and numbers on the treaty trips – although it may well reflect the exhausting physical labour they performed. Nonetheless, their presence underscores the role that First Nations and Metis peoples played in the reinscription of territory by generations of non-Indigenous explorers, surveyors, and, indeed, poets. "The Height of Land" would not have been possible without them.

Moreover, the poem's most powerful metaphysical elements establish a persistent connection between the land and its Indigenous inhabitants. In his solitary meditation, the poet feels the presence of two apparently separate powers, both of which are coloured "with a tinge of the indigenous."[58] First, there is the "spell" that brings him in touch with his primitive essence. Second – and even more resonant with a sense of looming Indigenous power – there is the "ancient disturber of solitude" who, while reminiscent of Wordsworthian inspiration, is also closely associated, if not identical, with the "region-spirit" that appears at line 68.[59] In its first appearance, the "ancient disturber" may simply signify the wind "[b]reath[ing] a pervasive sigh" through a landscape that has become animated again after a period of silence and stillness: "Now are there sounds walking in the wood, / And all the spruces shiver and tremble, / And the stars move a little in their courses." Like the spell, the "ancient disturber of solitude" turns the poet's mind to origins: it is in his presence that "the soul seems to hear / The gathering of the waters at their sources."[60] But later on, when he "stirs his ancestral potion in the gloom," the "ancient disturber" brings the universal essence to which Scott appeals into contact with the land and its Indigenous significance.[61] In his more haunting form, in fact, the ancient disturber strongly resembles the "lonely spirit" of the Albany that Scott describes in "The Last of the Indian Treaties": "It is ever-present, but at night it grows in power. Something is heard and yet not heard: it rises, and dwells, and passes mysteriously, like a suspiration immense and mournful, like the sound of wings, dim and enormous, folded down with weariness." The similarities between this indefinable yet ever-present "something" that "haunts" the river and "becomes an obsession" in "The Last of the Indian Treaties," and the "ancient disturber of solitude" that breathes his "pervasive sigh" through "The Height of Land" – not to mention the "mournful" and "weary" atmosphere that the poem also captures – suggest that the spiritual essence that inhabits his poem may, like the spirit of the Albany River, also derive from "sorcerers" and "wendigo[s]."[62] Through this appropriation, Scott's lonely north comes to be characterized by a diffuse Indigenous spirit of place that, without negating the land's apparent loneliness, certainly qualifies its apparent vacancy.

Not unlike the "aerial pulse" of a conjurer's drum that Scott recalls hearing from time to time along the treaty route, and that would "throb" more threateningly in his 1926 poem, "Powassan's Drum," this spirit has a pervasive presence that is indistinctly but nonetheless powerfully felt at various points in "The Height of Land."[63] Although less nightmarish than those of "Powassan's Drum," the Indigenous elements that haunt "The Height of Land" are, in Dragland's words, "extremely ambiguous."[64] They are particularly unsettling as they merge with a landscape aesthetic that stands in marked contrast with the poem's idealized visions. "Stir[ring] his ancestral potion in the gloom," the "ancient disturber of solitude" interrupts the poet's meditation on the "perfect beauty" that arises from the interpenetration of "deed and thought" and brings him back to earth – not to the peaceful scene of the sleeping campsite, but to a "dark wood ... stifled with the pungent fume / Of charred earth burnt to the bone / That takes the place of air."[65] Here the "disturber" becomes more than just a "slightly disquieting undertone"; he is an "alien element," trickster-like as he "prods the poet out of conventional Romantic epiphany."[66] The "ancient disturber of solitude" effectively shatters the poet's thoughts, clouding the previously "clear" air with smoke that brings back memories of a hideous landscape:

> Then sudden I remember when and where, –
> The last weird lakelet foul with weedy growths
> And slimy viscid things the spirit loathes,
> Skin of vile water over viler mud
> Where the paddle stirred unutterable stenches,
> And the canoes seemed heavy with fear,
> Not to be urged toward the fatal shore
> Where a bush fire, smouldering, with sudden roar
> Leaped on a cedar and smothered it with light
> And terror.[67]

Unique among the topographical descriptions that anchor this poem in the northern boreal wilderness, this terrain repels the speaker. The memory of it replaces his placid dreaming with a "terror" that – as the "foul" and "weedy" lake, with its "skin" of water and "unutterable stenches," suggests – derives not from the sublime appearance of the fire so much as from an intensely earthly (even bodily) experience of decay and destruction.

Scott's "weird lakelet" is a poetic rendering of the "marshy stream" that the treaty party paddled through on 7 August 1906; the bush fire was encountered later, on the return journey along this same route.[68] In the poem, both swamp and fire perform a metaphoric function as well as a mimetic one. Pervaded by gloom and smoky devastation, the scene as a whole catches something of the "Indian nature" that Scott felt was "smouldering and dying away in ashes" as Indigenous title was extinguished in the region.[69] The elegiac passage that follows brings the poem back around to the atmosphere of endings with which it began: "How strange the stars have grown," the poet muses, "The presage of extinction grows on their crests / And they are beautied with impermanence."[70] Could there be a link between the impermanence of stars and the impermanence of races and cultures? If this turn upward, towards the stars, pulls him out of his disturbing recollections of the swamp and the bush fire, it also amplifies their portent of ruin. The "strange" stars with their "presage of extinction" mingle with his recollections of the "weird lakelet" and its "fatal shore" to produce a sense of something dramatic coming to a close. That the stars are "beautied with impermanence" and will "survive the race of men" does not entirely allay the feelings of foreboding that the previous passage builds into the poem. Awakened by the "ancient disturber of solitude," and thus connected – at least in a loose, suggestive way – with the land's Indigenous history and spirit, these feelings encompass both metaphysical questions about the meaning and transience of life and also a vision of the north and its peoples. Is the bush fire's stifling smoke destined to become "the fading smoke" that, in "Indian Place-Names," augurs the eventual disappearance of Indigenous peoples from the land?[71] If such a reading is plausible, then the "blush sunrise" to which the poet looks in the final lines of the poem heralds the emergence of a new spirit and a new poetry of the north that has its source, not only in the "evolutionary optimism and questing heterodoxy" that has been identified here and elsewhere in the work of the Confederation Poets[72] but also in the transformation of Indigenous lands into Canadian territory.

The poet in "The Height of Land" cannot promise that the poet of the future will stand "with the deep fathomed, with the firmament charted"; yet he propels us towards a vision full of cartographic allure as, in the poem's final lines, he feels "the lulled earth, older in pulse and motion, / Turn the rich lands and the inundant oceans / To the flushed colour" of the sunrise, and hears "The thrill of life beat / up the planet's margin."[73] These words capture the world in a state of becoming. They speak of beginnings, and they link the northern wilderness to the "rich lands and the inundant oceans" of the entire "lulled earth." Yet, despite the "clear susurrus of deep joy / That echoes and reechoes in [his] being," this is a poem that ultimately registers "man's failure to comprehend."[74] Plagued by questions, the poet is unable to impose any sustained order on universe, and the "region-spirit" remains a haunting but elusive presence that disturbs the harmony of his thoughts.

Recent discussions of the poem posit that this disharmony has more to do with the land's Indigenous claims than had previously been supposed. McKay suggests, for instance, that by calling one of his guides Chees-que-ne-ne ("in fact, a shaman"), "Scott may have been welcoming into his epiphanic poem the very element that would disrupt its basic assumptions, disturbing the aesthetic solitude of its protagonist."[75] Disharmony indeed characterizes interactions between Indigenous and non-Indigenous interests in this region, in the decades leading up to the negotiation of Treaty 9 to the present, and the spiritual conflict that Scott records in "The Height of Land" resonates with this sense of the north as contested territory.[76] Indeed, the dramatic shift in tone that distinguishes these lines, with their "sudden roar" of rekindling flames, from the waning fires of the poem's first verse paragraph, suggests a threat that will not be so easily extinguished. Scott's poem presents the north as ripe for reimagining, but something of its spirit and history resists the poetic and national appropriation that is taking place. The product of oral agreements honouring the interests of First Nations as well as the emerging one, Treaty 9 created a landscape of overlapping voices and incomplete erasures. "Was it a trick or a treaty?" asks John S. Long in his penetrating historical study *Treaty No. 9: Making the Agreement to Share the Land in Far Northern Ontario in 1905*. The question, he shows, is a complicated one, but how we answer it will determine how we continue to dwell both physically and psychically in these spaces, sharing the land.[77] Whatever the answer, the fact that the Anishinaabeg and Mushkegowuk have successfully appealed to the treaty as a promise of their continuing land rights highlights the frailty of Scott's colonial ideals.[78]

Both "The Last of the Indian Treaties" and "The Height of Land" layer imagined geographies onto real ones. The setting of the most lyrical of Scott's northern poems is a mapped and mappable place. It entwines the poetic with the geographic in a way that embeds both the poem and its speaker in the politically charged context of a real place across which many stories converge and collide. Like a map, the poem adds its own territorial inscription to these stories. We read therein of the poet, meditating in solitude through the long, lonely night on the depth and burden of life's mysteries; and we read of Scott the author and treaty commissioner ascending the portage with the 1906 treaty party and a motley crew of guides, among his luggage a chest of treaty money and a copy of *The Oxford Book of English Verse*. If the poem did not also reside in the spaces of Treaty 9, we might become lulled by the beauty the poet conjures. It is to land and territory that literary cartography points, opening the possibility of reading this poem as an expression of the negotiation and refiguration of colonial space that Treaty 9 represented. To stand with Scott's speaker "on the uplands where the air is clear," then, is imaginatively to occupy, for a moment, a terrain whose contours were shifting beneath the pressures of expanding settlement, railroad construction, and resource demands from the south. This context, across which Scott's poetic musing charts its own intricate path, complicates both the poetic "homecoming" that takes place therein, and the sense of "region-spirit" to which Scott gestures. The poet's inability to reconcile himself to the terrain that he poetically maps has to do with his colonial relationship to the north. While he animates this place with his fleeting presence, he also remains at odds with it, a foreign presence unable to assimilate himself to its mysterious and ominous spirit. As is the case in each of the texts discussed in this book, "[h]ere" is laden with the encounters, negotiations, and contest over land that animated colonial Canada; it is the product of memories of elsewhere as well as of close attention to the here and now; it is landscape, treaty, and territory; it is a map.

Maps and Counter-Maps (On Getting Lost)

In Canada and other colonies like it, the nineteenth century was an age of surveying. As *Mapping with Words* underscores, the legacies of this age are literary as well as cartographic, and the map's gridded spaces – along with the enumeration of places, landmarks, and species – generated a cartographic poetics characterized by a palpable desire for symmetry, order, and visibility. Early Canadian literature is marked by settler preoccupations with orientation and emplacement, with mobility and accommodation, with not getting lost.

These preoccupations, as Paul Carter explains in *The Road to Botany Bay*, are future-oriented. Paraphrasing the nineteenth-century Australian surveyor Thomas Livingstone Mitchell, Carter writes: "Unlike the explorer who left hardly any trace of where he had been, and whose journey often seemed to leave the country emptier than before, the surveyor was a harbinger of civilization. He saw his task as preparing the path for orderly colonization. He was the means of transforming the dynamic space of travelling into the fixed and passive space of settlement. But he effected this transformation by positing a plausible place rather than by discovering it. He viewed the country he passed through as if with the eyes of the future."[1] In many ways, *Mapping with Words* charts the shift from this one sense of space to the other. Looking forward to the land's transformation – from woodland to farmland; from prairies into estates; from vast distances and impenetrable forests, marshes, and mountains to networks of roads and railways; from Indigenous territories into a patchwork blanket of treaties – the writers examined in this book contributed to the creation of a spatial order predicated on the future-oriented gaze of the surveyor rather than the explorer. They worked to produce a sense of fixed place: defined, articulated, and passive. They made their mark on the land. And yet, in those moments where they turn from visions of the future to the land as it actually was, these writers also resemble Mitchell's explorers. Indeed, it is when moving from the one to the other that they give us glimpses of counter-maps that resist or belie the easy inscription of monolithic, legible settler space. That the periods of exploration and colonization overlap in Canada's geographical and literary history, moreover, further blurs the lines between the two spatial sensibilities.

This book has suggested that through the lens of literary geography we can read colonial texts differently, training our eyes on the territoriality of this writing in order to expose and deconstruct cartographic strategies and bring into clearer view the counter-mappings that – to return to John Pickles's idea, cited in the introduction – have been with us all along, often embedded in the very narratives that were part of the culture of overwriting. Colonial spatiality is more nuanced and unsettled than metanarratives of conquering empty space would have us believe. This book's final arguments on this subject turn to another counter-map that has in many ways been with us all along: the writings of David Thompson, the fur trader, explorer, astronomer, map-maker, settler, and writer destined to become Canada's most celebrated land geographer.

Thompson's career intersects uncannily with key moments in this study, blurring the line between settler and explorer literary cartographies in ways that further complicate Anglo-colonial texts from this period. He arrived at Churchill Factory as a fourteen-year-old apprentice clerk to the Hudson's Bay Company in 1784, the same year that Captain James Cook published his map of the world that left the western interior of North America almost entirely blank. In 1789, the year that Thomas Cary's *Abram's Plains* first appeared, the young fur-trader broke his leg, an event that changed the course of his career when he spent his long recovery at Cumberland House learning surveying techniques from Philip Turnor. He began to chart the rivers and fur trade posts of the northwest, labouring to fill in much of the space that Cook had left unmapped. Over the course of nearly three decades in the region, working first for the Hudson's Bay Company and then for the North West Company, Thompson traversed more than 80,000 kilometres, and mapped approximately 1.9 million square kilometres, of terrain through Rupert's Land and the Pacific northwest. By the time Adam Hood Burwell penned *Talbot Road* in 1818, Thompson knew the northwest more intimately than did any other European.

This knowledge is captured by his monumental *Map of the North-West Territory of the Province of Canada*, commonly referred to as his Great Map (figure 10). Completed between 1812 and 1814, this map was the first unified cartographic representation of the northwest. Unparalleled in breadth and accuracy, it provided information from which cartographers would draw, often without acknowledgment, for the next century. Aaron Arrowsmith famously plagiarized Thompson's work in his own widely circulated maps of the northwest. Thompson himself gained very little acclaim for his Great Map beyond the North West Company post of Fort William where the first copy of it was housed.

Thompson left the northwest, and with it the life of the explorer, in 1812 with his Cree-Métis wife, Charlotte Small. They settled first in Terrebonne, near Montreal, moving three years later to Glengarry County, Upper Canada. Among other jobs, he worked on the International Boundary Survey, charting the line from St Regis, Ontario (near Cornwall) to the Northwest Angle on Lake of the Woods. After a period of prosperity, his fortunes began to decline when he lost his investments in the failed fur-trade firm McGillivray, Thain and Company in 1825. His financial situation worsened through the same economic downturn that brought new waves of settlers, among them Susanna Moodie and Catharine Parr Traill, to Canada. Between 1845 and 1850, an aging man with failing eyesight hoping for a new source of income, he wrote the manuscripts of his now famous *Travels* – a narrative based on his fur trade journals – with borrowed paper and ink. Unable to secure a publisher, he died in poverty and relative obscurity in Longueil in February of 1857, just four months before the Palliser Expedition set out across the northwest. Thompson's manuscripts languished until J.B. Tyrrell purchased them from Charles Lindsey[2] and published a first edition titled *David Thompson's Narrative of His Explorations in Western America* with the Champlain Society in 1916 – the year in which Duncan Campbell Scott's "The Height of Land" appeared in *Lundy's Lane*.

Thompson resides in the background of this study, then, in an oddly spectral way. He might well have been included among the "men" that William F. Butler described in 1870 as having "come and gone, leaving behind them no track, no vestige, of their presence" in the northwest.[3] Grant mentions the "celebrated traveller and astronomer" only briefly, and not in connection to the boundary survey or the river that Simon Fraser named after him in 1808, but in a discussion of climate conditions.[4] Although Thompson has since been memorialized by several geographical features named in his honour, in 1916 Tyrrell lamented that "there [was] not even a monument marking the last resting-place of this great geographer," and one reviewer observed that "his name does not even appear in the *Dictionary of National Biography*."[5] In many ways, Thompson's fate is consistent with the erasure of imperial trade infrastructures across the northwest during this period. Barbara Belyea notes that the fur trade "left so few physical marks that Dr James Hector of the Palliser Expedition wrote as if he were distanced by centuries rather than decades from its activity. Indeed, by the mid-nineteenth century a number of abandoned posts" – a number of which Thompson would have helped build – "could scarcely be located, portages had disappeared, and most of the North West Company's records had been lost or destroyed."[6] Thompson's disappearance both from the physical landscape and from public life is a remarkable element of a story that registers the shift from explorer to settler space that the writers featured in this study help to mark. Nonetheless, a look at his *Narrative* – in many ways, a counter-mapping that has been present all along – suggests how these categories, and their corresponding imaginaries, might be productively blurred.

When Tyrrell's edition appeared in 1916, *Narrative* drew Thompson into the spotlight as "one of those builders of empire to whom fell the work without the fame," as one reviewer put it.[7] As a contribution to the geographical imaginary of empire-building, however, *Narrative* is far from straightforward. It makes a dramatic counterpoint to Butler's representation of the prairie as an "ocean" of grass unmarked by history – a place with "no past."[8] Its descriptions of places, people, and natural history are the product of intense observation that was impossible for a traveller such as George Monro Grant to experience during three sunny months along the proposed Canadian Pacific Railway route (see chapter 4). Literary geography draws attention to the territorial implications of the diverse ecology, topography, and Indigenous cultures that he so richly elaborates in his book. Rather than a land "waiting for settlers," as the future-oriented Grant put it, Thompson reveals a place densely textured with social and ecological meaning, a living habitat for people and wildlife whose presence he attempted to map in his book. To bring this work to the fore is to conjure an image of the northwest before the numbered treaties extended their "blanket," as Scott calls it, across the prairies to the mountains; it is to recall, as readers would doubtless have had to do when the *Narrative* came out in 1916, the many and varied ways in which "Indians owned the land," as Tekahionwake (E. Pauline

Johnson) asserts in "A Cry from an Indian Wife," that the treaties negotiated and reshaped (see chapter 4).

Thompson's *Narrative* treads a fine line, then, between map and counter-map. In doing so, it both orients and disorients the reader. As he put it to George Simpson (in a rather trite phrase that was part of an unsuccessful appeal for publication), his *Narrative* recounts "a wild life in wild countries."[9] Far from presaging orderly colonization, this wild life resists the map's unifying force. It does very little to emplace the prospective settler; this is not their story, and Thompson is unconcerned with accommodating their interests. Formally, this is also the case. His *Narrative* is the product of a careful stitching together of words and maps, exemplifying a fine-tuned literary cartography intent on locating the terrain and its multiple meanings. Yet although this book hangs on a framework of surveyed coordinates, it is also a generically complex and nonlinear text-map in which the reader can easily get lost, encountering (as Thompson did) the limits of their knowledge and ways of seeing in the face of the land's heterogeneity and depth of meaning.

Orientation: The Narrative as Map

Following a trajectory that is spatial as well as temporal, Thompson's *Narrative* has been described as "the verbal counter-part of his great series of maps of northwestern North America" as well as a work of "imaginative mapping" in its own right.[10] Formally, the coordinates of latitude and longitude that punctuate the narrative connect it the most clearly to his maps. "It is tedious to the reader to attend to these calculations," Thompson admits, "and yet to the enquiring mind they are necessary that he may know the ground on which they are based. For the age of guessing has passed away, and the traveller is expected to give his reasons for what he asserts."[11] While a weary reader may well skim over these dry technical markers, regarding them as superfluous to the narrative trajectory of the book, Thompson encourages us to regard them as integral to its purpose and effect. As I.S. MacLaren points out, "the general *effect* of landscape, so central a concern in the eighteenth-century British aesthetic tradition which bred the Sublime and the Picturesque, is displaced in Thompson by the quest for the objective, even numerically measured, relations among landscape features."[12] When we recall how remote and little-known the northwest remained to colonial Canadians, not only when Thompson explored it between 1784 and 1812, but also when he wrote his manuscript several decades later with Red River still an "isolated settlement"[13] and the Palliser and Hind Expeditions not yet underway, his *Narrative* acquires significance as a text that – in a way that is different from, though related to, his graphic cartography – provided a form of orientation. Its geo-coding solidifies the relationship between exploration and topographical description on the one hand, and the technologies of surveying and mapping on the other.

It is hard not to see these geographical coordinates as subtly presaging the surveyor's transformative presence across the West. Attaching the hundreds of pages of observations and stories that make up his "imaginative mapping" to measured points on the earth, they embed the narrative in the geometrical order of Cartesian perspectivalism and logic, and thus in the global imperial network that this logic helped to forge. Ironically, by charting his dynamic travels through the land in this way, keeping an eye on the whole of the mapped earth beyond each individual measured point, Thompson became a "means of transforming the dynamic space of travelling into the fixed and passive space of settlement" as well as into the networks of global imperial trade.

Indeed, to a modern reader, there is something uncannily prescient about Thompson's description of how, when his companions discovered him observing the moon and stars with "brass Sextant, ... achromatic Telescope, ... Parallel glasses, ... quicksilver horizon, ... Compass, Thermometer, and other requisite instruments," they concluded that he must be "looking into futurity" rather than measuring their present position. Thompson protested that his "instruments" were not the occult props of a clairvoyant, but rather the practical tools of a surveyor, designed only "to determine the distance and direction from the place observed to other places."[14] Yet his companions were not far off when they suspected Thompson of peering into the future. The maps that he would draw from these measurements – maps that linked, for the first time, the territories of the northwest with Canada in the east – in effect presaged the expansionist movement that would transform these territories, some almost beyond recognition.

Thompson was well aware of the imaginative power of the map as an extension of perception. Upon reaching the mouth of the Columbia River, he describes looking at the Pacific Ocean for the first time: the "full view of the Pacific Ocean ... was to me a great pleasure," he recalls, "but my Men seemed disappointed; they had been accustomed to the boundless horizon of the Great Lakes of Canada, and their high rolling waves; from the Ocean they expected a more boundless view, a something beyond the power of their senses which they could not describe; and my informing them, that directly opposite to us, at the distance of five thousand miles was the Empire of Japan added nothing to their ideas, but a Map would."[15] The map's aesthetic potential lies in its ability to expand perception, to access that "something beyond the power of their senses." The cartographic imaginary, according to Thompson in this passage, traverses oceans.

Needless to say, this is a climactic moment in his narrative. Read in hindsight, it is the moment that connects the explorer's cartographic sensibility with future technological developments with the greatest clarity and force. Upon completing their trip across the continent some sixty years later, Grant would describe the Pacific Ocean "stretch[ing] unbroken to Japan and China" in similarly cartographic terms, as a "passage-way between the old world and the new": "[t]o our railway terminus will converge the products of Australia and Polynesia as well as of China and Japan," he anticipates.[16] Although a transcontinental railway had hardly been imagined yet, something happens for Thompson, too, as he reaches a destination tied to future hopes of westward expansion and trade. His language foreshadows the opening lines of E.J. Pratt's poem *Towards the Last Spike*, where the poet would describe "[t]he east-west cousinship, a nation's rise, / Hail of identity, a world expanding, / If not the universe: the feel of it."[17]

Literary Counter-Mapping and Disorientation

Allowing the eye to range unimpeded wherever it wishes to go, a map extends the faculty of sight and collapses time and space. In this sense, Thompson's cartographic legacy anticipated not only the east-to-west union of the country that Grant would help to solidify, but also the railways that would one day transfigure the land and how it would be experienced. Similarly, Thompson's graphic maps, with their diagrammatic rendering of an abstract and totalized geographical space, obscure the direct, physical encounters with land that map-making required. In his *Narrative*, however, the sense of wholeness that emerges from the culmination of his cartographic command of the continent that he helped to stitch together, point by point, route by route, recedes in the face of the multiplicity of landscapes and peoples he encountered. His *Narrative* is dominated by descriptive "regional vignettes" that underscore that the northwest is anything but monolithic. He builds an increasingly intricate and varied sense of the northwest as far more than a space traversed by imperial trade networks; it is also a place, inhabited by diverse peoples and wildlife. The geo-coded text gives these inhabitants a concrete presence in a precise patchwork of places to which Thompson attaches the authority of cartographic representation. Yet it is also the case that the significance of each regional description far exceeds the geographical import of his calculations.

Debates among scholars and critics about the role that these vignettes play in relation to the chronological narrative (with particular editions accentuating the one or the other) illuminate the generic complexity of Thompson's literary cartography.[18] In contrast with the persistent linearity of Grant's expansionist narrative, which does not stray from the prospective route of the Canadian Pacific Railway, Thompson's narrative circles and loops along many pathways that branch off from the chronological journey, and each vignette slows the narrative in order to mark its mapped spaces with precisely individuated places.[19] While one can feel comfortingly oriented by Thompson's graphic maps, one can also get wonderfully lost in his *Narrative* as it orients and emplaces a collection of stories and descriptions of the land's Indigenous inhabitants and native ecosystems, told in many voices and from many perspectives other than his own.

Although they are precisely framed by his surveys, these stories and voices mark the limits of Thompson's own geographical knowledge. From the beginning, he casts himself not as an authority, but as someone who has a lot to learn. His journey from Westminster, England, to Fort Churchill occasions a humbling discovery of the extent of his ignorance about the world. As he recounts, his education, enriched by stories such as *Robinson Crusoe* and *Gulliver's Travels*, had filled him with youthful confidence that he possessed "knowledge to say something of any place [he] might come to" – a confidence that quickly dissolves as even the Orkney Islands reveal "a new world" that baffles the young observer with its treeless topography.[20] Every place that he encounters thereafter becomes another source of geographical awakening that is frequently as disorienting as it is orienting, with Thompson an explorer in the truest sense of the word.

Nor did his remarkable talent for surveying obscure the superior navigational skills of his Indigenous companions. In the aforementioned passage where he describes his survey technique, he also notes that his was not the only way to understand the world: "I had always admired the tact of the Indian in being able to guide himself through the darkest pine forests to exactly the place he intended to go, his keen, constant attention on everything; the removal of the smallest stone, the bent, or broken twig; a slight mark on the ground all spoke plain language to him. I was anxious to acquire this knowledge, and often being in company with them, sometimes for several months, I paid attention to what they pointed out to me, and became almost equal to some of them; which became of great use to me."[21] At this moment the great cartographer casts his own achievements in the shadow of his Indigenous companions and guides, whose ability to read the land he longs to emulate. Thompson validates other kinds of geographical literacy more pointedly than Susanna Moodie implicitly does in the passage with which this book opened, when she describes her "Indian friends" coveting a map of Canada. Reversing the relationship, here it is Thompson who wants to learn to read the land's "plain language" through the Indigenous practice of "keen, constant attention."

Thompson looked to the stars in order to determine his position on the earth, but he also followed his companions' advice and "look[ed]" carefully "to the ground," which he interprets using natural history, religion, and ethnography. His *Narrative* accordingly moves in and out of several perspectives and spatial registers, some wide and sweeping and others intimate, to give a sense not only of the characteristics that unify large geographical regions and define them in relation to one another, but also of the minutest features of a particular stretch of terrain. For the literary geographer, the significance of these descriptions extends beyond the information that they provide to historians, anthropologists, and geographers about the environments and communities of the northwest. Effectively interrupting the main travel narrative, they tell their own geographical stories about Thompson's deepening knowledge, acquired by living in the land rather than simply passing through it.

Thompson's wonder and curiosity in his descriptions of everything from seal holes to mosquitoes gives him a kinship with the likes of Catharine Parr Traill, who would doubtless have appreciated his natural history articles in the *Montreal Herald* and the *Gazette*, although she did not live long enough to see the publication of his *Narrative*. In the process of building such detailed knowledge of the ground, Thompson also continues to chart the limits of his understanding: "[t]hese wild northern countries produce questions, difficult to answer," he admits. Indeed, uncertainty is a recurring motif in his *Narrative* as he finds himself at a loss to explain phenomena ranging from the origins of dwarf pines on the smooth rocky islands of Manito Lake to snow fleas to the aurora borealis.[22] He sometimes went to great lengths to find answers to the mysteries that confounded his understanding. Puzzled by "the excessive heat of the blood of the Rein Deer," for instance, he speculates that it may be related to the white moss that he finds in their stomachs: "I then traced the Deer to where they had been feeding," he recounts: "it was on a white crisp moss in a circular form, of about ten inches in diameter, each division distinct, yet close together. I took a small piece about the size of a nutmeg, chewed it, it had a mild taste. I swallowed it, and it became like a coal in my stomach. I took care never to repeat the experiment."[23]

Thompson also filled the gaps in his knowledge with lengthy quotations from other sources, both written and verbal. He combines a number of first-person accounts with his own discourse to create a collage of perspectives. As Moreau points out: "two aged Cree tell of the natural history of the beaver ... ; the Ojibway chief Sheshepaskut and the Nor'wester Jean-Baptiste Cadotte *fils* speak of warfare with the Cheyenne and the Sioux ... ; the Hudson's Bay Company trader Mitchell Oman relates tales of inland history and the smallpox epidemic of 1781–82 ... ; and a young Piegan describes a war party against the Snake. ... The ... narrative ... of Saukamappee ... is the finest of all; personal and intimate, it continues for some fifteen manuscript pages and extends recorded Piegan history back to 1730."[24] Giving over his own voice to others, Thompson truly embodies the explorer's stance as Mitchell defines it. As his voice recedes, others that we merely glimpse in Grant's text expand, leaving their own marks on the land. Although Moreau attributes the "apparent disjointedness" of *Narrative* to the "several roles" of "storyteller, interpreter, scholar, ... philosopher, ... [and] mediator" that Thompson assumed while writing,[25] the generic heterogeneity of his account as it moves between different registers of description and narrative is surely also a product of the distinct places and peoples that he encountered across such a vast region. Cartographically, the multiplicity of voices points to the linguistic and cultural diversity of a region defined by many ways of seeing.

Thompson is a quiet, self-effacing narrator who is as keen to expand on the habits of beavers, the properties of birch bark, and the culture, economies, and politics of particular Indigenous nations as he is to tell his own story. Yet, given the richness of description and the range of perspectives – especially Indigenous ones[26] – from which his *Narrative* draws, it would be hard to say that Thompson was an explorer whose "journey seemed to leave the country emptier than before." His

Narrative produces an impression not of emptiness, but of fullness that dispels the illusions of vacant space upon which settlers depended. Even when he notes a dearth of human inhabitants – for instance, when describing the area around Lake Winnipeg – "empty" is not an adjective that he tends to use: "There are but few, natives about this Lake, and they lead a hard life," he observes, and the "small" woods and "severe" climate around this lake are home to "few deer, and other animals; but," he adds, "the fish are good, and it's [*sic*] isles in the summer season are covered with the nests of the common Gull, the eggs of which are nearly as good as those of our common Fowls."[27]

The fullness of the land, however, does not beckon the settler. Despite having spent more than three decades in the region – during which time he married Small, to whom he remained devoted for the rest of his life – and despite the knowledge that he accumulated beyond any single nation's territory, the land is expressly framed as Indigenous. Not yet divided or contained by Canadian borders, the numbered treaties, or provincial boundaries, Inuit, Dene, Cree, Blackfoot, Piegan, Mandan, Fall, Sioux, Cheyenne, and Ojibway territories (among others) are each connected in shifting ways – sometimes peacefully, sometimes contentiously – with other nations and with the cultural networks of the fur trade. The closeness of Thompson's perspective, which makes the details of the land and its people large and immediate, enables readers to grasp the depth of living, of habitation, to which his counter-mappings point. Appealing frequently to Indigenous knowledge and emplacement, he makes it abundantly clear that they are the rooted ones, he the "Epic Wanderer" (as D'Arcy Jenish describes him in his biography of that title). This is literary cartography at its most vital.

Not unlike the other voices that he records throughout his journeys, Thompson's vignettes register the phenomenological depth of habitation as a bodily, material, and cultural attachment to land. In one striking passage, he describes an Ojibway wild rice harvest, worth quoting at length for the perspective it offers of what it means to inhabit a place. "The wild rice," Thompson begins,

> is fully ripe in the early part of September. The natives lay thin birch rind all over the bottom of the Canoe, a man lightly clothed, or naked places himself in the middle of the Canoe, and with a hand on each side, seizes the stalks and knocks the ears of rice against the inside of the Canoe, into which the rice falls, and thus he continues until the Canoe is full of rice; on coming ashore the Women assist in unloading. A canoe may hold from ten

> to twelve bushels. He smokes his pipe, sings a Song; and returns to collect another canoe load.
>
> And so plentifull is the rice, an industrious Man may fill his canoe three times in a day. Scaffolds are prepared about six feet from the ground made of small sticks covered with long grass; on this the rice is laid, and gentle clear fires kept underneath by the women, and turned until the rice is fully dried. The quantity collected is no more than the scaffolds can dry, as the rice is better on the stalk than on the ground. The rice when dried is pounded in a mortar made of a piece of hollow oak with a pestle of the same until the husk comes off. It is then put up in bags made of rushes and secured against animals. The Natives collect not only enough for themselves, but also as much as the furr traders will buy from them; Two or three Ponds of water can furnish enough for all that is collected.[28]

This passage exemplifies Thompson's unique prose: spare yet fresh and vividly fitted to his experiences and perceptions of the land. Yet while it exhibits the mix of "concreteness," "colloquial vitality," "precision," and the tremendous "power for exact scientific observation"[29] upon which many critics remark, much more emerges here than an accurate rendering of the processing of rice. Thompson's language echoes the rhythms of the place, his sentence structure and diction making it possible for the reader to hear the picking, the knocking of the stalks, and the sibilant fall of rice into the canoe as the harvester "seizes the stalks and knocks the ears of rice against the inside of the canoe." The repetition of "rice," accentuated by the "s" sounds, builds a sense of abundance that is more than just a visual rendering, as "thus he continues until the Canoe is full of rice." Thompson's words fold around the world that he describes, in both sound and sense.

His attention to the harvester's body not only makes concrete the physical activity of harvesting, but also strengthens the intimate locality of the ritual that takes place on two or three ponds of water, drawing from local materials (birch rind, small sticks, long grass, hollow oak, rushes) that make clear the connection between the harvesters and this specific place, where birch trees and rushes grow alongside the wild rice plants. Unlike Traill, Thompson does not explicitly lament or foresee settlers' encroachments on the wild rice habitat (see chapter 3), yet an implicit defence of the harvest, and the Anishinaabe territoriality that it signifies, emerges from the powerful presentness of the scene and its entanglement of language, land, and people. This vignette is one example among many that draw attention to Indigenous material and economic ties to particular locales, highlighting the resourcefulness and ingenuity with which people adapted to particular environments. Yet the relationship that he describes has dimensions beyond the economic. Rice gathering is also a cultural practice: its labour is broken up with smoking and singing, the routines of economic and material subsistence (which are bolstered in his *Narrative* by the description of maple sugar that follows) intertwined with literary and musical practice. Rice, Thompson shows, is more than just food, and the land is more than just land.

Indeed, as he makes abundantly clear throughout his *Narrative*, the land through which he travels is marked by creation stories, ceremonies, and rituals – such as the practice of leaving a bear's head "ashore ... with it's [*sic*] nose to the sea" after a kill, or of leaving offerings at sacred places such as Manito Fall – and infused with the widely shared belief that all beings have souls ("even a tree," he writes, "though it cannot stir from it's [*sic*] place").[30] Although at times the biases of his own Christian faith make him sceptical (if not outright dismissive) of Indigenous beliefs, in many cases he refrains from passing judgment, and recedes into the background of his text in a manner that allows the land to come into focus as a place of deep religious significance. Again, his most affecting literary cartography works on an intimate level, such as in the vignette describing the Nahathaway women's "dance to the Manito of the Martens." As he recalls it, the event took place in response to a mundane need for marten skins to trade for "Beads and Ribbons," yet he describes it with reverence: "it was a fine, calm, moonlight night," he writes; "the young men came with the Rattle and the Tambour, about nine women formed the dance, to which they sung with their fine voices, and lively they danced hand in hand in a half circle for a long hour." Thompson's astonishment that he can call to mind "this gay hour," even "many years" later, attests to the dance's impact on him.[31] Here again he is only an observer conjuring deceptively simple words that map the women's movements. Assonance and alliteration connect the dancers "hand in hand" in their "half circle," while the syntactic inversion in his phrase "lively they danced" catches something of the way in which such rituals intervene in and transform the spaces in which they are performed. In such scenes, the ground, which might have remained abstracted by his cartographic coordinates, is reanimated, even recreated, by the dance in the calm moonlight.

The intimate, affective union of Thompson's language with the places, people, and practices that he describes produces a counter-mapping that belies the imperial trope of the northwest as a space traversed by networks of trade. Instead, the land is made concretely – indeed, sensuously – meaningful as a collection of distinct topographical and ecological regions and complexly interrelated human territories. Detailed and alive, his regional vignettes intensify the impact of other signs of Indigenous habitation that he glimpses more fleetingly, from the many paths travelled "from time immemorial" to mnemonic landmarks such as "One Pine," a tree that stands as a monument to one family's suffering from smallpox.[32] The land, Thompson stresses, is important to those who call it home even if it does not always provide an easy life: as he writes of the Nahathaways, "[n]otwithstanding the hardships the Natives sometimes suffer, they are strongly attached to the country of Rivers, Lakes, and Forests."[33]

Embedded in an explicitly spatial narrative, vignettes, pathways, and monuments coalesce into counter-mappings that challenge what it means to settle in these places. The depth of attachment that they convey bolsters the language of possession, law, diplomacy, and economic relations that also defines the territoriality of distinct nations. Neither Thompson's oblique predictions that much of the good prairie would one day be taken up by farmers, nor his regret that Indigenous people were already being dispossessed of their lands either "by fraud or by force" by "White Men," shake his steadfast belief that substantial tracts such as the southern "great Plains," near the Mandan villages, had been "given by Providence to the Red Men for ever."[34] Reversing the colonial trope of God-given land (see chapters 1 and 4), this belief echoes an earlier description of the more northerly "Stony Region" (as he called the shield country) between Lake Winnipeg and Lake Athabasca, which "the Supreme Being, the Lord of the whole Earth" had "given to the Deer, and other wild animals; and to the Red Man forever."[35] Thompson is not naive about the impending expansion of colonial settlement that was fuelled by a desire for farmland as well as for a Pacific trade route. And it is largely those lands that "cannot become agricultural" that receive his stamp of providential protection, despite his knowledge that some nations, such as the Mandan, cultivated corn, beans, and squash.[36] "[T]he Stony Region," for example, is "an immense extent of country, on which the White Man cannot live; except by hunting, which he will not submit to," and so "the Red Man forever, here, as his fathers of many centuries have done ... may roam, free as the wind."[37]

With his echoing "forevers," Thompson projects a vision of the future that is solidly anchored in the present and the past. It is a vision that, while not divorced from colonial expansion, contrasts with the erasures and reinscriptions associated with the settler-surveyor – a vision that Grant only half-imagines when he writes of "the Ojibbeway ... at home in his canoe" and "the Cree ... at home on his horse,"[38] and that many others failed to imagine at all. As David Chisholme writes in his introduction to *The Canadian Magazine and Literary Repository* in 1823:

> Though the country which we inhabit still bears the impress of infancy on her brow, and the stamp of uncultivated wildness on her forehead – though her woods are interminable and her soil lying waste – though the bear, the wolf and the buffalo roam in all the untractability of their ferocious nature through all her regions – and though many of her *native* sons and daughters remain still unblest with the light of knowledge and Christianity – yet the time may come when her present condition will be remembered no more – when the wilderness shall give place to the calm serenity of cultivation – when the wild beasts of the fields shall fly at the voice of man, and give place to the busy hum of a cheerful and industrious population.[39]

Against Chisholme's paradigm of forgetting, Thompson reminds us that to map is not only to wipe the slate clean in order to inscribe utopian dreams for the future; it is also to grapple with individual perceptions of the present: it is to be an explorer rather than a surveyor, to accommodate oneself *to* – rather than just *in* – its layers of meaning and experience.

What would it mean to fully absorb this understanding of the land; to allow it to displace the colonial spatial metanarrative, and to become the text rather than the subtext of our literary cartography? Germaine Warkentin calls upon "the powerful tools of contemporary literary analysis" to "give utterance to the other voices" whose presence can be felt in explorer writings: "Even in the partial and limited way which these essentially European texts permit," she suggests, "what emerges is a picture of great richness and complexity, and a social scene which, if re-examined with these questions in mind, may hold the key to the afterlife of their narrative of conquest, which is a matter of great interest to all of us, since we are living it."[40] Literary geography can be added to these tools. Illuminating not just the territorial claims that writers make, but also the counter-claims that arise from the gestures, glimpses, traces, and signs that point to other modes of habitation, literary geography interprets the territoriality both of colonial literature and of "the afterlife" of which she speaks. It might help us, then, to reimagine how we continue to occupy and share land.

This book has argued for greater recognition of the role that cartographic aesthetics and strategies played in the discursive claiming of settler space and of literary cartography as a testament to the power of maps as models of orientation and appropriation. It has also tried to resist an oversimplified reading of the territorializing imperatives that maps and text-maps record, drawing attention to those forces, geographical and human, that challenge the colonial imaginary and its efforts to enclose, codify, and appropriate the land. Colonial text-maps are full of evidence of the contradictory impulses to possess and to understand, to erase and to represent, to inscribe and to reflect; as much as they are animated by the creation of settler space, they are also records of wonder and wondering, of anxious reading and listening. Interpreting such records as lenses through which other perspectives might emerge gives the settler imperative less, not more, power. That one map-maker's stories can chafe against others confirms their tenuous hold on the land. The world moves in and out of focus, the literary cartographer's lines merely spatial stories marked with others that fray the edges of the myths of emptiness, *terra nullius*, and wilderness wastes upon which colonial expansion relied. Thus the broad arguments of *Mapping with Words* lean not just towards orientation, but also towards disorientation: these texts are rich with the potential for getting lost in a place marked by other codes and other ways of seeing. Methodologically, acknowledging this potential moves us away from a literary-geographical perspective that examines each text-map in its singularity, and towards a geocritical one that decenters the single story, instead opting "for a plural point of view" of places as "located at the crossroads of distinct representations."[41] We loosen the individual writer's hold on a place, and look to others for direction.

At issue in all representations of land is the land itself: the topography that is being coded and recoded, claimed, contested, inhabited, and reshaped in accordance with the figures that inform our perceptions of it. The map is one such figure, but it is not the only one. As Julie Cruikshank notes: "Indigenous knowledge and the European scientific tradition present very different models for thinking about the world. For example, a scientist may link information about any point on the earth's surface to a series of numbers giving its *longitude*, its *latitude*, and its *altitude*. To people who live there, that place may have further dimensions."[42] In "We Are All in the Ojibway Circle," his address to the Royal Commission on the Northern Environment, Chief John Kelly reveals these dimensions by shifting the model from cartography to geometry. Refiguring the spatiality of the regions across which writers such as Scott, Grant, and Thompson travelled, Kelly draws attention to the ongoing material and economic consequences of many of the cartographic imaginaries that this book describes. "Mr Commissioner, welcome to the territory of Treaty No. 3," he begins, his articulation of protocol reminding us that we might read Souzie's similar gesture of welcome in *Ocean to Ocean* not as an assimilatory one, but as a marker of territory (see chapter 4). The story that Kelly goes on to tell is about this territory, negotiated in 1871 on lands adjoining what would become Treaty 9 in northwestern Ontario. He speaks about its creation, about the promises that were supposed to sustain it, and about the greed that is endangering it. The land is variously defined by the language of human relationships, sharing, sustenance, deceit, neglect, betrayal, theft, and dispute. But above all, it is defined by the spatial figure of the circle:

> [A]s the years go by, the circle of the Ojibway gets bigger and bigger. Canadians of all colours and religions are entering that circle. You might feel that you have roots somewhere else, but in reality, you are right here with us. I do not know if you feel the throbbing of the earth in your chest, and if you feel the bear is your brother with a spirit purer and stronger than yours, or if the elk is on a higher level of life than is man. You may not share my spiritual anguish as I see the earth ravaged by the stranger, but you can no longer escape my fate as the soil turns barren and the rivers poison.[43]

Kelly's appeal for the environment depends upon a new spatial vision of Treaty 3 territory. The gridded spaces of European maps are absent; instead, the land and its people are encompassed in an "Ojibway circle" that signals an alternative sensibility to which European models of ownership are anathema. "This land is so unique," Kelly insists, "so intolerant of disturbance, that it seems blasphemous even to think of it as property."[44] As he later makes clear, the alternative sensibility that the circle encapsulates entails more than just an alternative way to imagine people in the landscape; it will, he hopes, create a more sustainable relationship among humans and the environment. The aesthetic reinscription of the terrain is also, importantly, a practical reclamation of the spaces that he sees as endangered by the other "system of life" that the Europeans and their descendents "have been attempting to graft upon" them.[45]

All Canadians continue to live in places created by colonial maps and their attendant "system of life." The instability of settler maps, however, suggests how easily they might have adopted others and how we might do so now to reorient ourselves in and to the complexities of this place. That Kelly's address eventually appeared in Michael Ondaatje's anthology of "Canadian Stories," *From Ink Lake*, confirms that these territorial negotiations take place in the arena of stories as well as politics, that our maps are literary. Combining the depth that words afford with the far-reaching spatial imaginary of cartography, the text-map queries not just "Where Is Here," but what it means to be here: to map with words, and to be always writing new ones.

Appendix of Figures

Figure 1 Part of James Chewett's *Map of the Province of Upper Canada and the Adjacent Territories in North America Compiled by James G. Chewett, Assistant Draftsman under the Direction of Thomas Ridout, Esqr., Surveyor General of the Province Shewing the Districts, Counties and Townships in which Are Situated the Lands Purchased from the Crown by the Canada Company, Incorporated 1826. To His Most Excellent Majesty King George IV ... This Map Is Most Humbly Dedicated by the Canada Company*, Canada Company, 1826. (Library and Archives Canada, n0018562k_a2.)

This part of Chewett's map includes the districts where the Moodies lived. It also reveals the close ties between mapping and colonial settlement, as the surveyor's grid appears to creep northward into the unmapped (and apparently vacant) edges of the shield country, and towards the coat of arms that presides over the whole.

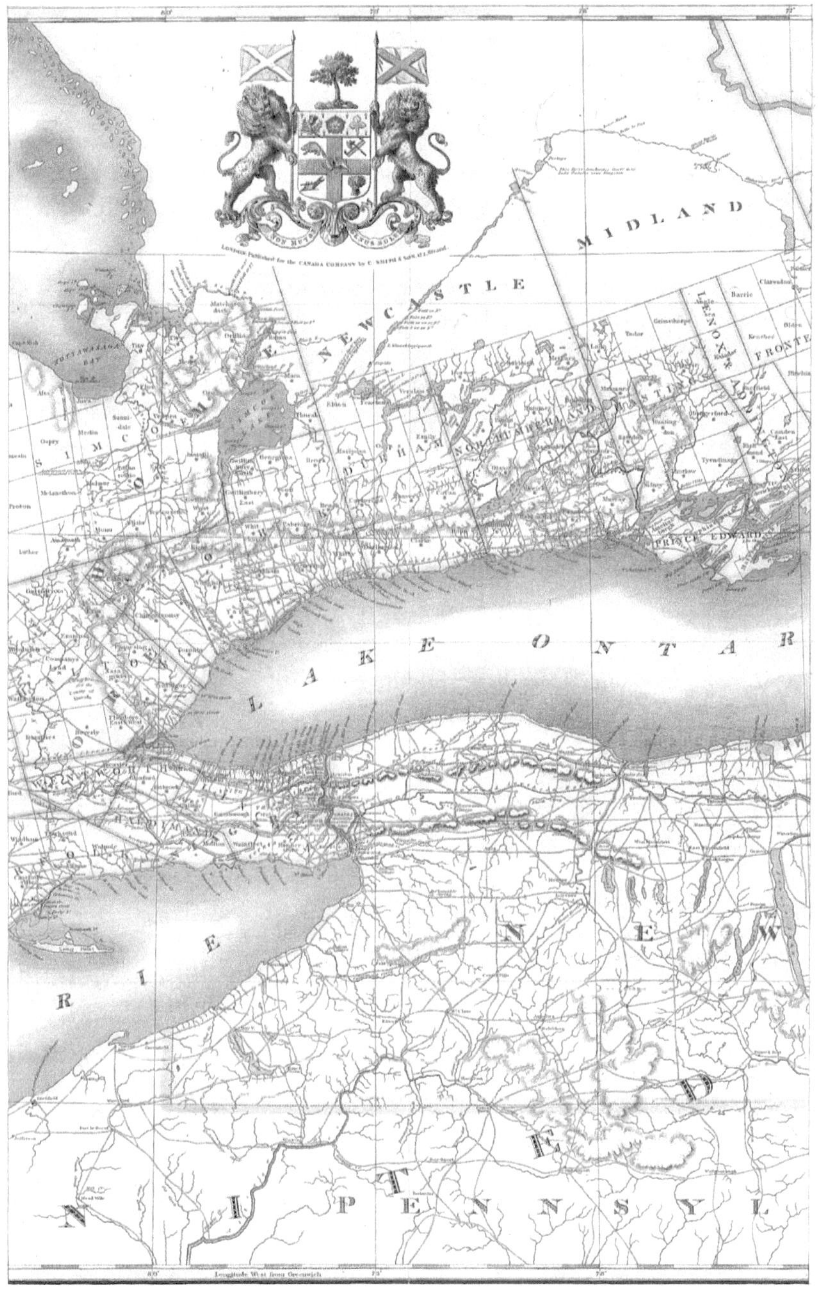
MIDLAND
NEWCASTLE
PRINCE EDWARD
LAKE ONTAR
E N
PENNSYL

Figure 2 *A New Map of North America, from the Latest Discoveries*, from Jonathan Carver's *Travels through the Interior Parts of North America, in the Years 1766, 1767, and 1768*, 3rd ed. (Courtesy of the David Rumsey Map Collection, David Rumsey Map Center, Stanford Libraries.)

Jonathan Carver's map of North America illustrates the limits of geographical knowledge in the late eighteenth century, when colonial settlement and surveys were concentrated in the eastern and southern parts of North America. It nevertheless also gives a sense of the emerging cartographic shape of what is now Canada, with the blank spaces beckoning map-makers north and west just a few years before David Thompson set out across this terrain (see figure 10).

A NEW MAP of NORTH AMERICA From the Latest Discoveries 1778.
Engraved for Carvers Travels.
BAFFINS BAY
Cumberland I
Efkimeaux
HUDSONS
BAY
Hudsons Straits
NEW NORTH WALES
NEW SOUTH WALES
LABRADOR
NEW BRITAIN
Criftinaux
Land of the Afsiniboils
WESTERN SEA
River of the West
NEW ALBION
Teguayo z Quivira
CANADA
LOUISIANA
NEW MEXICO
SOUTH CAROLINA
GULF OF MEXICO
New Bifcay
Panuco
Cape Florida
ATLANTIC OCEAN

Figure 3 Mahlon Burwell's December 1810 map of Delaware Township. (Archives of Ontario, F 501–1-0–0-6.)

This hand-drawn map (one of many large-scale maps that Burwell drew for Colonel Talbot, with the names of settlers written over each plot of land) exemplifies the aesthetic tension between the diagrammatic and topographic elements of the mapped landscape that Adam Hood Burwell's poem captures. The interplay of geometric and organic shapes, as the surveyor both responds to the land's irregularities and also subjugates them to his designs, illustrates the dual function of cartography to at once represent and create geographical space.

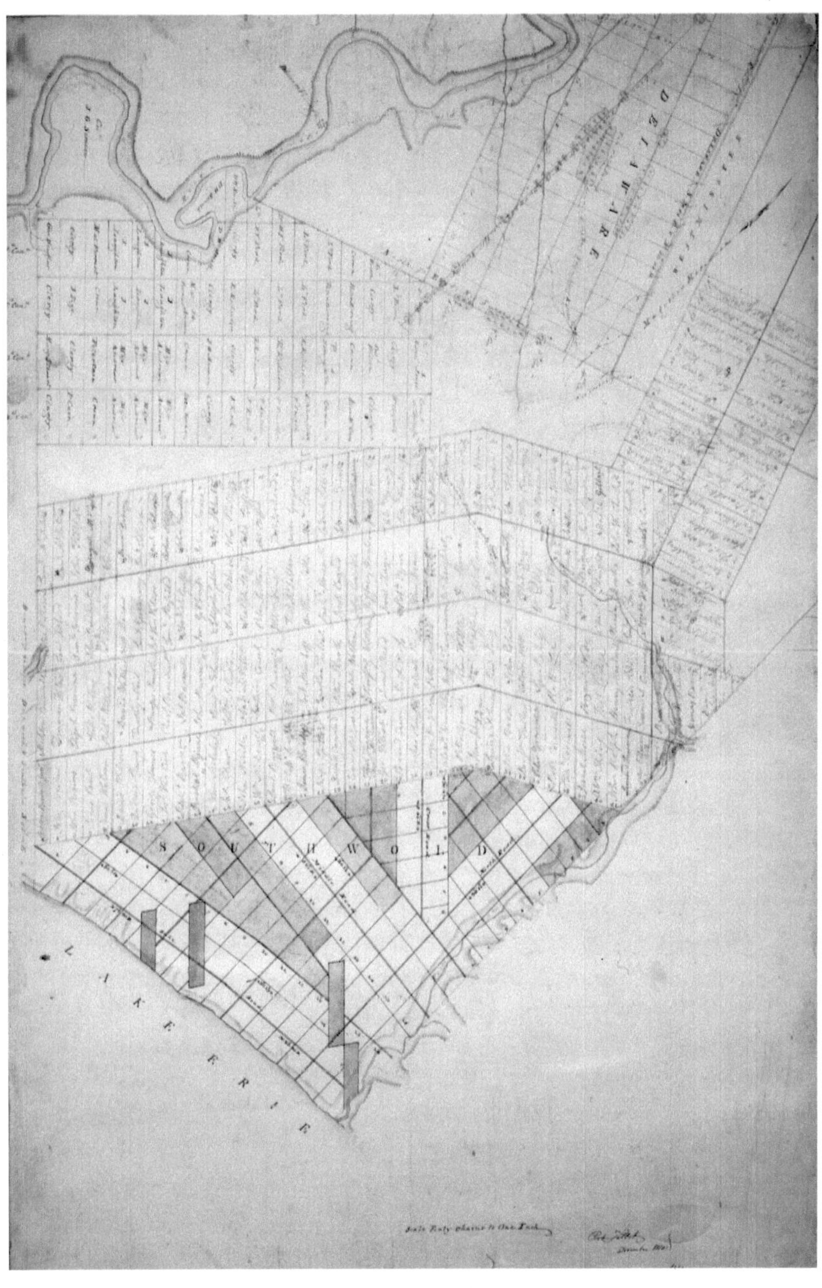
DELAWARE
SOUTHWOLD
LAKE ERIE

Figure 4 Henri Chatelain's *Carte Particulière du Fleuve Saint Louis Dressée sur les Lieux Avec les Noms des Sauvages du Païs*, c. 1719. (Archives of Ontario, C 279–0-0–0-16.)

Bordering this map of New France are lists of the region's animals, insects, fish, birds, trees, and fruits, suggesting the connection between natural history inventories and expanding geographical knowledge.

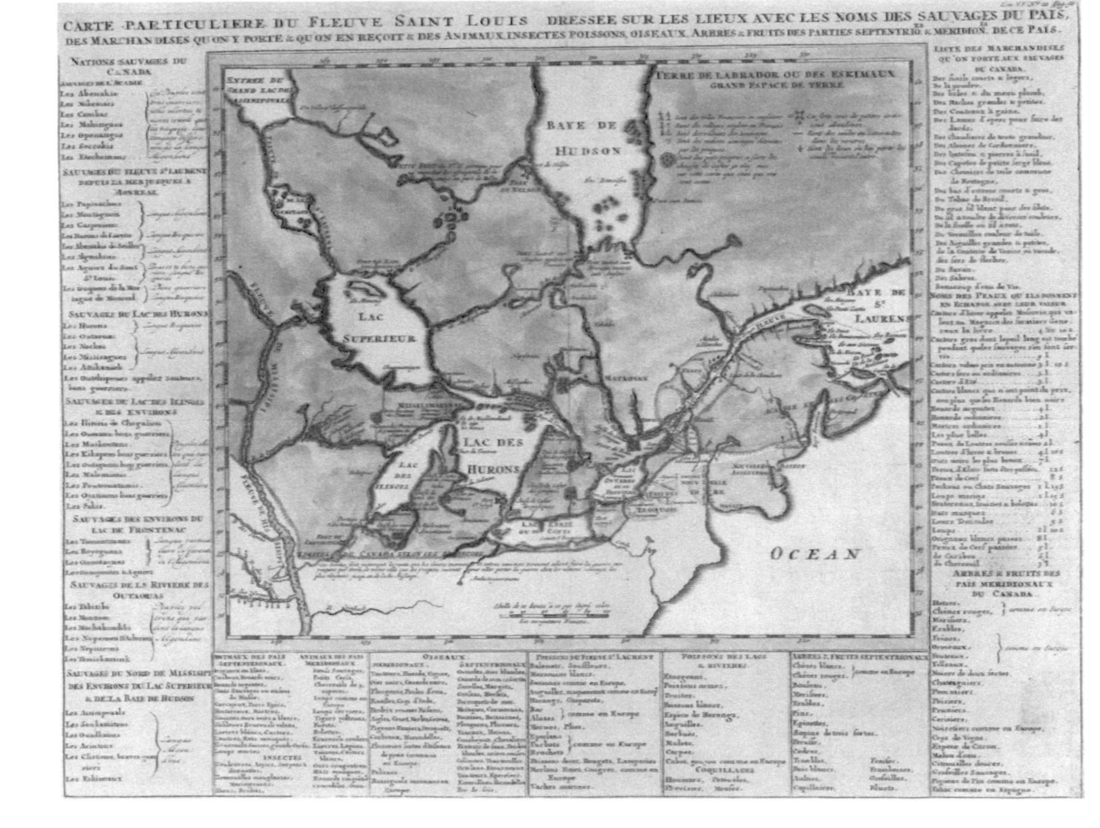
CARTE PARTICULIERE DU FLEUVE SAINT LOUIS DRESSEE SUR LES LIEUX AVEC LES NOMS DES SAUVAGES DU PAIS,
DES MARCHANDISES QU'ON Y PORTE & QU'ON EN REÇOIT & DES ANIMAUX, INSECTES, POISSONS, OISEAUX, ARBRES & FRUITS DES PARTIES SEPTENTRION.LES & MERIDION.LES DE CE PAIS.
NATIONS SAUVAGES DU CANADA
SAUVAGES DU FLEUVE S.T LAURENT DEPUIS LA MER JUSQUES A MONREAL
SAUVAGES DU LAC DES HURONS
SAUVAGES DU LAC DES ILINOIS & DES ENVIRONS
SAUVAGES DES ENVIRONS DU LAC DE FRONTENAC
SAUVAGES DE LA RIVIERE DES OUTAOUAS
SAUVAGES DU NORD DE MISSISIPI DES ENVIRONS DU LAC SUPERIEUR & DE LA BAIE DE HUDSON
ENTREE DU GRAND LAC DES ASSINIPOUALS
TERRE DE LABRADOR OU DES ESKIMAUX
GRAND ESPACE DE TERRE
BAYE DE HUDSON
LAC SUPERIEUR
LAC DES HURONS
LAC DES ILINOIS
LAC ERIE
BAYE DE S.T LAURENS
OCEAN
LISTE DES MARCHANDISES QU'ON PORTE AUX SAUVAGES DU CANADA
NOMS DES PEAUX QU'ILS DONNENT EN ECHANGE AVEC LEUR VALEUR
ARBRES & FRUITS DES PAIS MERIDIONAUX DU CANADA
ANIMAUX DES PAIS SEPTENTRIONAUX
ANIMAUX DES PAIS MERIDIONAUX
INSECTES
OISEAUX
POISSONS DU FLEUVE S.T LAURENT
POISSONS DES LACS & RIVIERES
COQUILLAGES
ARBRES & FRUITS SEPTENTRIONAUX

Figure 5 David William Smyth's *Map of the Province of Upper Canada, Describing all the New Settlements, Townships, &c. with the Countries Adjacent, from Quebec to Lake Huron*, 1818. (Library and Archives Canada, e008316611.)

One of the striking effects of this map is the way in which the hinterland spaces overwhelm the mapped ones. Against the Chippewa (Ojibway) Hunting Country to the north and east of Lake Huron (and the generalized "Indians" to the west of it), along with the unsurveyed Great Tract of Woodland that extends north and east of the Talbot settlement, the settler landscape that is Burwell's sole focus becomes a diminutive, almost insignificant feature of the larger geography. What is prominent on Smyth's map, however, is the international boundary, which, clearly marked, obscures the ease with which this imaginary line was breached in 1812. Considering Burwell's poem as a piece of literary cartography embedded within this small-scale map clarifies the effect of mapping on spatial experience and perspective, as the singular place that he describes becomes at once its own world and part of a larger cartographic whole.

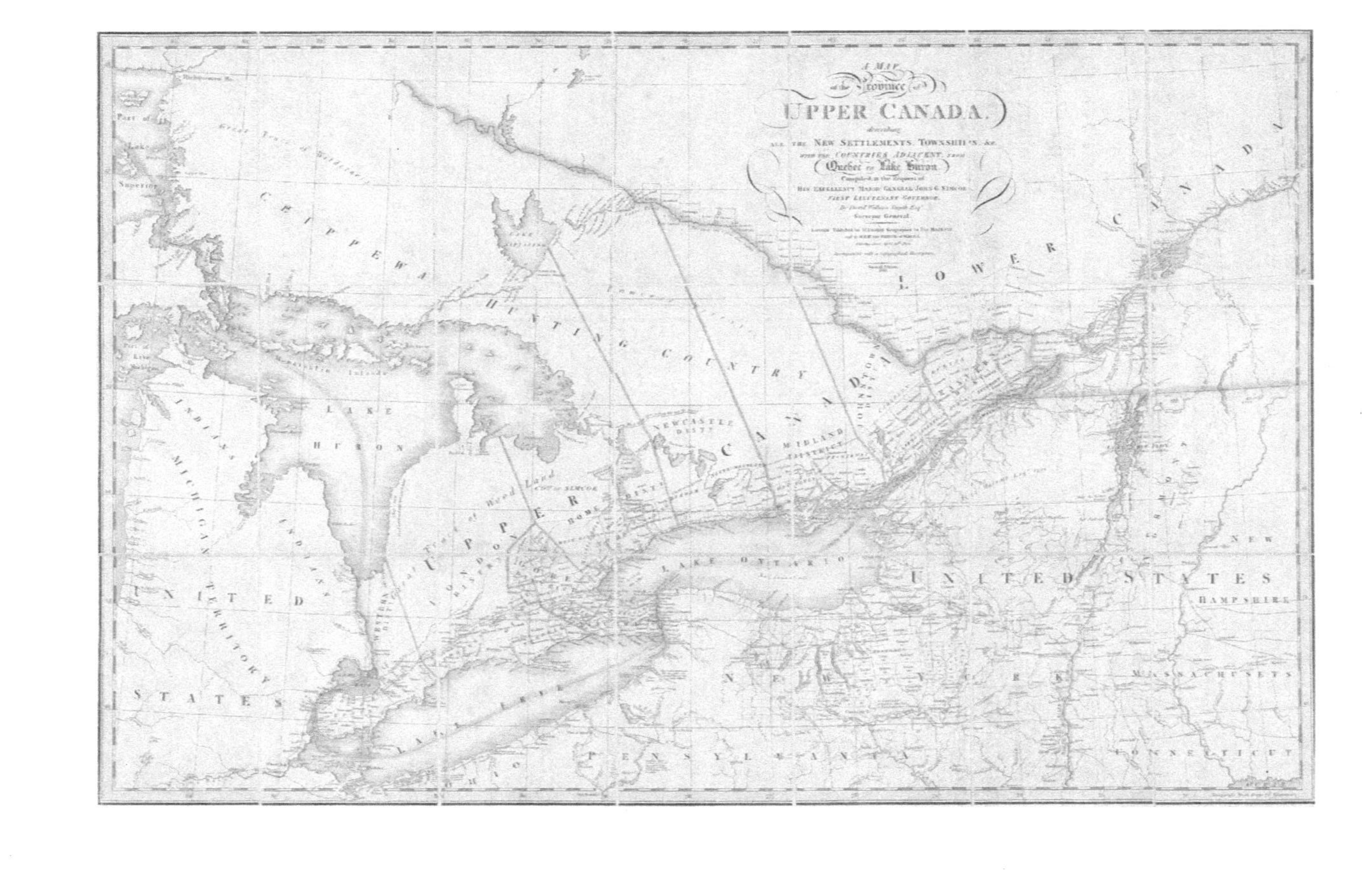
A MAP
of the Province of
UPPER CANADA.
describing
ALL THE NEW SETTLEMENTS, TOWNSHIPS, &c.
with the COUNTRIES ADJACENT, from
Quebec to Lake Huron.
Compiled at the Request of
HIS EXCELLENCY MAJOR GENERAL JOHN G. SIMCOE,
FIRST LIEUTENANT GOVERNOR.
Surveyor General.
LOWER CANADA
UPPER CANADA
CHIPPEWA HUNTING COUNTRY
LAKE HURON
LAKE ONTARIO
LAKE ERIE
NEWCASTLE DISTT
MIDLAND DISTRICT
UNITED STATES
MICHIGAN TERRITORY
INDIANS
NEW YORK
NEW HAMPSHIRE
MASSACHUSETS
CONNECTICUT
PENNSYLVANIA
OHIO

Figure 6 Frederick Preston Rubidge's *A Chart, Showing the Interior Navigation of the District of Newcastle, Upper Canada, and the Proposed Improvements on the Otonabee River etc.*, 1833. (Library and Archives Canada, n0003052.)

This map complements Traill's goal of providing guidance and accommodation through a more fully developed sense of "the geography of this portion of the country."[1] Emphasizing navigability, it frames and orders the territory that Traill "fills in" with her elaborate descriptions, not just in *The Backwoods* but in her later botanical writings as well.

1 Traill, *Backwoods*, 51.

A CHART, shewing the Interior Navigation of the ***DISTRICT***
of Newcastle, Upper Canada, and the proposed improvements on the Otanabee River &c.
Drawn by F.P.Rubidge, and engraved by T.Evans, for the Cobourg Star.

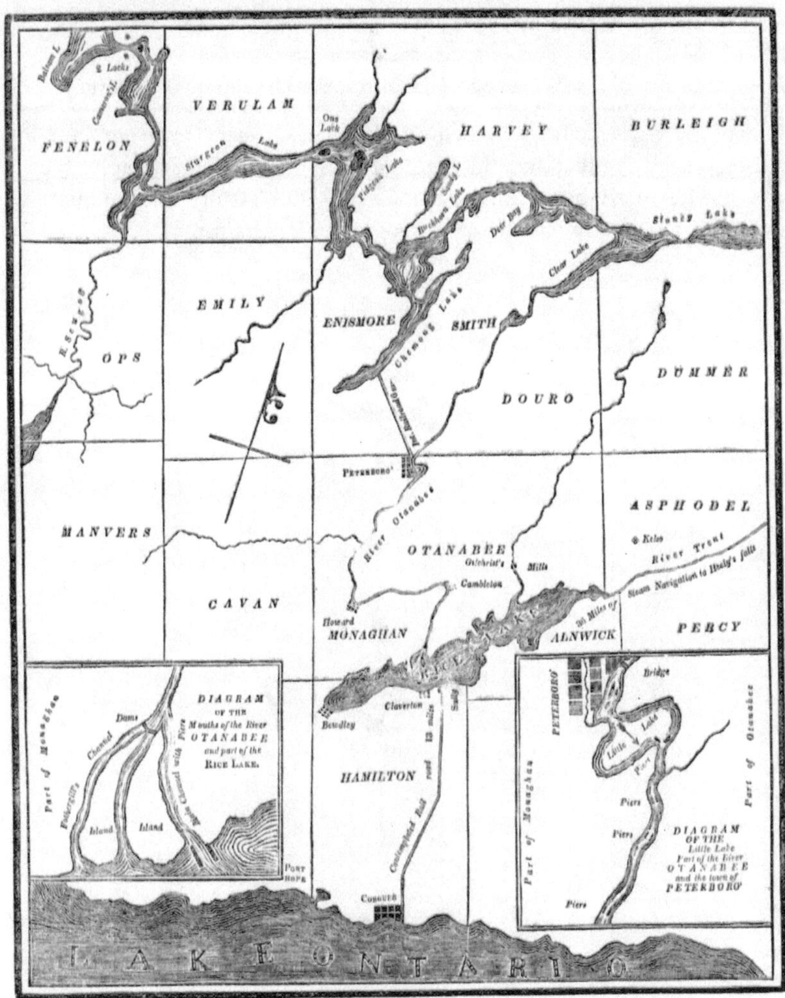

TABLE of DISTANCES.

COBOURG to RICE LAKE . . . . 18 Miles, Land carriage.
RICE LAKE to PETERBORO' . . . 25 By Steam-boat.
PETERBORO' to CHEMONG LAKE . . 7 Miles Land carriage.

CHEMONG thro' SMITH, ENNISMORE, HARVEY, VERULAM,OPS, CARTWRIGHT and FENELON, 81 Miles by Steam-boat.
RICE LAKE to Healey's falls in Seymour,35 Miles, by Steam-boat.

Figure 7 Map showing Fort Pitt to Fort Edmonton from Grant's *Ocean to Ocean*. (Image courtesy of Bruce Peel Special Collections, University of Alberta.)

Many of the maps included in the first edition of *Ocean to Ocean* are Captain Palliser's. Layering text over the graphic rendering of the topography, they showcase the interwoven practice of mapping land, history, and colonial desire as they converge on the same geographical terrain.

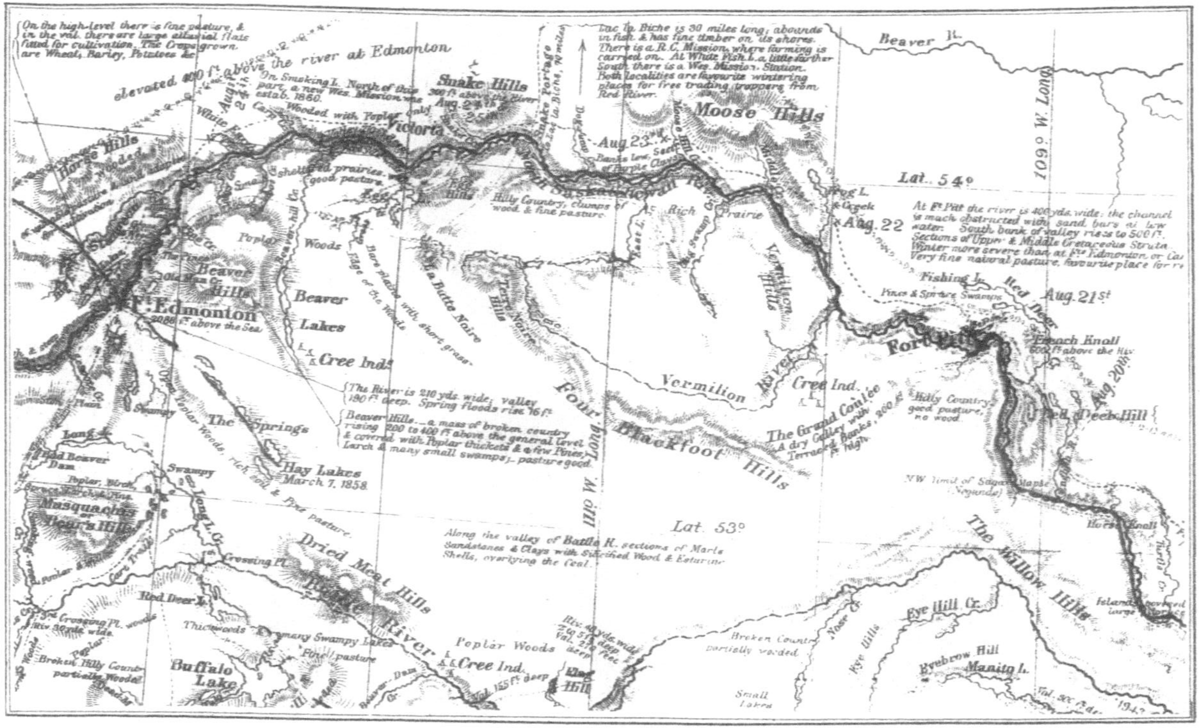

FORT PITT TO FORT EDMONTON.

Figure 8 *Skull of the Headless Indian* from Grant's *Ocean to Ocean*. (Image courtesy of Bruce Peel Special Collections, University of Alberta.)

SKULL OF THE HEADLESS INDIAN.

Figure 9 Map No. 20a showing the Indian treaties in Ontario from James L. Morris's *Map of the Province of Ontario: Dominion of Canada*, Ontario: Department of Surveys, 1931. (Archives of Ontario, F 1060–1-0–51.)

This map illustrates both the "patch-work" of treaties that Scott describes and the contrast that he also marks, in "The Height of Land," between the concentration of people in the densely settled south and the purportedly empty shield and muskeg to the north. That Morris drew the coloured treaty boundaries over an existing provincial map illuminates the cartographic project of reimagining the land blanketed by treaty territories lying "edge to edge."

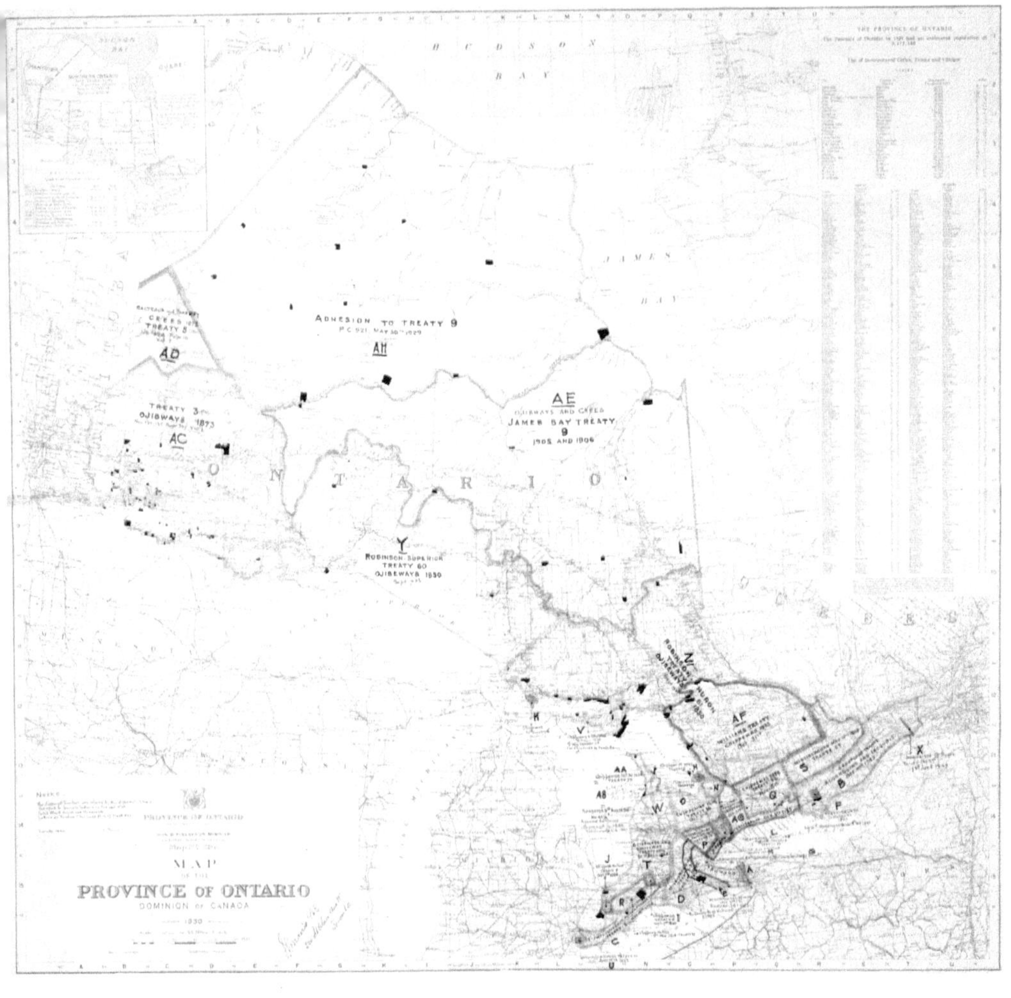
HUDSON BAY
JAMES BAY
CREES
TREATY 5
AD
ADHESION TO TREATY 9
AH
TREATY 3
OJIBWAYS 1873
AC
AE
OJIBWAYS AND CREES
JAMES BAY TREATY
9
1905 AND 1906
ONTARIO
Y
ROBINSON SUPERIOR
TREATY 60
OJIBWAYS 1850
AF
MAP
PROVINCE OF ONTARIO
DOMINION OF CANADA
1930

Figure 10 Two details (including the Peace and Athabasca rivers and the Columbia River to the Pacific Ocean) from the *Map of the North-West Territory of the Province of Canada from Actual Survey during the Years 1792 to 1812 ... 1813 and 1814 ... by David Thompson, Astronomical Surveyor.* (Historical Atlas of Canada, Library and Archives Canada/NMC R/701/1813–1814.)

Thompson's Great Map, the first to visually link the northwest with Canada in the east (at Lake Superior), transformed the colonial spatial imaginary and anticipated the expansion of the Dominion westward. At the same time, the Indigenous nations and toponyms that he records mark the cultural significance of this vast region that his *Narrative* would go on to fill in in remarkable detail.

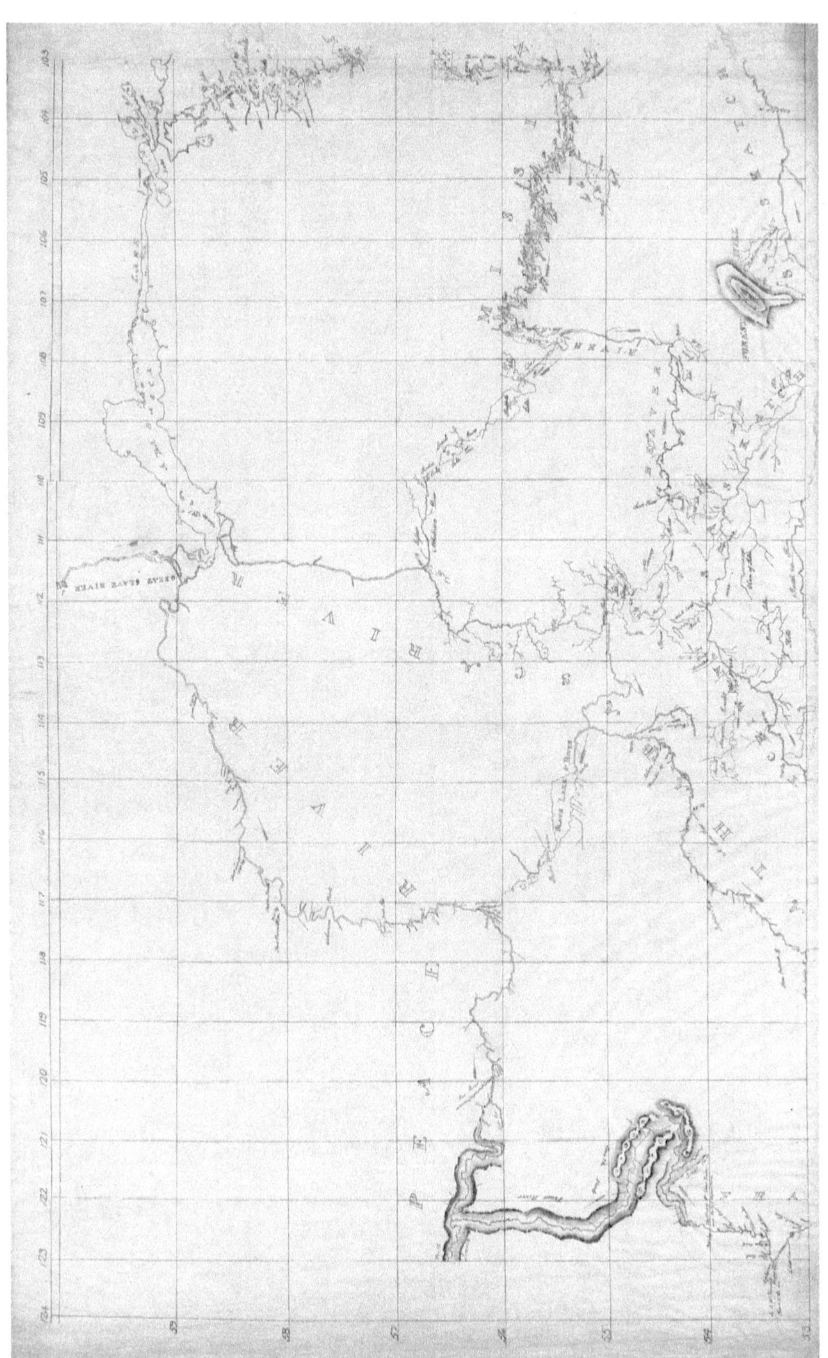

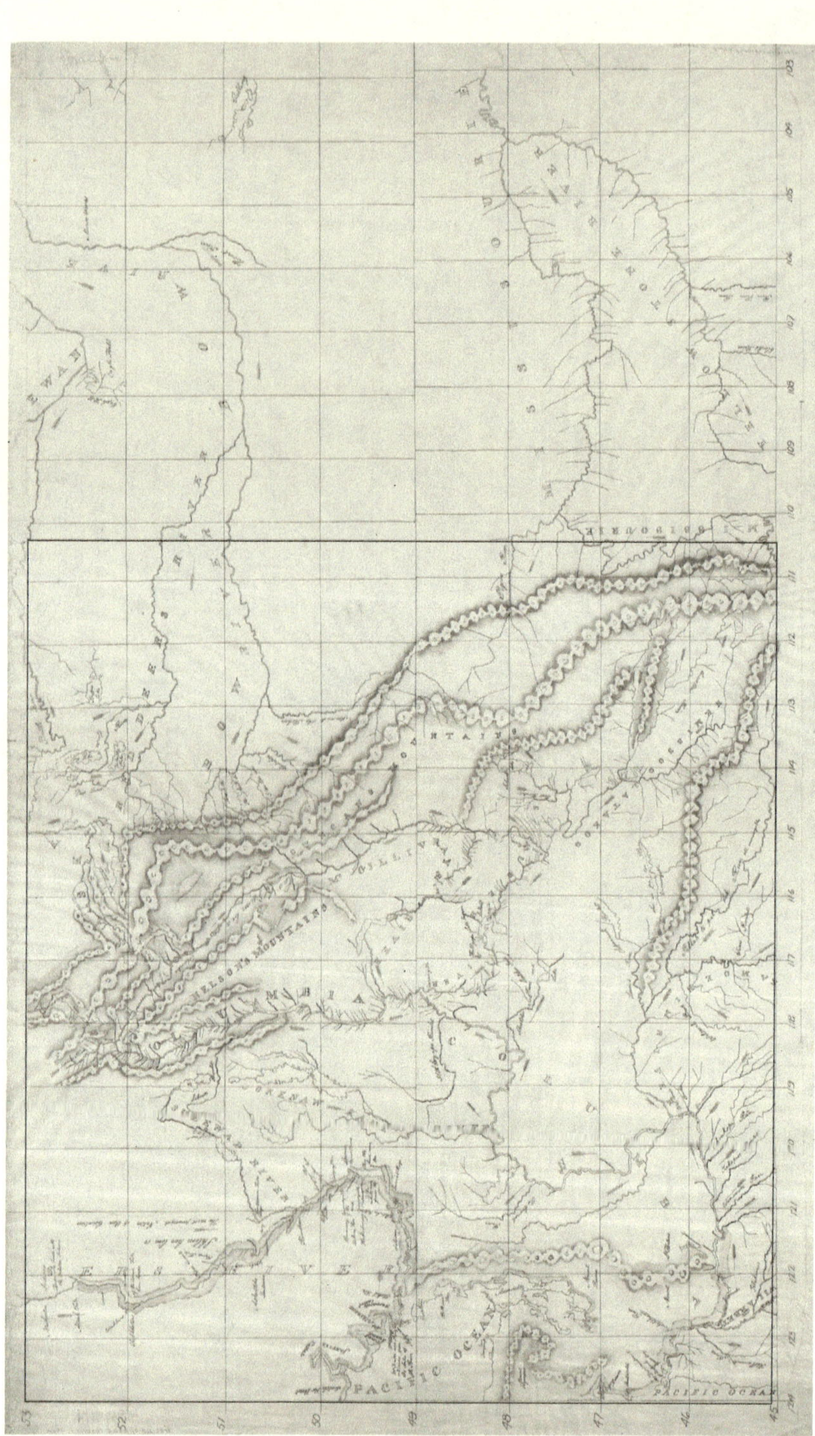

Notes

Introduction

1 Susanna Moodie, *Roughing It in the Bush* (1852), ed. Michael A. Peterman (New York: Norton, 2007), 187.
2 Tom Conley, *The Self-Made Map: Cartographic Writing in Early Modern France* (Minneapolis: University of Minnesota Press, 1996), 303.
3 John Pickles, *A History of Spaces: Cartographic Reason, Mapping and the Geo-coded World* (London: Routledge, 2004), 5; Geoff King, *Mapping Reality: An Exploration of Cultural Cartographies* (New York: St Martin's, 1996), 15.
4 Catharine Parr Traill, *The Backwoods of Canada: Being Letters from the Wife of an Emigrant Officer, Illustrative of the Domestic Economy of British America*, 1836, ed. David Staines (Toronto: McClelland & Stewart, 1989), 161–2.
5 Moodie, *Roughing It*, 178.
6 Florence Stratton, "Cartographic Lessons: Susanna Moodie's *Roughing It in the Bush* and Thomas King's *Green Grass, Running Water*," *Canadian Literature* (Summer 1999): 84.
7 I understand the distinction between space and place primarily through Yi Fu Tuan's theorizing of these concepts and experiences. "Space is transformed into place as it acquires definition and meaning," Tuan writes, adding that "the attempt to impose a spatial order by means of a grid of cardinal directions" – such as are found on many maps – "results in the establishment of a pattern of significant places, including the cardinal points and center." Yi Fu Tuan, *Space and Place: The Perspective of Experience* (Minneapolis: University of Minnesota Press, 1977), 136.
8 Henry Dearborn qtd. in James Belich, *Replenishing the Earth: The Settler Revolution and the Rise of the Angloworld, 1783–1939* (Oxford: Oxford University Press, 2009), 183.

9 See John Warkentin, introduction to *So Vast and Various: Interpreting Canada's Regions in the Nineteenth and Twentieth Centuries*, ed. John Warkentin (Montreal: McGill-Queen's University Press, 2010), 3–38.

10 For a concise explanation of the ways in which maps created illusions of tabula rasa and established colonial property in Canada, see Cole Harris, "How Did Colonialism Dispossess? Comments from an Edge of Empire," *Annals of the Association of American Geographers* 9.1 (2004): 165–82, 175–6; see also Stephen J. Hornsby, *Surveyors of Empire: Samuel Holland, J.F.W. Des Barres, and the Making of the* Atlantic Neptune (Montreal: McGill-Queen's University Press, 2011).

11 Belich, *Replenishing*, 279.

12 Common in the early period of settlement under John Graves Simcoe, these town plans (detailed down to the locations of public buildings and parks) were drawn and used as advertisements to emigrants before the land was actually surveyed. Several of these paper towns never materialized – a fact that highlights the fictional as well as anticipatory qualities of maps. See Jacob Spelt, *Urban Development in South-Central Ontario* (Toronto: McClelland & Stewart, 1972), 21.

13 J.B. Harley, *The New Nature of Maps: Essays in the History of Cartography* (Baltimore: Johns Hopkins University Press, 2001), 190. See also G. Malcolm Lewis, *Cartographic Encounters: Perspectives on North American Mapmaking and Map Use* (Chicago: University of Chicago Press, 1998), 58; Theodore Binnema, "How Does a Map Mean? Old Swan's Map of 1801 and the Blackfoot World," in *From Rupert's Land to Canada*, ed. Theodore Binnema et al. (Edmonton: University of Alberta Press, 2001), 201–24.

14 John MacTaggart, *Three Years in Canada: An Account of the Actual State of the Country in 1826-7-8 Comprehending its Resources, Productions, Improvements, and Capabilities; and Including Sketches of the State of Society, Advice to Emigrants, &c.*, vol. 1 (London: Colburn, 1829), vi.

15 Carl Berger, *Science, God, and Nature in Victorian Canada* (Toronto: University of Toronto Press, 1983), 16.

16 Lisa Brooks, *The Common Pot: The Recovery of Native Space in the Northeast.* (Minneapolis: Minnesota University Press, 2008), xix–xlvi.

17 For a description of literary geography, see Robert T. Tally, *Spatiality* (New York: Routledge, 2013), 79–80.

18 Pickles, *History*, 4–5, 109, 12, 22, 21.

19 Harley, *New Nature*, 53.

20 Tuan, *Space and Place*, 77.

21 Tally, *Spatiality*, 2. See also Christina Ljungberg, *Creative Dynamics: Diagrammatic Strategies in Narrative* (Amsterdam: John Benjamins, 2012), 1.

22 From Frye's "garrison" thesis, to D.M.R. Bentley's baseland and hinterland model of "ecological fitness," to W.H. New's exegesis of "space, presence, and power," to Laurie Ricou's bioregional readings of the Pacific northwest, to Margery Fee's recent study of the complexity and diversity of "literary land claims" in Canada, the spatial turn resonates in Canadian literary criticism, with neologisms such as "langscapes" and "architexts" attesting to a keen critical interest in articulating the close bond between literature and the physical spaces that it at once reflects and creates. The literary maps and atlases that have been drawn of this country illustrate this profound connection. Places, they remind us, are the products of writers, just as writers are the products of places. See Northrop Frye, *The Bush Garden: Essays on the Canadian Imagination*, intro. Linda Hutcheon (Concord, ON: Anansi, 1995), 222; D.M.R. Bentley, *The Gay]Grey Moose: Essays on the Ecologies and Mythologies of Canadian Poetry, 1690–1990* (Ottawa: University of Ottawa Press, 1992); W.H. New, *Land Sliding: Imagining Space, Presence, and Power in Canadian Writing* (Toronto: University of Toronto Press, 1997); Laurie Ricou, *The Arbutus/Madrone Files: Reading the Pacific Northwest* (Edmonton: NeWest Press, 2002); Margery Fee, *Literary Land Claims: The "Indian Land Question" from Pontiac's War to Attawapiskat* (Waterloo, ON: Wilfrid Laurier University Press, 2015); Gaile McGregor, *The Wacousta Syndrome: Explorations in the Canadian Langscape* (Toronto: University of Toronto Press, 1985); D.M.R. Bentley, *Canadian Architexts: Essays on Literature and Architecture in Canada: 1759–2006* (London, ON: Canadian Poetry Press, 2009).

23 Graham Huggan, *Territorial Disputes: Maps and Mapping Strategies in Contemporary Canadian and Australian Fiction* (Toronto: University of Toronto Press, 1994), 31, 32, 39.

24 Fee, *Literary Land Claims*, 38.

25 Huggan, *Territorial Disputes*, xv.

26 See Jean Baudrillard, *Simulacra and Simulation*, trans. Sheila Faria Glaser (Ann Arbor: University of Michigan Press, 1994), 1; Geoff King qtd. in Pickles, *A History*, 31.

27 Harley, *New Nature*, 159.

28 Gilles Deleuze and Felix Guattari, *A Thousand Plateaus: Capitalism and Schizophrenia*, trans. Brian Massumi (Minneapolis: University of Minnesota Press, 1987), 12.

29 Pickles, *A History*, 184, 189 (ellipses in original).

30 Fee, *Literary Land Claims*, 226; Dwayne Trevor Donald, "Forts, Curriculum, and Indigenous Métissage: Imagining Decolonization of

Aboriginal-Canadian Relations in Educational Contexts," *First Nations Perspectives* 2.1 (2009): 1–24, 9.

31 Adele Perry, *On the Edge of Empire: Gender, Race, and the Making of British Columbia, 1849–1871* (Toronto: University of Toronto Press, 2001), 7.

32 Aritha Van Herk, *A Frozen Tongue* (Sydney, Australia: Dangaroo, 1992), 27.

33 See Paul Carter, *The Road to Botany Bay: An Exploration of Landscape and History* (Minneapolis: University of Minnesota Press, 2010); William Cronon, *Changes in the Land: Indians, Colonists, and the Ecology of New England* (New York: Hill and Wang, 1983).

34 Denis Cosgrove, prologue to *Envisioning Landscapes, Making Worlds: Geography and the Humanities*, ed. Stephen Daniels et al. (New York: Routledge, 2011), xxiii.

35 Some of these contemporary literary-cartographic trajectories are explored in Sarah Wylie Krotz, "Place and Memory: Rethinking the Literary Map of Canada," *English Studies in Canada* 40.2–3 (June/September 2014): 133–54.

1. Illuminating the Horizon

1 Thomas Cary, *Abram's Plains* (London, ON: Canadian Poetry Press, 1986), 1–2.

2 See Bentley, introduction to *Abram's Plains*, by Thomas Cary (London, ON: Canadian Poetry Press, 1986), xxix.

3 Adam Hood Burwell, *Talbot Road: A Poem*, intro. D.M.R. Bentley (London, ON: Canadian Poetry Press, 1991), 93–4.

4 See Bentley, introduction to *Talbot Road*, by Adam Hood Burwell (London, ON: Canadian Poetry Press, 1991), xii.

5 Michael Williams, "Burwell, Adam Hood," *Dictionary of Canadian Biography*, vol. 6, University of Toronto/Université Laval, 2003–, http://www.biographi.ca/en/bio/burwell_adam_hood_7E.html. See also Daniel Gauvin, "Cary, Thomas (1751–1823)," *Dictionary of Canadian Biography*, vol. 6, University of Toronto/Université Laval, 2003–, http://www.biographi.ca/en/bio/cary_thomas_1751_1823_6E.html.

6 Established by John Denham in *Cooper's Hill* (1642), topographical poems generally follow Dr Johnson's definition of "local poetry," taking as their "fundamental subject ... some particular landscape ... poetically described, with the addition of such embellishment as may be described by historical retrospection and incidental meditation.'" Samuel Johnson, *Lives of the English Poets*, vol. 1 (London: Oxford University Press, 1933), 54, qtd. in Bentley, introduction to *Talbot Road*, xiii.

7 See Fee, *Literary Land Claims*; Henry Kelsey, "Now Reader Read..." in *Early Long Poems on Canada*, ed. D.M.R. Bentley (London, ON: Canadian Poetry Press, 1993), 5–7, lines 83–5. See also D.M.R. Bentley, *Mnemographia Canadensis: Essays on Memory, Community, and Environment in Canada*, vol. 1, *Muse and Recall* (London, ON: Canadian Poetry Press, 1999), 49, 50.
8 Oliver Goldsmith, "The Rising Village," 1834, ed. Gerald Lynch (in Bentley, *Early Long Poems on Canada*, 199–216), 31, 42.
9 Hornsby, *Surveyors of Empire*, 6. See also Hornsby, *Surveyors of Empire*, ch. 6; Don W. Thomson, *Men and Meridians: The History of Surveying and Mapping in Canada*, vol. 1 (Ottawa: Queen's University Press, 1966), 98, 107.
10 Jonathan Carver, *The New Universal Traveller* (London: Robinson Press, 1779), 625.
11 Ibid.
12 Burwell, *Talbot Road*, 485–6.
13 D.M.R. Bentley, *Mimic Fires: Accounts of Early Long Poems on Canada* (Montreal: McGill-Queen's University Press, 1994), 30; Bentley, introduction to *Talbot Road*, xxxvi.
14 Susan Glickman, *The Picturesque and the Sublime: A Poetics of the Canadian Landscape* (Montreal: McGill-Queen's Univeristy Press, 1998), 23.
15 Cary, *Abram's Plains*, 492.
16 Ibid., 2–14.
17 Ibid., 15–16.
18 Ibid., 454–66.
19 Ibid., 64–8.
20 Royal Proclamation of 7 October 1763, qtd. in Thomson, *Meridians*, 212.
21 Belich, *Replenishing*, 3; R. Cole Harris, *The Reluctant Land: Society, Space, and Environment in Canada before Confederation* (Vancouver: University of British Columbia Press, 2008), 232.
22 Cary, *Abram's Plains*, 21–30.
23 Bentley, *Mimic*, 30.
24 Cary, *Abram's Plains*, 29–39.
25 Moodie, *Roughing It*, 351.
26 Cary, *Abram's Plains*, 196–211.
27 Ibid., 222–3.
28 Oliver Goldsmith, "The Deserted Village," 1770, in *The Norton Anthology of English Literature*, 6th ed., vol. 1, ed. M.H. Abrams (New York: W.W. Norton & Co., 1993), 2484–93, lines 360–5.
29 Ibid., 351–8.
30 Cary, *Abram's Plains*, 116–21.

31 Ibid., 126–7.

32 See Bentley, *Mimic*, 34; Cary, *Abram's Plains*, 126–7.

33 Bentley, introduction to *Abram's Plains*, xxxiii. For further discussion of the relation between *Abram's Plains* and its eighteenth-century English models, see Glickman, *Picturesque*, 20–31.

34 Smaro Kamboureli, *On the Edge of Genre: The Contemporary Canadian Long Poem* (Toronto: University of Toronto Press, 1991), 17.

35 Lawrence Buell, *The Environmental Imagination: Thoreau, Nature Writing, and the Formation of American Culture* (Cambridge, MA: Belknap Press, 1995), 253.

36 Cary, *Abram's Plains*, 59–63.

37 Ibid., 33–47; as the historian Donald B. Smith recounts, these figures are documented on pictographs and were part of the oral literary tradition of this vast area. Donald B. Smith, *Mississauga Portraits: Ojibwe Voices from Nineteenth-Century Canada* (Toronto: University of Toronto Press, 2013), 42–4.

38 Cary, *Abram's Plains*, 54–5, 130–1.

39 Ibid., 99–109.

40 Ibid., 220–1.

41 Ibid., 66.

42 Ibid., 43–9.

43 As Robert Pogue Harrison observes, Western thought is steeped in the long-entrenched idea that forests were "an obstacle to visibility" and thus to civilization. Harrison, *Forests: The Shadow of Civilization* (Chicago: University of Chicago Press, 1993), 10. Cary, *Abram's Plains*, 50.

44 Cary, *Abram's Plains*, 434.

45 Ibid., 398–407, 363–436.

46 Harley, *New Nature*, 37, 146, 37, 54.

47 Mark Monmonier, *How to Lie with Maps* (Chicago: University of Chicago Press, 1991).

48 Goldsmith, "The Rising Village," 110.

49 Cary, *Abram's Plains*, 56–61.

50 Ibid., 190.

51 Bentley, *Mimic*, 34.

52 Cary, *Abram's Plains*, 414–17

53 Ibid., 147–53.

54 Qtd. in Smith, *Mississauga Portraits*, 41n53.

55 Goldsmith, "The Rising Village," 81–8.

56 Harris, *Reluctant Land*, 286.

57 Duncan Cambell Scott, *Selected Poems of Duncan Campbell Scott* (Toronto: Ryerson Press, 1951), 37.

58 Cary, *Abram's Plains*, 458–69.
59 Hornsby, *Surveyors*, 26–7.
60 Harley, *New Nature*, 62.
61 Bentley, introduction to *Talbot Road*, xxxv.
62 Burwell, *Talbot Road*, "Argument."
63 Burwell, *Talbot Road*, 485–6.
64 Thomson, *Meridians*, 236.
65 James H. Coyne, ed., *The Talbot Papers . . .* (Transactions of the Royal Society of Canada, 1909), 189–90. See also Thomson, *Meridians*, 239.
66 Pickles, *History*, 81.
67 Burwell, *Talbot Road*, 114, 548–63.
68 Tim Ingold, *Lines: A Brief History* (New York: Routledge, 2007), 81; Burwell, *Talbot Road*, 491; Ingold, *Lines*, 81.
69 Burwell, *Talbot Road*, 11–12 (my emphasis), 5.
70 Ibid., 95–6.
71 Ibid., 24.
72 Ibid., 301–8.
73 Ibid., 227, 287, 212.
74 J. Edward Chamberlin, *If This Is Your Land, Where Are Your Stories? Finding Common Ground* (Toronto: Knopf, 2003), 28.
75 Ibid., 28; Bentley, *Mnemographia*, 47.
76 Burwell, *Talbot Road*, 20–7, 91.
77 Thomson, *Meridians*, 237. See also Ron Brown, *The Lake Erie Shore: Ontario's Forgotten South Coast* (Toronto: Dundurn, 2009), 105.
78 Burwell, *Talbot Road*, 13–14.
79 Ibid., 13–22.
80 Harley, *New Nature*, 81; Anna Brownell Jameson, *Winter Studies and Summer Rambles in Canada*, 1838, afterward by Clara Thomas (Toronto: McClelland & Stewart, 1990), 239; Adam Kidd, *The Huron Chief*, in Bentley, *Early Long Poems on Canada*, 293–369; Burwell, *Talbot Road*, 374.
81 Burwell, *Talbot Road*, 14–28.
82 Ibid., 31–8.
83 Ibid., 69, 77–84.
84 Ibid., 86.
85 Ibid., 105–8. Although it might be the case that, as Bentley suggests, the poet's choice of the verb "swarm" (which he repeats at line 442) "partly undercuts his celebration of the new settlers," this verb also arguably works to convey the dramatic effect of the sudden arrival of large numbers of emigrants (around 20,000 by 1826) in the area. Bentley, introduction to Burwell, *Talbot Road*, xxxiv. See also Howison's use of the

term at n16. John Howison, *Sketches of Upper Canada: Domestic, Local, and Characteristic*, 1821 (Toronto: Coles, 1970), n16.

86 Burwell, *Talbot Road*, 36–40.

87 See Gray et al., *Inventory of the Thomas Talbot Papers* (Archives of Ontario: June 1993), 1. Bentley, *Gay]Grey Moose*, 125.

88 Burwell, *Talbot Road*, "Argument," 14, 89.

89 Ibid., 103–4, 16. See also 125–6, 452.

90 Ibid., 117, 159, 222.

91 Ibid., 271; Wood, *Making Ontario*, 8.

92 Burwell, *Talbot Road*, 145, 97–8.

93 Chamberlin, *If This*, 29.

94 Burwell, *Talbot Road*, 435–42.

95 Wood, *Making Ontario*, 9. Catharine Parr Traill, *The Backwoods of Canada*, 162. As Anna Brownell Jameson would bluntly put it, "[a] Canadian settler *hates* a tree, regards it as his natural enemy, as something to be destroyed, eradicated, annihilated by all and any means." Jameson, *Winter*, 64.

96 Burwell, *Talbot Road*, 165, 278–301.

97 Ibid., 305, 621–2, 647.

98 Wood, *Making Ontario*, 12.

99 Burwell, *Talbot Road*, 450–1, 287; Wood, *Making Ontario*, 287.

100 Burwell, *Talbot Road*, 114, 205–10.

101 Ibid., 395, 411–18, 429–42.

102 Cornwall Bayley, "Canada," in Bentley, *Early Long Poems on Canada*, 77–103; Frye, *Bush Garden*, 227.

103 Said, qtd. in Huggan, *Territorial Disputes*, 19–20.

104 Goldsmith, "The Rising Village," 59, 60, 96, 81; Joseph Howe, *Acadia*, ed. M.G. Parks, in Bentley, *Early Long Poems on Canada*, 367–400, lines 510, 513, 521.

105 Michael Williams, editorial emendations and explanatory notes in Burwell, *Talbot Road*, 31.

106 Michael Smith, *A Geographical View of the Province of Upper Canada* (Trenton, NJ: Moore and Lake, 1813), 5; see also Bentley, introduction to *Talbot Road*, xlii; Bentley, *Mnemographia*, 101.

107 Burwell, *Talbot Road*, 444–54.

108 Ibid., 487–523.

109 Ibid., 487–92.

110 Ibid., 517–22.

111 Bentley, *Moose*, 203.

112 Burwell, *Talbot Road*, 526.

113 Bentley, *Moose*, 203; Burwell, *Talbot Road*, 487–583.

114 Burwell, *Talbot Road*, 617–18, 301–2, 310. See Raymond Williams, *The Country and the City* (Oxford: Oxford University Press, 1975), esp. 120–41.

115 Burwell, *Talbot Road*, 573–82.

116 Ibid., 607–11. John Howison's account of the Talbot settlement in his *Sketches of Upper Canada* (1821) suggests that Burwell's optimism was not unfounded, and that his predictions were being fulfilled: "[Talbot] encountered all those difficulties that invariably occur under similar circumstances, and was likewise strenuously opposed by some of the minions of the Provincial government," Howison concedes, "however, he has accomplished his object; for that tract of country, which, ten or twelve years ago, hardly knew the foot of man, now swarms with thousands of active settlers." Nonetheless, Howison saw room for further improvement; it was his hope "that its present occupants [would] henceforth gradually disappear, and be succeeded by a population of a superior kind. That this will be the case seems highly probable; for emigrants of some capital now begin to make their appearance in the Province." It may be that behind Burwell's predictions of future commercial and cultural prosperity in the Talbot settlement lie similar, if unarticulated, hopes for such a demographic turnover in the region. Howison, *Sketches of Upper Canada*, 78, 170–1.

117 Burwell, *Talbot Road*, 615–16.

118 John Young qtd. in Bentley, *Mnemographia*, 82.

119 Harrison, *Forests*, 6.

2. The Land up Close

1 Moodie, *Roughing It*.

2 Ibid., 10.

3 William Cattermole, *Emigration: The Advantages of Emigration to Canada …*, 1831 (Toronto: Coles, 1970), 3.

4 Moodie, *Roughing It*, 187.

5 Laura Smyth Groening, *Listening to Old Woman Speak: Natives and AlterNatives in Canadian Literature* (Montreal: McGill-Queen's University Press, 2004), 64.

6 Review qtd. in Elizabeth Thompson, "An Early Review of *Roughing It in the Bush*," *Canadian Literature* 151 (Winter 1996): 202–4.

7 Moodie, *Roughing It*, 347.

8 Wood, *Making Ontario*, 20.

9 Glickman, *Picturesque*, 63.

10 Susanna Moodie, *Life in the Clearings versus the Bush,* 1853 (Toronto: McClelland & Stewart, 1989), 297.
11 See Thomson, *Meridians,* 219; MacTaggart, *Three Years,* 49.
12 Moodie, *Roughing It,* 14, 9.
13 Janet Giltrow, "'Painful Experience in a Distant Land': Mrs Moodie in Canada and Mrs Trollope in America," *Mosaic* 14.2 (1981): 133.
14 John Thurston, *The Work of Words: The Writing of Susanna Strickland Moodie* (Montreal: McGill-Queen's University Press, 1996), 85. See also David Jackel, "Mrs Moodie and Mrs Traill, and the Fabrication of a Canadian Tradition," *The Compass* 6 (Spring 1979): 4.
15 Moodie, *Roughing It,* 19, 25, 24.
16 Michel de Certeau, *The Practice of Everyday Life,* trans. Steven Rendall (Berkeley: University of California Press, 1988), 92.
17 Moodie, *Roughing It,* 25.
18 de Certeau, *Everyday Life,* 93.
19 Ibid., 91–110; see also Ron Broglio, *Technologies of the Picturesque: British Art, Poetry, and Instruments, 1750–1830* (Lewisberg: Bucknell University Press, 2008), 59.
20 Moodie, *Roughing It,* 19.
21 Ibid., 37, 24, 20, 28.
22 The likelihood that Moodie read Howison's work is suggested by, among other things, her sister Catharine Parr Traill's familiarity with it; see Traill, *The Backwoods of Canada,* 50.
23 Howison, *Sketches,* 169–70.
24 Bentley, *Mnemographia,* 102.
25 Moodie, *Roughing It,* 61.
26 Ibid., 174, 179.
27 Ibid., 180.
28 Ibid., 368.
29 Ibid., 361.
30 Ibid., 357.
31 Heather Murray, "Women in the Wilderness," in *A Mazing Space: Writing Canadian Women Writing,* ed. Shirley Newman and Smaro Kamboureli (Edmonton: Longspoon Press, 1986), 77–9.
32 Moodie, *Roughing It,* 61, 59, 59, 61.
33 Thurston, *Work,* 69.
34 Moodie, *Roughing It,* 88.
35 Ibid., 59.
36 MacTaggart, *Three Years,* 200.

37 Gerald M. Craig, *Upper Canada: The Formative Years 1784–1841*, 1963 (Toronto: McClelland & Stewart, 1979), 141.
38 For New's suggestive linking of these terms, see *Land Sliding*, 82–3.
39 Moodie, *Roughing It*, 132. Here Moodie alludes to the English jurist and common lawyer Sir Edward Coke's famous dictum, "[a] man's home is his castle, *et domus sua cuique est tutissimum refugium*." Coke qtd. in Bentley, *Mnemographia*, 63.
40 Henri Lefebvre, *The Production of Space*, trans. Donald Nicholson-Smith (Oxford: Blackwell Press, 1991), 56–7.
41 Moodie, *Roughing It*, 69.
42 Ibid., 54.
43 Ibid., 109, 91.
44 Jeremy Bentham, *The Works of Jeremy Bentham*, vol. 4 (New York: Russell & Russell, 1962), 44–5.
45 Moodie, *Roughing It*, 91.
46 Thurston, *Work*, 143. See Moodie, *Roughing It*, 74–5.
47 Moodie, *Roughing It*, 122–4.
48 Frye, *Bush Garden*, 239; Moodie, *Roughing It*, 123.
49 Moodie, *Roughing It*, 124.
50 Ibid., 61.
51 For example, Bina Freiwald illuminates the extent to which, throughout *Roughing It*, "Moodie not only brings into textual existence a universe populated by mothers and their offspring, but is *always also* ... marked herself/marks herself as a figure of mothering." Indeed, her responsibility as a mother inflects her self-representation in the anxious scene I just described. Bina Freiwald, "'The Tounge of Woman': The Language of Self in Susana Moodie's *Roughing It in the Bush*," in *Re(dis) covering Our Foremothers: Nineteenth-Century Canadian Women Writers*, ed. Lorraine McMullen (Ottawa: University of Ottawa Press, 1988), 156. See also Shelley Boyd, *Garden Plots: Canadian Women Writers and Their Literary Gardens* (Montreal: McGill-Queen's University Press, 2013), ch. 1 and 2.
52 Moodie, *Roughing It*, 121, 122, 124.
53 Ibid., 186.
54 Ibid., 42 (my emphasis).
55 Ibid., 155; Thurston, *Work*, 68.
56 Moodie, *Roughing It*, 113–14. In *The Backwoods of Canada*, Traill remarks the prevalence of "household graves" throughout the colony, and notes that "when a farm is disposed of to a stranger, the right of burying their dead is generally stipulated by the former possessor." Traill, *Backwoods*, 49.

57 Moodie, *Roughing It*, 89.

58 Ibid., 84.

59 For a cartographic illustration of settlement patterns in relation to traditional Indigenous lands, see "Native Canada, ca, 1820" in vol. 1 of the *Historical Atlas of Canada*. This map depicts the increasing pressure that settlers placed on traditional economies. Upper Canada is included in a vast area "of declining and depleted game and fur resources," and the writers note an "increasing dependence on fish and small game" among Indigenous peoples who suffered "frequent food shortages." Conrad E. Heidenreich and Robert M. Galois, "Native Canada, ca. 1820," in Matthews, *Historical Atlas*, vol. 1, 69.

60 Moodie, *Roughing It*, 221.

61 Ibid., 196, 178. Traill also famously wrote: "As to ghosts or spirits they appear totally banished from Canada. This is too matter-of-fact country for such supernaturals to visit. Here there are no historical associations, no legendary tales of those that come before us." Traill, *Backwoods*, 128. In Cynthia Sugars's interpretation, the Indigenous ghosts that do surface in settler narratives are "a reminder that the settler, however much he/she might wish it, can never be the true inheritor of the land's legacy, which always makes of the settler (or settler descendant) a kind of illegitimate Gothic interloper." Sugars, *Canadian Gothic: Literature, History, and the Spectre of Self-Invention* (Cardiff: University of Wales Press, 2014), 37.

62 Moodie, *Roughing It*, 200.

63 Smith, *Mississauga Portraits*, 167–8. See also H.A. McCue, "The Kawartha Lakes Indians: A Brief History 1800–1850," in Cole, *Kawartha*, 12. The Moodies' friend Peter Nogan was chief of "the Mud (later Curve) Lake band," the members of which resisted "the agricultural mode of life that the reserve was designed to promote" and continued to frequent "the lands of the white settlers," including those that the Moodies occupied. Ballstadt, "Explanatory Notes," in *Roughing It in the Bush: Or, Life in Canada*, by Susanna Moodie (Ottawa: Carleton University Press, 1995), 580.

64 Moodie, *Roughing It*, 187.

65 Donald B. Smith, *Mississauga Portraits*, 169.

66 Moodie, *Roughing It*, 228.

67 Ibid., 172.

68 Janet Floyd, *Writing the Pioneer Woman* (Columbia: University of Missouri Press, 2002), 49.

69 Moodie, *Roughing It*, 172.

70 Moodie, *Life in the Clearings*, 295–6.

71 Moodie, *Roughing It*, 164.

72 Ibid., 165.
73 Ibid., 183. See also Michael Peterman, *This Great Epoch of Our Lives: Susanna Moodie's Roughing It in the Bush* (Toronto: Entertainment Culture Writing Press, 1996), 76–7; John Witham, "Building the Trent-Severn: A Summary," in Cole, *Kawartha*, 29.
74 Moodie, *Roughing It*, 172–3.
75 Ibid., 213, 229.
76 Peterman, *This Great Epoch*, 82.
77 Smith, *Mississauga Portraits*, 168.
78 Moodie, *Roughing It*, 173, 174.
79 Ibid., 174–5.
80 Ibid., 175.
81 Ibid., 24, 20.
82 Ibid. (emphasis original).
83 Ibid., 21.
84 Ibid., 20.
85 Ibid., 119.
86 Suzanne Zeller, *Inventing Canada: Early Victorian Science and the Idea of a Transcontinental Nation* (Toronto: University of Toronto Press, 1987), 258, 193.
87 Samuel Strickland qtd. in Zeller, *Inventing Canada*, 193.
88 Moodie, *Roughing It*, 296 (emphasis original).
89 Ibid., 299.
90 Ibid., 301.
91 Helen M. Buss, *Mapping Our Selves: Canadian Women's Autobiography in English* (Montreal: McGill-Queen's University Press, 1993), 92.
92 Moodie, *Roughing It*, 297, 304.
93 Ibid., 308.
94 Ibid., 306–7.
95 Ibid., 309; Thomas Moore, *Moore's Poetical Works, Complete in One Volume* (London: Longman, 1854), 109.
96 Moodie, *Roughing It*, 20.
97 Ibid., 178.
98 Thurston, *Work*, 149.
99 Moodie, *Roughing It*, 321–2.

3. The Intimate Geography of Wilderness

1 Traill, *Backwoods*, 48.
2 Carter, *The Road to Botany Bay*, 8 (emphasis original).

3 Traill, *Backwoods*, 10.
4 Ibid., 13.
5 Ibid., 87.
6 See Charlotte Gray, *Sisters in the Wilderness: The Lives of Susanna Moodie and Catharine Parr Traill* (Toronto: Penguin Books, 1999), 8, 288. Additionally, Ballstadt mentions Comte de Buffon's *Natural History of Birds, Fish, Insects and Reptiles* (1793) and Hector St John de Crèvecœur's *Letters from an American Farmer* (1782) as texts that influenced Traill early in her life. Carl P.A. Ballstadt, "Catharine Parr Traill," in *Canadian Writers and Their Works*, Fiction Series, vol. 1, ed. Robert Lecker, Jack David, and Ellen Quigley (Toronto: Entertainmet Culture Writing Press, 1983), 156.
7 Traill, *Backwoods*, 68.
8 Thomas R. Dunlap, *Nature and the English Diaspora: Environment and History in the United States, Canada, Australia, and New Zealand* (Cambridge: Cambridge University Press, 1999), 28.
9 MacTaggart, *Three Years in Canada*, 171–2.
10 Catharine Parr Traill, *Canadian Wild Flowers. Painted and Lithographed by Agnes Fitzgibbon; with Botanical Descriptions by C.P. Traill* (Montreal: Lovell, 1868), 7; Traill, *Backwoods*, 168.
11 See, e.g., "Ramblings by the River" (first published as no. 6 in the Forest Gleanings series in *Anglo-American Magazine* 2 [1853]), "Rice Lake Plains – The Wolf Tower" (first published as no. 3 in the same series in *Anglo-American Magazine* 1 [1852]), and "A Walk to Railway Point" (first published as no. 12 in the same series in *Anglo-American Magazine* 3 [1853]).
12 Marianne Gosztonyi Ainley, "Science in Canada's Backwoods: Catharine Parr Traill," in *Natural Eloquence: Women Reinscribe Science*, ed. Barbara T. Gates and Ann B. Shteir (Madison: University of Wisconsin Press, 1997), 79–97, 89.
13 Jackel, "Mrs Moodie," 4, 17.
14 Traill, *Backwoods*, 53.
15 Ballstadt, "Catharine," 170–2.
16 Marian Fowler dismisses Traill's natural history as "babbling" that serves only "to cover up the awful silence, her general unease in the presence of Nature, [and] her sense of exile" or as a means by which Traill averts her eyes from "the overwhelming size and mass, the raw, undigested quality of the Canadian landscape." Similarly, McGregor represents Traill's natural history either as an "avoidance strategy" that disguises a state of "paranoia," or as a domesticating tool for "cutting nature down to size." While such interpretations elucidate certain dimensions of Traill's work,

they reveal more clearly Frye's lasting influence on critical perceptions of settlers and the wilderness. Moreover, their limited scope works to the detriment of a more complete understanding of the meaningful ways in which her nature writing engages with and appreciates the wilderness. Most harmfully, they maintain the wilderness versus civilization dichotomy that Traill actively resisted. As Shelley Boyd also argues about Traill's gardens, Traill's botanical writings reveal a woman not turning away from wild nature but acquainting herself with it in an unflinchingly direct encounter that continually blurs the boundary between the human and the natural worlds. Marian Fowler, *The Embroidered Tent: Five Gentlewomen in Early Canada* (Toronto: Anansi Press, 1982), 73–6; McGregor, *Wacousta*, 39–41; Boyd, *Garden*.

17 Catharine Parr Traill, *Studies of Plant Life in Canada; or, Gleanings from Forest, Lake and Plain* (Ottawa: Woodburn, 1885), 74.
18 Traill, *Wild Flowers*, 13.
19 Traill, *Studies*, 215.
20 Ibid., i.
21 Michel Foucault, *The Order of Things: An Archaeology of the Human Sciences* (London: Tavistock Press, 1970), 141.
22 Derek Gregory, *Geographical Imaginations* (Oxford: Blackwell, 1994), 22, 40.
23 Mary Louise Pratt, *Imperial Eyes: Travel Writing and Transculturation*, 1992 (London: Routledge, 2008), 36–8.
24 Zeller, *Inventing Canada*, 214.
25 Traill, *Studies*, 15, 40.
26 Christoph Irmscher, "Nature Writing," in *The Cambridge Companion to Canadian Literature* (Cambridge: Cambridge University Press, 2006), 101.
27 Milton Freeman, "The Nature and Utility of Traditional Ecological Knowledge," in *Consuming Canada: Readings in Environmental History*, ed. Chad Gaffield and Pam Gaffield (Toronto: Copp Clark Company, 1995), 39.
28 Gilbert White, *The Natural History of Selborne; With Observations on Various Parts of Nature, and the Naturalist's Calendar*, ed. Thomas Brown (London: 1875), 205.
29 Traill, *Studies*, 52.
30 Ibid., 81.
31 Ibid., 1.
32 Ibid., iii.
33 Traill, *Wild Flowers*, 62.
34 Traill, *Studies*, 114.
35 Ibid., 13.
36 Ibid., 32.

37 Ibid., 2.
38 Ibid., 149, 151.
39 Ibid., 166.
40 Ibid., 245.
41 S.T. Wood, *Rambles of a Canadian Naturalist* (Toronto: Dent, 1916), 194, 109, 65.
42 See Bentley, *Confederation*, 177–203.
43 See Traill, *Backwoods*, 46, 49, 80, 67.
44 Ibid., 81–2.
45 Cronon, *Changes in the Land*, vii.
46 Traill, *Wild Flowers*, 55; see also Traill, *Studies*, 126.
47 Traill, *Studies*, 52.
48 Ibid., 48, 40.
49 Traill, *Backwoods*, 72.
50 Traill, *Wild Flowers*, 61–2.
51 Traill, *Backwoods*, 3–4.
52 Ibid., 69.
53 Natural theology was defined in the seventeenth-century most notably by John Ray in *The Wisdom of God Manifested in the Works of Creation* (1691) and reiterated for nineteenth-century readers by William Paley in his *Natural Theology; or, Evidences of the Existence and Attributes of the Deity Collected from the Appearances of Nature* (1802). The influence of natural theology is apparent in the work of Canadian naturalists such as Philip Henry Gosse and John Keast Lord and poets such as Cornwall Bayley. See Bentley, *Mimic*, 54–6; for an extended discussion on natural history's religious significance in Canada, see Berger, *Science*, 31–50.
54 Berger, *Science*, 35; James Fletcher qtd. in Gray, *Sisters*, 329.
55 Lynn Merrill, *The Romance of Victorian Natural History* (Oxford: Oxford University Press, 1989), 157, 255.
56 Fletcher qtd. in Gray, *Sisters*, 330, 329.
57 Fletcher qtd. in Peterman, "Splendid," 176.
58 Traill, *Wild Flowers*, 8.
59 Traill, *Backwoods*, 68.
60 Traill, *Wild Flowers*, 67.
61 Traill, *Studies*, 112.
62 Traill, *Backwoods*, 107.
63 Traill, *Studies*, 217.
64 This is a common trope throughout her writing: the preface of *Canadian Wild Flowers* refers readers to "[n]ature's own book"; the language shifts only slightly on the first page of *Studies of Plant Life* to direct them to "the

great volume of Nature which lies open before us." Traill, *Wild Flowers*, 7; Traill, *Studies*, 1.

65 Traill, *Backwoods*, 110–12.

66 Victoria Dickenson, *Drawn from Life: Science and Art in the Portrayal of the New World* (Toronto: University of Toronto Press, 1998), 225.

67 Traill, *Wild Flowers*, 7.

68 Traill, *Studies*, 12.

69 Ibid., 88.

70 Traill, *Backwoods*, 88; Traill, *Studies*, 241.

71 Traill, *Backwoods*, 104; Traill, *Wild Flowers*, 7–8.

72 Ballstadt, "Catharine," 157.

73 Merrill, *Romance*, viii, 255.

74 Foucault, *Order*, 134, 161.

75 Traill, *Studies*, 60, 70. Her call for more "poetical" practices in naming also reinforces the link between nature and God, for poetry, as she recalls an elderly gardener telling her, "was the language in which God spake to man through the tongues of angels and prophets." 70.

76 Foucault, *Order*, 135.

77 Traill, *Studies*, 184.

78 Ibid., 70.

79 Ibid., 60.

80 Ibid., 5.

81 Catharine Parr Traill, *Pearls and Pebbles*, 1894, ed. Elizabeth Thompson (Toronto: Natural Heritage Press, 1999), 27.

82 See, e.g., Traill, *Studies*, 23.

83 Ibid., 103.

84 Traill, *Wild Flowers*, 84, 45; Traill, *Pearls*, 103.

85 The four stages theory was, as Bentley explains in *Mnemographia*, a common component of Enlightenment thought promulgated by Adam Smith and others; it presupposed that all societies develop through four distinct stages, each defined by its mode of subsistence: (1) a savage stage based on hunting and gathering; (2) a barbaric (or pastoral) stage based on herding; (3) an agricultural stage based on farming; and (4) a commercial stage based on trading. Of these four stages, the first two were held – in the buzz words of the day – to be "rough" and "rude," and the second two "polished" and "refined." Bentley, *Mnemographia*, 53.

Although Traill, along with many of her contemporaries, was doubtless influenced by this pervasive theory, her sense of progress and refinement do not always accord with its rigid categories.

86 Traill, *Pearls*, 27, 23, 57, 104.

87 Ibid., 105.

88 Traill, *Studies*, 103–5.

89 Fowler, *Embroidered*, 65.

90 Traill, *Studies*, 105, 24–5.

91 Ibid., 141, 189.

92 Ibid., 104, 179. For a map of reserves in eastern Canada prior to 1900, see plates 32 and 33 of Geoffrey J. Matthews, *Historical Atlas of Canada*, vol. 2, *The Land Transformed: 1800–1891*, ed. Louis R. Gentilcore (Toronto: University of Toronto Press, 1993).

93 Traill, *Studies*, 183.

94 Traill qtd. in Thompson, "Something," 146; Thompson, "Something," 147; see also Rebecca Raglon, "Little Goody Two-Shoes: Reassessing the Work of Catharine Parr Traill," in *This Elusive Land: Women and the Canadian Environment*, ed. Melody Hessing, Rebecca Raglon, and Catriona Sandilands (Vancouver: University of British Columbia Press, 2005), 13.

95 Traill, *Backwoods*, 11, 67.

96 Ibid., 168, 211.

97 Traill, *Studies*, 253.

98 Ibid., 156.

99 Ibid., 253.

100 See Ainley, "Science," 92. J. David Wood provides useful elaboration on this point; he explains that "combatting nature was an integral part of progress in the nineteenth-century mind, and anything that could be labelled 'progress' automatically won out over preserving a corner of the natural world." Other historians note that, at the same time, "many contemporaries were well aware of the environmental degradation" that followed in the wake of progress. Wood, *Making Ontario*, 10; Gaffield, *Consuming Canada*, 94.

101 Traill, *Studies*, 213.

102 Ibid., 217.

103 In Ontario, agriculture was "replac[ing] a neatly integrated woodland ecology with a simpler and largely exotic – in the sense that most of the crops were not native and the biological diversity was lower on cropland – land use regimen." Wood, *Making Ontario*, 8; see also Alfred W. Crosby's "Ecological Imperialism: The Overseas Migration of Western Europeans as a Biological Phenomenon" in Gaffield and Gaffield, *Consuming Canada*, 49–61; Ramsay Cook, "1492 and All That: Making a Garden out of the Wilderness," in Gaffield and Gaffield, *Consuming Canada*, 73.

104 Traill, *Studies*, 165.

105 Ibid., 152. This was a common belief among emigrants, although many, taking their cues from Edward Gibbon's widely read *History of the Decline and Fall of the Roman Empire* (1776), thought that such artificial change would be more a benefit than a harm. See Zeller, *Inventing Canada*, 122, 140, 172.
106 Traill, *Studies*, 153.
107 Berger, *Science*, 3.
108 Stephen Greenblatt, *Marvelous Possessions: The Wonder of the New World* (Chicago: University of Chicago Press, 1991), 24.
109 Traill, *Studies*, ii.
110 Ibid.
111 Traill, *Pearls*, 5.
112 Wood, *Making Ontario*, xx.
113 MacTaggart, *Three Years*, 93.
114 Traill, *Studies*, 222, 152.

4. Writing and Reading the Northwest

1 Traill, *Studies*, 104.
2 William Lawson Grant and Frederick Hamilton, *George Monro Grant* (Toronto: Morang, 1905), 143.
3 Collins qtd. in Bentley, "Shadows," 753n2; Elizabeth Waterston, "Travel Books," in *Literary History of Canada: Canadian Literature in English*, vol. 1, 2nd ed., ed. Carl F. Klinck (Toronto: University of Toronto Press, 1977), 361–79; David Jackel, "*Ocean to Ocean*: G.M. Grant's 'Round Unvarnish'd Tale,'" *Canadian Literature* 81 (Summer 1979): 7–23, 7.
4 William Lawson Grant, *Ocean to Ocean: Sandford Fleming's Expedition through Canada in 1872*, 1873 (Toronto: Coles, 1970), 352. Unless otherwise specified, citations to Grant, *Ocean* refer to this first edition.
5 Ibid., 9, 353.
6 Strachan qtd. in Doug Owram, *Promise of Eden: The Canadian Expansionist Movement and the Idea of the West 1856–1900* (Toronto: University of Toronto Press, 1980), 7.
7 William F. Butler, *The Great Lone Land: A Tale of Travel and Adventure in the North-West of America*, 1872 (Toronto: Macmillan, 1910), 200–1.
8 Grant, *Ocean*, 351.
9 Ibid., 6; Grant and Hamilton, *George Monro Grant*, 131–2.
10 Grant, *Ocean*, "To the Public."
11 Grant, *Ocean*, 215.
12 Ibid., preface; Jackel, "*Ocean*," 7.
13 Grant, *Ocean*, 127, 114; Greenblatt, *Marvelous Possessions*, 132.

14 Grant, *Ocean*, 365.
15 Ibid., 123; Jackel, "*Ocean*," 18 (my emphasis).
16 Grant, *Ocean*, 206.
17 Kelsey, "generally credited with being the first European to set his foot and make his mark on the Canadian prairies," has been suggestively called an "ancestor of ... the (rail)road builder." Bentley, *Mnemographia*, 2; Bentley, *Gay*, 78; Grant, *Ocean*, 83–5.
18 Bentley, *Mnemographia*, 51.
19 Grant, *Ocean*, 243.
20 Ibid., 1.
21 Ann Baker, "Word, Image, and Geography: Panorama Pamphlets and Manifest Destiny," in *American Literary Geographies: Spatial Practice and Cultural Production 1500–1900*, ed. Martin Brückner and Hsuan L. Hsu (Newark: University of Delaware Press, 2007), 89–110, 89, 90; Stephan Oettermann qtd. in Baker, "Word," 90; Baker, "Word," 90.
22 Grant, *Ocean*, 1.
23 Ibid., 313.
24 Ibid., 11.
25 Ibid., 310.
26 Ibid., 301, 87.
27 Ibid., 342.
28 Zeller, *Inventing Canada*, 9.
29 Berger, *Science*, 16.
30 Grant, *Ocean*, 29, 186.
31 Ibid., 107. Grant echoes Thomas Carlyle's denunciation, in "Chartism," of British poverty "in a world where Canadian forests stand unfelled, boundless Plains and Prairies unbroken with the plough; on the west and on the east green desert spaces never yet made white with corn; and to the overcrowded little western nook of Europe, our Terrestrial Planet, nine-tenths of it yet vacant or tenanted by nomads, is still crying, Come and till me, come and reap me!" Carlyle, *The Works of Thomas Carlyle*, vol. 4, *The French Revolution: A History III*, ed. Henry Duff Traill (Cambridge: Cambridge University Press, 2010), 203.
32 Canada gained significant international attention, for instance, from events such as the Great Exhibition in London's Crystal Palace in 1851, in which samples of natural resources were put on display. See Zeller, *Inventing Canada*, 78–84.
33 Grant, *Ocean*, 85. See also I.S. MacLaren, with Eric Higgs and Gabrielle Zezulka-Mailloux, *Mapper of Mountains: M.P. Bridgland in the Canadian Rockies 1902–1930* (University of Alberta Press, 2005), 9–10.

34 Grant, *Ocean*, 366, 365.
35 Ibid., 118.
36 Ibid., 20, 21, 77, 80, 229.
37 MacLaren et al., *Mapper*, 19, 18.
38 Grant, *Ocean*, 6.
39 Ibid., 33, 106.
40 Butler, *Great Lone Land*, 200.
41 Ibid., 107.
42 Ibid., 45, 146.
43 Theodore Binnema, "How Does a Map Mean?," 208; see also 218. Henry Youle Hind, *Narrative of the Canadian Red River Exploring Expedition of 1857 and of the Assinniboine and Saskatchewan Exploring Expedition of 1858*, 1860 (Edmonton: Hurtig, 1971), 370; George Monro Grant, *Ocean to Ocean: Sandford Fleming's Expedition through Canada in 1872*, enl. and rev. ed., Toronto: 1879 (Rutland, Vermont: Tuttle, 1967), 47.
44 Grant, *Ocean*, 118, 122.
45 Butler, *Great Lone Land*, 217–18. Compounding this elegiac image, shortly before describing the prairie strewn with buffalo bones Butler describes another cause of the tragic decimation of Indigenous populations: "Small-pox, in its most aggravated type, had passed from tribe to tribe, leaving in its track depopulated wigwams and vacant council-lodges; thousands (and there are not many thousands, all told) had perished on the great sandy plains that lie between the Saskatchewan and the Missouri" (202). See also James Daschuk, *Clearing the Plains: Disease, Politics of Starvation, and the Loss of Aboriginal Life* (Regina: University of Regina Press: 2013).
46 Grant, *Ocean*, 122.
47 Ibid., 107.
48 Harley, *New*, 81.
49 Grant, *Ocean*, 176.
50 de Certeau, *Practice*, 107
51 Grant, *Ocean*, 17.
52 Ibid., 145, 196. For a description of the ritual and multivocal significance of lobsticks, see Carolyn Podruchny, Frederic W. Gleach, and Roger Roulette, "Putting up Poles: Power, Navigation, and Cultural Mixing in the Fur Trade," in *Gathering Places: Aboriginal and Fur Trade Histories*, ed. Carolyn Podruchny and Laura Peers (Vancouver: University British Columbia Press, 2010), 25–47.
53 Susan Naramore Maher, *Deep Map Country: Literary Cartography of the Great Plains* (Lincoln: University of Nebraska Press, 2014), 6; Neil Campbell qtd. in Maher, *Deep Map Country*, 7; Maher, *Deep Map Country*, 11.

54 See Wallace Stegner, *Wolf Willow: A History, a Story, and a Memory of the Last Plains Frontier*, intro. Page Stegner (New York: Penguin, 2000).
55 Pickles, *History*, 121, 122.
56 Grant, *Ocean*, 52.
57 George Copway, *The Traditional History and Characteristic Sketches of the Ojibway Nation*, 1850, afterward by Shelley Hulan (Waterloo, ON: Wilfrid Laurier Press, 2014), 11.
58 Grant, *Ocean*, 147.
59 Ibid., 52.
60 Catherine Soneegoh Sutton, "Letter," in *An Anthology of Native Literature in English*, 2nd ed., ed. Daniel David Moses and Terry Goldie (Oxford: Oxford University Press, 1997), 26–7.
61 Grant, *Ocean*, 97.
62 Ibid., 147.
63 See Fee, *Literary Land Claims*, ch. 4.
64 Ibid., 47.
65 Ibid., 47–8.
66 In his *Second Treatise of Government* (1690), Locke describes "the right of annexation through labour," one of the "three principles of land ownership that had – and have – enormous consequences for Canada and all its peoples." Bentley, *Mnemographia*, 52–3, 47. This principle defines property as the product of human industry: "[w]hatsoever [man] removes out of the state that nature hath provided," Locke explains, "he hath mixed his labour with ... and thereby makes it his property." According to this theory, agriculture was a definitive marker of ownership, for "[a]s much land as a man tills, plants, improves, cultivates, and can use the product of, so much is his property." For further discussion of this principle, see chapter 1. John Locke, "Second Treatise of Government," 1690, in *The Selected Political Writings of John Locke*, ed. Paul E. Sigmund (New York: Norton, 2005), 17–125, 28, 30.
67 Grant, *Ocean*, 33–4.
68 Ibid., 34, 48.
69 Ibid., 288.
70 Ibid., 122.
71 Daniel Coleman, *White Civility: The Literary Project of English Canada* (Toronto: University of Toronto Press, 2006), 29.
72 Grant, *Ocean*, 250.
73 Ibid., 250.
74 Ibid., 275.

75 Gerald Friesen, *The Canadian Prairies: A History* (Toronto: University of Toronto Press, 1987), 113; Grant, *Ocean*, 111.

76 Grant, Ocean, 96. "Scrofulous" refers here not to moral degeneracy, but to a form of tuberculosis, a disease that swept across the northwest with the arrival of Europeans, and was exacerbated in Indigenous populations by malnutrition resulting from the extirpation of the bison. James Daschuk observes that in the late nineteenth century, "tuberculosis was increasingly seen as a hereditary disease" resulting "from the indigenous way of life," and it was not uncommon for both "government officials" and "the Canadian public" to view "the suffering as nature taking its course." Daschuk, *Clearing*, xxii.

77 Grant, *Ocean*, 96–7, 144.

78 Ibid., 34.

79 Ibid., 340–1.

80 Ibid., 344.

81 See Penelope Edmonds, "From Bedlam to Incorporation: Whiteness and the Racialisation of Colonial Urban Space in Victoria, British Columbia and Melbourne, Victoria, 1840s–1880s," in *Exploring the British World: Identity, Cultural Production, Institutions*, ed. Kate Darian-Smith et al. (Melbourne: RMIT Publishing, 2004), 60–90.

82 Grant, *Ocean*, 67, 310, 323.

83 Grant consolidates his thoughts on treaties into a sustained argument in an appendix to the enlarged and revised edition of *Ocean to Ocean*, which levels a pointed critique of British Columbia's circumvention of the treaty process (see 393–6); nonetheless, the scattered references to treaties are an important feature of the literary cartography of the first edition.

84 Ibid., 97; James (Sákéj) Youngblood Henderson, "The Context of the State of Nature," in *Reclaiming Indigenous Voice and Vision*, ed. Marie Battiste (Vancouver: University of British Columbia Press, 2000), 11–38, 24.

85 Grant, *Ocean*, 67, 95.

86 Irene Spry, "The Tragedy of the Loss of the Commons in Western Canada," in *As Long as the Sun Shines and Water Flows: A Reader in Canadian Native Studies*, ed. Ian A.L. Getty and Antoine S. Lussier (Vancouver: UBC Press, 1983), 222.

87 Grant, *Ocean*, 365–6.

88 Ibid., 97–8.

89 Grant, *Ocean*, rev. and enl. ed., 392.

90 Qtd. in Donald B. Smith, *Mississauga*, 44.

91 Chief Peguis (William King), "To the Aboriginal Protection Society," in *A Few Acres of Snow: Documents in Pre-Confederation Canadian History*,

ed. Thomas Thorner with Thor Frohn-Nielsen (Toronto: University of Toronto Press, 2009), 291–3, 292.

92 E. Pauline Johnson, *E. Pauline Johnson, Tekahionwake: Collected Poems and Selected Prose*, ed. and intro. Carole Gerson and Veronica Strong-Boag (Toronto: University of Toronto Press, 2002), 14.

93 Wolfgang Schivelbusch, *The Railway Journey: The Industrialization of Time and Space in the 19th Century* (Berkeley: University of California Press, 1986), 53.

94 Qtd. in Owram, *Promise*, 47.

5. The Poet in Treaty Territory

1 Brian Titley, *A Narrow Vision: Duncan Campbell Scott and the Administration of Indian Affairs in Canada* (Vancouver: Univeristy of British Columbia Press, 1986), 14.

2 Scott, *Selected Poems*, 37.

3 The most (in)famous of these include the frequently anthologized sonnets "The Onondaga Madonna" (1894) and "Watkwenies" (1898), which portray Indigenous subjects in decline (although others such as "Powassan's Drum" [1926] convey a more ambivalent position). See especially Stan Dragland, *Floating Voice: Duncan Campbell Scott and the Literature of Treaty 9* (Concord, ON: Anansi Press, 1994); Lisa Salem-Wiseman, "Verily, the White Man's Ways Were the Best': Duncan Campbell Scott, Native Culture, and Assimilation," *Studies in Canadian Literature* 21.1 (1996); Laura Smyth Groening, *Listening to Old Woman Speak: Natives and AlterNatives in Canadian Literature* (Montreal: McGill-Queen's University Press, 2004); D.M.R Bentley, "Shadows in the Soul: Racial Haunting in the Poetry of Duncan Campbell Scott," *University of Toronto Quarterly* 75.2 (Spring 2006): 752–70.

4 See Dragland, *Floating*, 252.

5 Tracy Ware, "D.C. Scott's 'The Height of Land' and the Greater Romantic Lyric," *Canadian Literature* 111 (Winter 1986): 14.

6 Patrick Macklem, "The Impact of Treaty 9 on the Resource Development in Northern Ontario," in *Aboriginal and Treaty Rights in Canada: Essays on Law, Equality and Respect for Difference*, ed. Michael Asch (Vancouver: University of British Columbia Press, 1997), 105.

7 Ware, "D.C. Scott," 21.

8 Ibid., 15, 18, 20.

9 Bentley, *Gay*, 4. Don McKay, introduction to *Open Wide a Wilderness*, ed. Nancy Holmes (Waterloo, ON: Wilfrid Laurier University Press, 2009), 1.

10 Dragland, *Floating*, 234, 236. The poem's precise setting had already been the subject of some speculation. In *Canadian Literary Landmarks*, Colombo, perhaps inferring from the fact that "Potàn the Wise" (one of the guides referred to in "The Height of Land") also appears in "Spring on Mattagami," locates the poem on the Mattagami River. John Robert Colombo, *Canadian Literary Landmarks* (Willowdale, ON: Hounslow Press, 1984).
11 Kathy Mezei, "From Lifeless Pools to the Circle of Affection: The Significance of Space in the Poetry of D.C. Scott," in *The Duncan Campbell Scott Symposium*, ed. K.P. Stich (Ottawa: University of Ottawa Press, 1980), 28.
12 Duncan Campbell Scott, "The Last of the Indian Treaties," in *Duncan Campbell Scott: Addresses, Essays, Reviews*, vol. 1, ed. Leslie Ritchie, intro. Stan Dragland (London, ON: Canadian Poetry Press, 2000), 83.
13 Scott, "Indian Affairs," 188. Scott was not the first to use this metaphor for what many at the time considered an obstacle to colonial progress. John S. Long notes that "in 1905, when Treaty No. 9 was first signed, aboriginal title was considered to be an inconvenient annoyance. Frank Pedley, deputy superintendent general of Indian Affairs, referred, in his 1904 correspondence with Ontario commissioner of Crown lands E.J. Davis, to the mere 'shadow of Indian title.'" John Long, *Treaty No. 9: Making the Agreement to Share the Land in Far Northern Ontario in 1905* (Montreal: McGill-Queen's University Press, 2010), 3; see 4–5 for further historical contextualization of contemporary government views of Indigenous title and rights to land.
14 Duncan Campbell Scott, "The Height of Land," in Scott, *Selected*, lines 1–4, 25–40.
15 See, e.g., the entry qtd. in Long, *Treaty*, 152.
16 Scott, "Height," 19, 37, 107, 28, 33–4, 120.
17 Ibid., 36–9, 100–3.
18 Ibid., 41–8.
19 W.K. Keith, *Literary Images of Ontario* (Toronto: University of Toronto Press, 1992), 130.
20 Gordon Johnston, "The Significance of Scott's Minor Poems," in Stich, *Duncan*, 14.
21 Bentley, *Gay*, 4.
22 By 1912, Ontario's northern boundary had moved from the Albany River to the shore of Hudson Bay; Treaty 9 expanded to cover the new provincial territory by the end of that decade. W. Robert Wightman and Nancy M. Wightman, *The Land Between: Northwestern Ontario Resource*

Development, 1800 to the 1900s (Toronto: University of Toronto Press, 1997), 190.

23 Scott, "Last," 90; Wightman and Wightman, *Land*, 109.

24 Harley, *New*, 81. See also Morris's map (figure 9), which similarly depicts northern Ontario as an expanse of blank space.

25 Scott, "Height," 30.

26 See Titley, *Narrow*; Dragland, *Floating*; Macklem, "Impact."

27 Canada, The James Bay Treaty: Treaty No. 9 (Made in 1905 and 1906) and Adhesions Made in 1929 and 1930, 1931 (Ottawa: Queen's Printer, 1964).

28 Canada, James Bay. Hunting and fishing rights, which the treaty protected, would also be subject to federal laws and further restricted as "settlement, mining, lumbering, trading or other purposes" dictated. Canada, James Bay. For subsequent erosions of Indigenous treaty rights, see Titley, *Narrow*; Dragland, *Floating*; Wightman and Wightman, *Land*, 211. Scott, "Last," 83.

29 Canada, James Bay. This pernicious trope is one half of a contradiction that lies at the core of settler-colonial culture, and that J. Edward Chamberlin critiques in *If this Is Your Land, Where Are Your Stories?*: "Aborigines, who know the names of every plant and the location of all the water holes, as perpetual nomads? Europeans in a place ten thousand miles from home, as settlers? It doesn't make sense" (29–30).

30 Canada, James Bay; Dunlap, *Nature*, 3.

31 Scott, "Height," 17–18.

32 Ibid., 65–6.

33 Ibid., 51–5.

34 Dragland, *Floating*, 249.

35 For an elaboration of mythopoeic elements in Canadian poetry, see Frye, *Bush*, 181, and for the postcolonial implications of such elements, see Devereux, "Search."

36 Dragland, *Floating*, 30; Scott qtd. in Titley, *Narrow*, 70.

37 Scott, "Height," 148–51.

38 Ibid., 50–2; William Wordsworth, "Lines Written a Few Miles above Tintern Abbey," *Lyrical Ballads*, William Wordsworth and Samuel Taylor Coleridge, 1798, ed. W.J.B. Owen, 2nd ed. (Oxford: Oxford University Press, 1996), 111–17, lines 95–102; Scott, "Height," 64; Wordsworth, "Lines," 94–5.

39 See Sandra Campbell, "A Fortunate Friendship: Duncan Campbell Scott and Pelham Edgar," in Stich, *Duncan*, 120.

40 Armand Garnet Ruffo, "Poem for Duncan Campbell Scott," in *Opening in the Sky* (Penticton: Theytus Press, 1994), 25.

41 Ibid., 25. *Opening in the Sky* was named for his great great grandfather, who signed Treaty 9.
42 Scott, "Indian," 212; Scott, "Last," 92.
43 Scott, "Height," 7–11.
44 Ibid., 11–15.
45 Scott, "Last," 82.
46 Scott, "Height," 7, 4.
47 Ibid., 19–22.
48 Dragland, *Floating*, 252.
49 Scott, *Selected*, 37, 133. For a discussion of this frequent trope in Scott's poetry, see Groening, *Listening*.
50 Scott, "Height," 73–92.
51 Johnston, "Significance," 13, 15.
52 Scott, "Height," 81, 85, 89, 91, 138–9.
53 Wordsworth, "Tintern," 52–3.
54 Bentley, "Shadows," 753.
55 Ware, "Lyric," 15.
56 Scott, "Height," 25.
57 Scott, "Last," 84.
58 Dragland, *Floating*, 252.
59 Scott, "Height," 51–5, 63, 93.
60 Ibid., 60–6.
61 Ibid., 94.
62 Scott, "Last," 90.
63 Ibid.; Scott, *Selected*, 66.
64 Dragland, *Floating*, 251.
65 Scott, "Height," 85–98.
66 Dragland, *Floating*, 250; McKay, *Open*, 5.
67 Scott, "Height," 93–108.
68 Dragland, *Floating*, 236.
69 Scott, "Last," 82.
70 Scott, "Height," 114–16.
71 Scott, *Selected*, 37.
72 Scott, "Height," 129. Bentley, *Confederation*, 239; see also D.M.R. Bentley, "A Deep Influx of Spirit: Maurice Maeterlinck and Duncan Campbell Scott," in *Criticism on Duncan Campbell Scott*, http://www.uwo.ca/english/canadianpoetry/confederation/DCScott/criticism/maurice.htm.
73 Scott, "Height," 138, 146–50.
74 Ibid., 150; Ware, "Lyric," 17; see also Misao Dean, *Inheriting a Canoe Paddle: The Canoe in Discourses of English-Canadian Nationalism* (Toronto: Toronto University Press, 2013), 36.

75 McKay, *Open*, 6.
76 Disharmony certainly marks the language of conquest and cultural genocide with which the Chiefs of Grand Council Treaty 9 have described non-Indigenous incursions into this territory. Long, *Treaty*, 3. See also Wightman and Wightman, *Land*, 26–7, 52–4, 96–101.
77 Long, *Treaty*, 4. For a detailed discussion of how difficulties communicating and translating different views of the treaty and its promises – not only between languages and cultures, but also between oral and written traditions – has led to ongoing challenges with interpreting the treaty, see Long, *Treaty*, ch. 23. For further discussion of the legacies of Treaty 9 see also Alanis Obomsawin's feature documentary film *Trick or Treaty?*, dir. Alanis Obomsawin (National Film Board of Canada, 2014).
78 Macklem, "Impact," 105, 111, 115. Recognizing the partiality of the government commissioners' views of the treaty, the Supreme Court of Canada has since stipulated that its "terms are to be interpreted in a manner sensitive to Aboriginal expectations." Macklem, "Impact," 100.

Conclusion

1 Carter, *Road*, 119–20.
2 As Tyrrell notes, Lindsey "made a partial use of it in preparing an account of the 'Extent of Country which the North-West Company occupied' in his *Investigation of the Unsettled Boundaries of Ontario*." Tyrrell, introduction to David Thompson, *David Thompson's Narrative of His Explorations in Western America, 1784–1812*, ed. J.B. Tyrrell (Toronto: Champlain Society, 1916), xvii–xviii.
3 Butler, *Great Lone Land*, 200.
4 Grant, *Ocean*, 357.
5 Tyrrell, introduction, xix; E.A.B. [Ernest Alfred Benians], review of *David Thompson's Narrative of His Explorations in Western America, 1784–1812, English Historical Review* 31.4 (Oct. 1916): 671.
6 Barbara Belyea, introduction to David Thompson, *Columbia Journals*, ed. Barbara Belyea (Montreal: McGill-Queen's University Press, 2007), xxv.
7 E.A.B., review of *David Thompson's Narrative*, 671. Although there have been several editions since Tyrrell's, unless otherwise specified, I refer primarily to this edition, which appeared at the end of the period under consideration in this study.
8 Butler, *Great Lone Land*, 200.
9 Thompson qtd. in Moreau, introduction to David Thompson, *The Writings of David Thompson*, vol. 1, *The Travels, 1850 Version*, ed. William E. Moreau (Montreal: McGill-Queen's University Press, 2009), xli.

10 T.D. MacLulich, "The Explorer as Sage: David Thompson's Narrative," *Journal of Canadian Fiction* 4.4 (1976): 99; I.S. MacLaren, "David Thompson's Imaginative Mapping of the Canadian Northwest, 1784–1812," *Ariel* 15 (1984): 89–106.
11 Thompson, *Narrative*, 288.
12 MacLaren, "David Thompson," 92.
13 Thompson, *Narrative*, 251.
14 Ibid., 104–5.
15 Ibid., 501.
16 Grant, *Ocean*, 342, 346.
17 E.J. Pratt, *Selected Poems*, ed. Sandra Djwa et al. (Toronto: University of Toronto Press, 2000), 28–30.
18 See Moreau, introduction, xliii.
19 Thompson seems, on the whole, impervious to the pressure that the form of the travel narrative exerted upon the writer to move forward – as it does, for example, on Butler when he curtails his description of places of Indigenous spiritual significance on Lake of the Woods with the explanation that "all these things are too long to dwell upon now; I must haste along my way." Butler, *Great Lone Land*, 160.
20 Thompson, *Narrative*, 5, 6.
21 Ibid., 105–6.
22 Ibid., 140, 157, 139, 157, 160.
23 Ibid., 159.
24 Moreau, introduction, xlv. Tyrrell omitted the textual excerpts that Thompson copied into his manuscripts from the 1916 version, but Moreau includes them in his edition of the *Travels* – see, e.g., John Richardson's observations of igloo building and of the Inuit's use of driftwood for kayak frames, homes, and fuel. Thompson, *Writings*, 21–3.
25 Moreau, introduction, xliii, xliv.
26 As MacLaren notes, Thompson "assimilated ... many Indian customs and myths in the course of his development and travels," and his best landscape descriptions bring together European and Indigenous perspectives, with no single view – scientific, aesthetic, mythic, or fanciful – prevailing. MacLaren, "David Thompson," 91.
27 Thompson, *Narrative*, 182.
28 Ibid., 275.
29 Victor Hopwood, introduction to *David Thompson: Travels in Western North America, 1784–1812*, by David Thompson (Toronto: Macmillan, 1971), 1–39, 20.
30 Thompson, *Narrative*, 33, 144, 204.

31 Ibid., 92.
32 Tyrrell in Thompson, *Narrative*, 142n1; Thompson, *Narrative*, 324.
33 Ibid., 127.
34 Ibid., 142, 241.
35 Ibid., 142.
36 Ibid., 241.
37 Ibid., 142.
38 Grant, *Ocean*, 365.
39 David Chisholme, "Introduction to *The Canadian Magazine and Literary Repository*," *Towards a Canadian Literature: Essays, Editorials & Manifestos*, vol. 1, *1752–1940*, ed. Douglas M. Daymond and Leslie G. Monkman (Ottawa: Tecumseh, 1984), 17.
40 Germaine Warkentin, introduction to the first edition, *Canadian Exploration Literature*, ed. Germaine Warkentin (Toronto: Dundurn, 2006), 19–34, 22.
41 Bertrand Westphal, *Geocriticism: Real and Fictional Spaces*, trans. Robert T. Tally Jr. (New York: Palgrave, 2011), 114.
42 Julie Cruikshank, *Reading Voices / 'Dan Dha Ts'edenintth'e: Oral and Written Interpretations of the Yukon's Past* (Vancouver: Douglas and McIntyre, 1991), 11.
43 John Kelly, "We Are All in the Ojibway Circle," in *From Ink Lake: Canadian Stories*, ed. Michael Ondaatje (New York: Viking, 1990), 579–90, 585.
44 Ibid., 589.
45 Ibid., 588.

Bibliography

Ainley, Marianne Gosztonyi. "Science in Canada's Backwoods: Catharine Parr Traill." In *Natural Eloquence: Women Reinscribe Science*, edited by Barbara T. Gates and Ann B. Shteir, 79–97. Madison: University of Wisconsin Press, 1997.

Baker, Ann. "Word, Image, and Geography: Panorama Pamphlets and Manifest Destiny." In *American Literary Geographies: Spatial Practice and Cultural Production 1500–1900*, edited by Martin Brückner and Hsuan L. Hsu, 89–110. Newark: University of Delaware Press, 2007.

Ballstadt, Carl P.A. "Catharine Parr Traill." In *Canadian Writers and Their Works*, Fiction Series, vol. 1, edited by Robert Lecker, Jack David, and Ellen Quigley, 149–88. Toronto: Entertainment Culture Writing Press, 1983.

Ballstadt, Carl P.A., ed. *Roughing It in the Bush: Or, Life in Canada*. By Susanna Moodie. Ottawa: Carleton University Press, 1995.

Baudrillard, Jean. *Simulacra and Simulation*. Translated by Sheila Faria Glaser. Ann Arbor: University of Michigan Press, 1994.

Bayley, Cornwall. "Canada." In Bentley, *Early Long Poems on Canada*, 77–103.

Belich, James. *Replenishing the Earth: The Settler Revolution and the Rise of the Angloworld, 1783–1939*. Oxford: Oxford University Press, 2009.

Belyea, Barbara. Introduction to *Columbia Journals* by David Thompson, edited by Barbara Belyea, xi–xxx. Montreal: McGill-Queen's University Press, 2007.

Bentham, Jeremy. *The Works of Jeremy Bentham*. Vol. 4. New York: Russell & Russell, 1962.

Bentley, D.M.R. *Canadian Architexts: Essays on Literature and Architecture in Canada: 1759–2006*. London, ON: Canadian Poetry Press, 2009.

– *The Confederation Group of Canadian Poets, 1880–1897*. Toronto: University of Toronto Press, 2004.

– "A Deep Influx of Spirit: Maurice Maeterlinck and Duncan Campbell Scott." *Criticism on Duncan Campbell Scott.* http://www.uwo.ca/english/canadianpoetry/confederation/DCScott/criticism/maurice.htm.

Bentley, D.M.R., ed. *Early Long Poems on Canada.* London, ON: Canadian Poetry Press, 1993.

– "Explanatory Notes." Cary, *Abram's Plains,* 25–43.

– *The Gay]Grey Moose: Essays on the Ecologies and Mythologies of Canadian Poetry, 1690–1990.* Ottawa: University of Ottawa Press, 1992.

– "Introduction." Cary, *Abram's Plains,* xi–xlviii.

– "Introduction." Burwell, *Talbot Road,* xi–xlviii.

– *Mimic Fires: Accounts of Early Long Poems on Canada.* Montreal: McGill-Queen's University Press, 1994.

– *Mnemographia Canadensis: Essays on Memory, Community, and Environment in Canada.* Vol. 1, *Muse and Recall.* London, ON: Canadian Poetry Press, 1999.

– "Shadows in the Soul: Racial Haunting in the Poetry of Duncan Campbell Scott." *University of Toronto Quarterly* 75.2 (Spring 2006): 752–70.

Berger, Carl. *Science, God, and Nature in Victorian Canada.* Toronto: University of Toronto Press, 1983.

Binnema, Theodore. "How Does a Map Mean? Old Swan's Map of 1801 and the Blackfoot World." In *From Rupert's Land to Canada,* edited by Binnema et al., 201–24. Edmonton: University of Alberta Press, 2001.

Boyd, Shelly. *Garden Plots: Canadian Women Writers and Their Literary Gardens.* Montreal: McGill-Queen's University Press, 2013.

Broglio, Ron. *Technologies of the Picturesque: British Art, Poetry, and Instruments, 1750–1830.* Lewisberg: Bucknell University Press, 2008.

Brooks, Lisa. *The Common Pot: The Recovery of Native Space in the Northeast.* Minneapolis: Minnesota University Press, 2008.

Brown, Ron. *The Lake Erie Shore: Ontario's Forgotten South Coast.* Toronto: Dundurn, 2009.

Buell, Lawrence. *The Environmental Imagination: Thoreau, Nature Writing, and the Formation of American Culture.* Cambridge, MA: Belknap, 1995.

Burwell, Adam Hood. *Talbot Road: A Poem.* 1818. Edited by Michael Williams. Introduction by D.M.R. Bentley. London, ON: Canadian Poetry Press, 1991.

Burwell, Mahlon. *Map of Delaware Township.* December, 1810.

Buss, Helen M. *Mapping Our Selves: Canadian Women's Autobiography in English.* Montreal: McGill-Queen's University Press, 1993.

Butler, William F. *The Great Lone Land: A Tale of Travel and Adventure in the North-West of America.* 1872. Toronto: Macmillan, 1910.

Campbell, Sandra. "A Fortunate Friendship: Duncan Campbell Scott and Pelham Edgar." In Stich, *The Duncan Campbell Scott Symposium,* 113–26.

Canada. The James Bay Treaty: Treaty No. 9 (Made in 1905 and 1906) and Adhesions Made in 1929 and 1930. 1931. Ottawa: Queen's Printer, 1964. http://www.aadnc-aandc.gc.ca/eng/1100100028863/1100100028864#chp3.

Carlyle, Thomas. *The Works of Thomas Carlyle*. Vol. 4, *The French Revolution: A History III*, edited by Henry Duff Traill. Cambridge: Cambridge University Press, 2010.

Carter, Paul. *The Road to Botany Bay: An Exploration of Landscape and History*. Minneapolis: University of Minnesota Press, 2010.

Carver, Jonathan. "A New Map of North America, from the Latest Discoveries." 1778. *Travels through the Interior Parts of North America, in the Years 1766, 1767, and 1768*. 3rd ed. London, 1781. http://www.davidrumsey.com/maps5917.html.

– *The New Universal Traveller*. London: Robinson, 1779.

Cary, Thomas. *Abram's Plains: A Poem*. 1789. Edited by D.M.R. Bentley. London, ON: Canadian Poetry Press, 1986.

Catermole, William. *Emigration: The Advantages of Emigration to Canada, Being the Substance of Two Lectures, Delivered at the Town-Hall, Colchester, and the Mechanics' Institution, Ipswich*. 1831. Toronto: Coles, 1970.

Chamberlin, J. Edward. *If this Is Your Land, Where Are Your Stories? Finding Common Ground*. Toronto: Knopf, 2003.

Chatelain, Henri. *Carte Particulière du Fleuve Saint Louis Dressée sur les Lieux avec les Noms des Sauvages du Païs*. L'Honore et Chatelain, c. 1719.

Chewett, James. *A Map of the Province of Upper Canada and the Adjacent Territories in North America Compiled by James G. Chewett, Assistant Draftsman under the Direction of Thomas Ridout, Esqr., Surveyor General of the Province Shewing the Districts, Counties and Townships in which Are Situated the Lands Purchased from the Crown by the Canada Company, Incorporated 1826. To His Most Excellent Majesty King George IV … This Map Is Most Humbly Dedicated by the Canada Company*. Canada Company, 1826. Library and Archives Canada, n0018562k_a2.

Chisholme, David. "Introduction to *The Canadian Magazine and Literary Repository*." In *Towards a Canadian Literature: Essays, Editorials & Manifestos*, edited by Douglas M. Daymond and Leslie G. Monkman. Vol. 1, *1752–1940*. Ottawa: Tecumseh, 1984.

Cole, A.O.C., and Jean Murray Cole, eds. *Kawartha Heritage: Proceedings of the Kawartha Conference, 1981*. Peterborough, ON: Peterborough Historical Atlas Foundation, 1981.

Coleman, Daniel. *White Civility: The Literary Project of English Canada*. Toronto: University of Toronto Press, 2006.

Colombo, John Robert. *Canadian Literary Landmarks*. Willowdale, ON: Hounslow, 1984.

Conley, Tom. *The Self-Made Map: Cartographic Writing in Early Modern France.* Minneapolis: University of Minnesota Press, 1996.

Cook, Ramsay. "1492 and All That: Making a Garden out of the Wilderness." In Gaffield and Gaffield, *Consuming Canada*, 62–80.

Copway, George. *The Traditional History and Characteristic Sketches of the Ojibway Nation*. 1850. Afterward by Shelley Hulan. Waterloo, ON: Wilfrid Laurier Press, 2014.

Cosgrove, Denis. Prologue to Daniels et al., *Envisioning Landscapes, Making Worlds*, xxii–xxv.

Coyne, James H., ed. *The Talbot Papers, Including Those Left by the Honorable Colonel Thomas Talbot at His Death, His Letters to the Honourable Peter Robinson, Commissioner of Crown Lands, and Some Letters Written by Him to the Hon. William Allan*. Transactions of the Royal Society of Canada: 1909.

Craig, Gerald M. *Upper Canada: The Formative Years 1784–1841*. 1963. Toronto: McClelland & Stewart, 1979.

Cronon, William. *Changes in the Land: Indians, Colonists, and the Ecology of New England*. New York: Hill and Wang, 1983.

Crosby, Alfred W. "Ecological Imperialism: The Overseas Migration of Western Europeans as a Biological Phenomenon." In Gaffield and Gaffield, *Consuming Canada*, 49–61.

Cruikshank, Julie. *Reading Voices / 'Dan Dha Ts'edenintth'e: Oral and Written Interpretations of the Yukon's Past*. Vancouver: Douglas and McIntyre, 1991.

Daniels, Stephen, Dydia DeLyser, J. Nicholas Entrikin, and Douglas Richardson. *Envisioning Landscapes, Making Worlds: Geography and the Humanities*. New York: Routledge, 2011.

Daschuk, James. *Clearing the Plains: Disease, Politics of Starvation, and the Loss of Aboriginal Life*. Regina: University of Regina Press: 2013.

Dean, Misao. *Inheriting a Canoe Paddle: The Canoe in Discourses of English-Canadian Nationalism*. Toronto: University of Toronto Press, 2013.

de Certeau, Michel. *The Practice of Everyday Life*. Translated by Steven Rendall. Berkeley: University of California Press, 1988.

Deleuze, Gilles, and Felix Guattari. *A Thousand Plateaus: Capitalism and Schizophrenia*. Translated by Brian Massumi. Minneapolis: University of Minnesota Press, 1987.

Desy, Pierrette, and Frederic Castel. "Native Reserves of Eastern Canada to 1900." In Matthews, *Historical Atlas*, vol. 2, 32.

– "Native Reserves: Names and Descriptions." In Matthews, *Historical Atlas*, vol. 2, 33.

Devereux, Cecily. "The Search for a Livable Past: Frye, Crawford, and the Healing Link." In *ReCalling Early Canada: Reading the Political in Literary and Cultural Production*, edited by Jennifer Blair et al., 281–300. Edmonton: University of Alberta Press, 2005.

Dickenson, Victoria. *Drawn from Life: Science and Art in the Portrayal of the New World*. Toronto: University of Toronto Press, 1998.

Donald, Dwayne Trevor. "Forts, Curriculum, and Indigenous Métissage: Imagining Decolonization of Aboriginal-Canadian Relations in Educational Contexts." *First Nations Perspectives* 2.1 (2009): 1–24.

Dragland, Stan. *Floating Voice: Duncan Campbell Scott and the Literature of Treaty 9*. Concord, ON: Anansi, 1994.

Dunlap, Thomas R. *Nature and the English Diaspora: Environment and History in the United States, Canada, Australia, and New Zealand*. Cambridge: Cambridge University Press, 1999.

Edmonds, Penelope. "From Bedlam to Incorporation: Whiteness and the Racialisation of Colonial Urban Space in Victoria, British Columbia and Melbourne, Victoria, 1840s–1880s." In *Exploring the British World: Identity, Cultural Production, Institutions*, edited by Kate Darian-Smith, Patricia Grimshaw, Lindsey Kiera, and Stuart Mcintyre, 60–90. Melbourne: RMIT Publishing, 2004.

Fee, Margery. *Literary Land Claims: The "Indian Land Question" from Pontiac's War to Attawapiskat*. Waterloo, ON: Wilfrid Laurier University Press, 2015.

Floyd, Janet. *Writing the Pioneer Woman*. Columbia: University of Missouri Press, 2002.

Foucault, Michel. *The Order of Things: An Archaeology of the Human Sciences*. London: Tavistock, 1970.

Fowler, Marian. *The Embroidered Tent: Five Gentlewomen in Early Canada*. Toronto: Anansi, 1982.

Freeman, Milton. "The Nature and Utility of Traditional Ecological Knowledge." In Gaffield and Gaffield, *Consuming Canada*, 39–46.

Freiwald, Bina. "'The Tongue of Woman': The Language of Self in Susana Moodie's *Roughing It in the Bush*." In McMullen, *Re(dis)covering Our Foremothers*, 155–72.

Friesen, Gerald. *The Canadian Prairies: A History*. Toronto: University of Toronto Press, 1987.

Frye, Northrop. *The Bush Garden: Essays on the Canadian Imagination*. Introduction by Linda Hutcheon. Concord, ON: Anansi, 1995.

Gaffield, Chad, and Pam Gaffield, eds. *Consuming Canada: Readings in Environmental History*. Toronto: Copp Clark, 1995.

Gauvin, Daniel. "Cary, Thomas (1751–1823)." *Dictionary of Canadian Biography*. Vol. 6. University of Toronto/Université Laval, 2003. http://www.biographi.ca/en/bio/cary_thomas_1751_1823_6E.html.

Giltrow, Janet. "'Painful Experience in a Distant Land': Mrs Moodie in Canada and Mrs Trollope in America." *Mosaic* 14.2 (1981): 131–44.

Glickman, Susan. *The Picturesque and the Sublime: A Poetics of the Canadian Landscape.* Montreal: McGill-Queen's Univeristy Press, 1998.

Goldman, Marlene. *Paths of Desire: Images of Exploration and Mapping in Canadian Women's Writing.* Toronto: University of Toronto Press, 1997.

Goldsmith, Oliver. "The Deserted Village." 1770. In *The Norton Anthology of English Literature.* 6th ed. Vol.1, edited by M.H. Abrams, 2484–93. New York: Norton, 1993.

Goldsmith, Oliver. "The Rising Village." 1834. Edited by Gerald Lynch. In Bentley, *Early Long Poems on Canada*, 199–216.

Grant, George Monro. "The North-West: Winnipeg to Rocky Mountains." *Picturesque Canada; The Country as It Was and Is.* c. 1883. Vol. 1, edited by George Monro Grant. Secaucus, NJ: Welfleet Press, 1988.

– *Ocean to Ocean: Sandford Fleming's Expedition through Canada in 1872.* 1873. Toronto: Coles, 1970.

– *Ocean to Ocean: Sandford Fleming's Expedition through Canada in 1872.* Enlarged and revised edition. Toronto: 1879. Rutland, VT: Tuttle, 1967.

Grant, William Lawson, and Frederick Hamilton. *George Monro Grant.* Toronto: Morang, 1905.

Gray, Carolyn, Donna Prystupa, and Corrado Santoro. *Inventory of the Thomas Talbot Papers.* Archives of Ontario: June 1993.

Gray, Charlotte. *Sisters in the Wilderness: The Lives of Susanna Moodie and Catharine Parr Traill.* Toronto: Penguin, 1999.

Greenblatt, Stephen. *Marvelous Possessions: The Wonder of the New World.* Chicago: University of Chicago Press, 1991.

Gregory, Derek. *Geographical Imaginations.* Oxford: Blackwell, 1994.

Groening, Laura Smyth. *Listening to Old Woman Speak: Natives and AlterNatives in Canadian Literature.* Montreal: McGill-Queen's University Press, 2004.

Harley, J.B. *The New Nature of Maps: Essays in the History of Cartography.* Baltimore: Johns Hopkins University Press, 2001.

Harris, Cole. "How Did Colonialism Dispossess? Comments from an Edge of Empire." *Annals of the Association of American Geographers* 94.1 (2004): 165–82.

Harris, R. Cole. *The Reluctant Land: Society, Space, and Environment in Canada before Confederation.* Vancouver: University of British Columbia Press, 2008.

Harrison, Robert Pogue. *Forests: The Shadow of Civilization.* Chicago: University of Chicago Press, 1993.

Heidenreich, Conrad E., and Robert M. Galois. "Native Canada, ca. 1820." In Matthews, *Historical Atlas*, vol. 1, 69.

Henderson, James (Sákéj) Youngblood. "The Context of the State of Nature." In *Reclaiming Indigenous Voice and Vision*, edited by Marie Battiste, 11–38. Vancouver: University of British Columbia Press, 2000.

Henderson, Jennifer. *Settler Feminism and Race Making in Canada*. Toronto: University of Toronto Press, 2003.

Hind, Henry Youle. *Narrative of the Canadian Red River Exploring Expedition of 1857 and of the Assinniboine and Saskatchewan Exploring Expedition of 1858*. 1860. Edmonton: Hurtig, 1971.

Hopwood, Victor. Introduction to *David Thompson: Travels in Western North America, 1784–1812*, by David Thompson, 1–39. Toronto: Macmillan, 1971.

Hornsby, Stephen J. *Surveyors of Empire: Samuel Holland, J.F.W. Des Barres, and the Making of the* Atlantic Neptune. Montreal: McGill-Queen's University Press, 2011.

Howison, John. *Sketches of Upper Canada: Domestic, Local, and Characteristic*. 1821. Toronto: Coles, 1970.

Huggan, Graham. *Territorial Disputes: Maps and Mapping Strategies in Contemporary Canadian and Australian Fiction*. Toronto: University of Toronto Press, 1994.

Ingold, Tim. *Lines: A Brief History*. New York: Routledge, 2007.

Irmscher, Christoph. "Nature Writing." In *The Cambridge Companion to Canadian Literature*, 94–114. Cambridge: Cambridge University Press, 2006.

Jackel, David. "Mrs Moodie and Mrs Traill, and the Fabrication of a Canadian Tradition." *The Compass* 6 (Spring 1979): 1–22.

– "*Ocean to Ocean*: G.M. Grant's 'Round Unvarnish'd Tale.'" *Canadian Literature* 81 (Summer 1979): 7–23.

Jameson, Anna Brownell. *Winter Studies and Summer Rambles in Canada*. 1838. Afterward by Clara Thomas. Toronto: McClelland & Stewart, 1990.

Johnson, Pauline. *E. Pauline Johnson, Tekahionwake: Collected Poems and Selected Prose*. Edited and introduced by Carole Gerson and Veronica Strong-Boag. Toronto: University of Toronto Press, 2002.

Johnson, Samuel. *Lives of the English Poets*. Vol. 1. London: Oxford University Press, 1933.

Johnston, Gordon. "The Significance of Scott's Minor Poems." In Stich, *The Duncan Campbell Scott Symposium*, 11–21.

Kamboureli, Smaro. *On the Edge of Genre: The Contemporary Canadian Long Poem*. Toronto: University of Toronto Press, 1991.

Keith, W.J. *Literary Images of Ontario*. Toronto: University of Toronto Press, 1992.

Kelly, John. "We Are All in the Ojibway Circle." In *From Ink Lake: Canadian Stories*, edited by Michael Ondaatje, 579–90. New York: Viking, 1990.

King, Geoff. *Mapping Reality: An Exploration of Cultural Cartographies*. New York: St Martin's, 1996.

Klinck, Carl F., ed. *Literary History of Canada: Canadian Literature in English*. Vol. 1. 2nd ed. Toronto: University of Toronto Press, 1977.

Krotz, Sarah Wylie. "Place and Memory: Rethinking the Literary Map of Canada." *English Studies in Canada* 40.2–3 (June/September 2014): 133–54.

Lee, Robert C. *The Canada Company and the Huron Tract, 1826–1853*. Toronto: Natural Heritage, 2004.

Lefebvre, Henri. *The Production of Space*. Translated by Donald Nicholson-Smith. Oxford: Blackwell, 1991.

Lewis, G. Malcolm. *Cartographic Encounters: Perspectives on North American Mapmaking and Map Use*. Chicago: University of Chicago Press, 1998.

Ljungberg, Christina. *Creative Dynamics: Diagrammatic Strategies in Narrative*. Amsterdam: John Benjamins, 2012.

Locke, John. "Second Treatise of Government." 1690. In *The Selected Political Writings of John Locke*, edited by Paul E. Sigmund, 17–125. New York: Norton, 2005.

Long, John. *Treaty No. 9: Making the Agreement to Share the Land in Far Northern Ontario in 1905*. Montreal: McGill-Queen's University Press, 2010.

McKay, Don. Introduction to *Open Wide a Wilderness*. Edited by Nancy Holmes. Waterloo, ON: Wilfrid Laurier University Press, 2009.

Macklem, Patrick. "The Impact of Treaty 9 on the Resource Development in Northern Ontario." In *Aboriginal and Treaty Rights in Canada: Essays on Law, Equality and Respect for Difference*, edited by Michael Asch, 97–134. Vancouver: University of British Columbia Press, 1997.

MacLulich, T.D. "The Explorer as Sage: David Thompson's Narrative." *Journal of Canadian Fiction* 4.4 (1976): 97–107.

MacTaggart, John. *Three Years in Canada: An Account of the Actual State of the Country in 1826–7–8 Comprehending its Resources, Productions, Improvements, and Capabilities; and Including Sketches of the State of Society, Advice to Emigrants, &c.* Vol. 1. London: Colburn, 1829.

MacLaren, I.S. "David Thompson's Imaginative Mapping of the Canadian Northwest, 1784–1812." *Ariel* 15 (1984): 89–106.

MacLaren, I.S., with Eric Higgs and Gabrielle Zezulka-Mailloux. *Mapper of Mountains: M.P. Bridgland in the Canadian Rockies 1902–1930*. Edmonton: University of Alberta Press, 2005.

Maher, Susan Naramore. *Deep Map Country: Literary Cartography of the Great Plains*. Lincoln: University of Nebraska Press, 2014.

Matthews, Geoffrey J. *Historical Atlas of Canada*. Vol. 1, *From the Beginning to 1800*, edited by Cole Harris. Toronto: University of Toronto Press [c. 1987].

– *Historical Atlas of Canada*. Vol. 2, *The Land Transformed: 1800–1891*, edited by Louis R. Gentilcore. Toronto: University of Toronto Press, 1993.
McCue, H.A. "The Kawartha Lakes Indians: A Brief History 1800–1850." In Cole and Cole, *Kawartha Heritage*, 3–12.
McGregor, Gaile. *The Wacousta Syndrome: Explorations in the Canadian Langscape*. Toronto: University of Toronto Press, 1985.
McLuhan, Marshall. *Understanding Media: The Extensions of Man*. Introduction by Lewis H. Lapham. Cambridge, MA: MIT Press, 1999.
McMullen, Lorraine. *Re(dis)covering Our Foremothers: Nineteenth-Century Canadian Women Writers*. Ottawa: University of Ottawa Press, 1990.
Merrill, Lynn. *The Romance of Victorian Natural History*. Oxford: Oxford University Press, 1989.
Mezei, Kathy. "From Lifeless Pools to the Circle of Affection: The Significance of Space in the Poetry of D.C. Scott." In Stich, *The Duncan Campbell Scott Symposium*, 23–35.
Milton, Viscount, and W.B. Cheadle. *The North-West Passage by Land: Being the Narrative of an Expedition from the Atlantic to the Pacific, Undertaken with the View of Exploring a Route across the Continent to British Columbia through British Territory, by One of the Northern Passes in the Rocky Mountains*. 1865. Toronto: Coles, 1970.
Monkman, Leslie. *A Native Heritage: Images of the Indian in English-Canadian Literature*. Toronto: University of Toronto Press, 1981.
Monmonier, Mark. *How to Lie with Maps*. Chicago: University of Chicago Press, 1991.
Moodie, Susanna. *Life in the Clearings versus the Bush*. 1853. Toronto: McClelland & Stewart, 1989.
– *Roughing It in the Bush*. 1852. Edited by Michael A. Peterman. New York: Norton, 2007.
Moore, Thomas. *Moore's Poetical Works, Complete in One Volume*. London: Longman, 1854.
Moretti, Franco. *Atlas of the European Novel, 1800–1900*. London: Verso, 1998.
– *Graphs, Maps, Trees: Abstract Models for a Literary History*. London: Verso, 2005.
Morris, James L. *Map of the Province of Ontario: Dominion of Canada*. Ontario: Department of Surveys, 1931.
Murray, Heather. "Women in the Wilderness." In *A Mazing Space: Writing Canadian Women Writing*, edited by Shirley Newman and Smaro Kamboureli, 74–83. Edmonton: Longspoon, 1986.
New, W.H. *Land Sliding: Imagining Space, Presence, and Power in Canadian Writing*. Toronto: University of Toronto Press, 1997.
Nicholson, N.L., and L.M. Sebert. *The Maps of Canada: A Guide to Official Canadian Maps, Charts, Atlases and Gazetteers*. Kent: Archon, 1981.

Nuttall, Thomas. *The Genera of North American Plants and a Catalogue of the Species to the Year 1817*. Philadelphia: Heartt, 1818.

Obomsawin, Alanis. *Trick or Treaty?* Film. Directed by Alanis Obomsawin. 2014. National Film Board of Canada.

Omhovère, Claire. *Sensing Space: The Poetics of Geography in Contemporary English-Canadian Writing*. Brussels: P.I.E. Peter Lang, 2007.

Owram, Doug. *Promise of Eden: The Canadian Expansionist Movement and the Idea of the West 1856–1900*. Toronto: University of Toronto Press, 1980.

Padrón, Ricardo. *The Spacious Word: Cartography, Literature, and Empire in Early Modern Spain*. Chicago: University of Chicago Press, 2004.

Peguis, Chief (William King). "To the Aboriginal Protection Society." In *A Few Acres of Snow: Documents in Pre-Confederation Canadian History*, edited by Thomas Thorner with Thor Frohn-Nielsen, 291–93. Toronto: University of Toronto Press, 2009.

Perry, Adele. *On the Edge of Empire: Gender, Race, and the Making of British Columbia, 1849–1871*. Toronto: University of Toronto Press, 2001.

Peterman, Michael. *This Great Epoch of Our Lives: Susanna Moodie's Roughing It in the Bush*. Toronto: Entertainment Culture Writing Press, 1996.

– "'Splendid Anachronism': The Record of Catharine Parr Traill's Struggles as an Amateur Botanist in Nineteenth-Century Canada." In McMullen, *Re(dis)covering Our Foremothers*, 173–85.

Peterman, Michael, and Carl Ballstadt, eds. *Forest and Other Gleanings: The Fugitive Writings of Catharine Parr Traill*. Ottawa: University of Ottawa Press, 1994.

Pickles, John. *A History of Spaces: Cartographic Reason, Mapping and the Geo-coded World*. London: Routledge, 2004.

Podruchny, Carolyn, Frederic W. Gleach, and Roger Roulette. "Putting up Poles: Power, Navigation, and Cultural Mixing in the Fur Trade." In *Gathering Places: Aboriginal and Fur Trade Histories*, edited by Carolyn Podruchny and Laura Peers, 25–47. Vancouver: University British Columbia Press, 2010.

Pratt, E.J. *Selected Poems*. Edited by Sandra Djwa et al. Toronto: University of Toronto Press, 2000.

Pratt, Mary Louise. *Imperial Eyes: Travel Writing and Transculturation*. London: Routledge, 2008.

Raglon, Rebecca. "Little Goody Two-Shoes: Reassessing the Work of Catharine Parr Traill." In *This Elusive Land: Women and the Canadian Environment*, edited by Melody Hessing, Rebecca Raglon, and Catriona Sandilands, 4–18. Vancouver: University of British Columbia Press, 2005.

Ricou, Laurie. *The Arbutus/Madrone Files: Reading the Pacific Northwest*. Edmonton: NeWest Press, 2002.

Ritchie, Leslie, ed. *Duncan Campbell Scott: Addresses, Essays, Reviews*. Vol. 1. Introduction by Stan Dragland. London, ON: Canadian Poetry Press, 2000.

Roy, Wendy. *Maps of Difference: Canada, Women, and Travel*. Montreal: McGill-Queen's University Press, 2005.

Rubidge, Frederick Preston. "A Chart, Showing the Interior Navigation of the District of Newcastle, Upper Canada, and the Proposed Improvements on the Otonabee River etc. Drawn by F.P. Rubidge and engraved by T. Evans, for the Coburg Star." 1833.

Ruffo, Armand Garnet. *Opening in the Sky*. Penticton: Theytus, 1994.

Said, Edward. *Culture and Imperialism*. New York: Vintage, 1994.

Salem-Wiseman, Lisa. "Verily, the White Man's Ways Were the Best': Duncan Campbell Scott, Native Culture, and Assimilation." *Studies in Canadian Literature* 21.1 (1996): 120–42.

Sandalack, Beverly A. "Prairie Towns: Process and Form." In *Place and Replace: Essays on Western Canada*, edited by Adele Perry, Esyllt W. Jones, and Leah Morton, 271–97. Winnipeg: University of Manitoba Press, 2013.

Schivelbusch, Wolfgang. *The Railway Journey: The Industrialization of Time and Space in the 19th Century*. Berkeley: University of California Press, 1986.

Scott, Duncan Campbell. "The Last of the Indian Treaties." In Ritchie, *Duncan Campbell Scott*, 82–93.

– "The Height of Land." In Scott, *Selected Poems of Duncan Campbell Scott*, 11–15.

– "Indian Affairs, 1867–1912." In Ritchie, *Duncan Campbell Scott*, 186–215.

– *Lundy's Lane and Other Poems*. Toronto: McClelland, Goodchild and Stewart, 1916.

– *Selected Poems of Duncan Campbell Scott*. Toronto: Ryerson, 1951.

Smith, Donald B. *Mississauga Portraits: Ojibwe Voices from Nineteenth-Century Canada*. Toronto: University of Toronto Press, 2013.

Smith, Michael. *A Geographical View of the Province of Upper Canada and Promiscuous Remarks on the Government, in Two Parts, with an Appendix: Containing a Complete Description of the Niagara Falls, and Remarks Relative to the Situation of the Inhabitants Respecting the War, and a Concise History of its Progress to the Present Date*. Trenton, NJ: Moore and Lake, 1813.

Smyth, David William. *A Map of the Province of Upper Canada, Describing All the New Settlements, Townships, &c. with the Countries Adjacent, from Quebec to Lake Huron*. London: Faden, 1818.

Soja, Edward W. *Thirdspace: Journeys to Los Angeles and Other Real-and-Imagined Places*. Oxford: Blackwell, 1996.

Spelt, Jacob. *Urban Development in South-Central Ontario*. 1955. Toronto: McClelland & Stewart, 1972.

Spry, Irene. "The Tragedy of the Loss of the Commons in Western Canada." In *As Long as the Sun Shines and Water Flows: A Reader in Canadian Native Studies*, edited by Ian A.L. Getty and Antoine S. Lussier, 203–28. Vancouver: University of British Colombia Press, 1983.

Stegner, Wallace. *Wolf Willow: A History, a Story, and a Memory of the Last Plains Frontier*. Introduction by Page Stegner. New York: Penguin, 2000.

Stich, K.P. *The Duncan Campbell Scott Symposium*. Ottawa: University of Ottawa Press, 1980.

Stratton, Florence. "Cartographic Lessons: Susanna Moodie's *Roughing It in the Bush* and Thomas King's *Green Grass, Running Water*." *Canadian Literature* (Summer 1999): 82–104.

Sugars, Cynthia. *Canadian Gothic: Literature, History, and the Spectre of Self-Invention*. Cardiff: University of Wales Press, 2014.

Sutton, Catherine Soneegoh. "Letter." In *An Anthology of Native Literature in English*, edited by Daniel David Moses and Terry Goldie, 26–7. 2nd ed. Oxford: Oxford University Press, 1997.

Tally, Robert T. Jr. *Spatiality*. New York: Routledge, 2013.

Talman, James J., and Ruth Talman. "The Canadas 1763–1812." In Klinck, *Literary History of Canada*, 83–91.

Thompson, David. *David Thompson's Narrative of His Explorations in Western America, 1784–1812*. Edited by J.B. Tyrrell. Toronto: Champlain Society, 1916.

– "Map of the North-West Territory of the Province of Canada." 1843.

– *The Writings of David Thompson, Volume I: The Travels, 1850 Version*. Edited by William E. Moreau. Montreal: McGill-Queen's University Press, 2009.

Thompson, Elizabeth. *The Backwoods of Canada*. Afterward by D.M.R. Bentley. Toronto: McClelland & Stewart, 1989.

– "Catharine Parr Traill's 'Something Gathers up the Fragments.'" *Canadian Poetry: Studies, Documents, Reviews* 42 (Spring/Summer 1998): 140–52.

– "An Early Review of *Roughing It in the Bush*." *Canadian Literature* 151 (Winter 1996): 202–4.

– "Illustrations for *The Backwoods of Canada*." *Studies in Canadian Literature* 19.2 (1994): 30–56.

– *The Pioneer Woman: A Canadian Character Type*. Montreal: McGill-Queen's University Press, 1991.

Thomson, Don W. *Men and Meridians: The History of Surveying and Mapping in Canada*. Vol. 1. Ottawa: Queen's University Press, 1966.

Thrower, Norman J.W. *Maps and Man: An Examination of Cartography in Relation to Culture and Civilization*. New Jersey: Prentice-Hall, 1972.

Thurston, John. *The Work of Words: The Writing of Susanna Strickland Moodie*. Montreal: McGill-Queen's University Press, 1996.

Titley, Brian. *A Narrow Vision: Duncan Campbell Scott and the Administration of Indian Affairs in Canada*. Vancouver: University of British Columbia Press, 1986.

Traill, Catharine Parr. *The Backwoods of Canada: Being Letters from the Wife of an Emigrant Officer, Illustrative of the Domestic Economy of British America*. 1836. Edited by David Staines. Toronto: McClelland & Stewart, 1989.

– *The Canadian Crusoes: A Tale of the Rice Lake Plains*. 1852. Ottawa: Carleton University Press, 1995.

– *Canadian Wild Flowers*. Painted and lithographed by Agnes FitzGibbon with botanical descriptions by C.P. Traill. Montreal: Lovell, 1868.

– *Lady Mary and Her Nurse; or, a Peep into the Canadian Forest*. A. Hall, 1856.

– *Pearls and Pebbles*. 1894. Edited by Elizabeth Thompson. Toronto: Natural Heritage, 1999.

– "Ramblings by the River." 1853. In Peterman and Ballstadt, *Forest and Other Gleanings*, 161–7.

– "Rice Lake Plains – The Wolf Tower." 1852. In Peterman and Ballstadt, *Forest and Other Gleanings*, 203–13.

– *Studies of Plant Life in Canada; or, Gleanings from Forest, Lake and Plain*. Ottawa: Woodburn, 1885.

– "A Walk to Railway Point." 1853. In Peterman and Ballstadt, *Forest and Other Gleanings*, 215–23.

Tuan, Yi Fu. *Space and Place: The Perspective of Experience*. Minneapolis: University of Minnesota Press, 1977.

Tyrrell, J.B. Introduction to David Thompson, *David Thompson's Narrative*, edited by J.B. Tyrrell, xxiii–lxiv.

Van Herk, Aritha. *A Frozen Tongue*. Sydney, Australia: Dangaroo, 1992.

Ware, Tracy. "D.C. Scott's 'The Height of Land' and the Greater Romantic Lyric." *Canadian Literature* 111 (Winter 1986): 10–25.

Warkentin, Germaine. Introduction to the first edition of *Canadian Exploration Literature*, edited by Germaine Warkentin, 19–34. Toronto: Dundurn, 2006.

Warkentin, John. Introduction to *So Vast and Various: Interpreting Canada's Regions in the Nineteenth and Twentieth Centuries*, edited by John Warkentin, 3–38. Montreal: McGill-Queen's University Press, 2010.

Waterston, Elizabeth. "Travel Books." In Klinck, *Literary History of Canada*, 361–79.

Westphal, Bertrand. *Geocriticism: Real and Fictional Spaces*. Translated by Robert T. Tally Jr. New York: Palgrave, 2011.

White, Gilbert. *The Natural History of Selborne; with Observations on Various Parts of Nature, and the Naturalist's Calendar*. Edited by Thomas Brown. London: 1875.

Wightman, W. Robert, and Nancy M. Wightman. *The Land Between: Northwestern Ontario Resource Development, 1800 to the 1900s*. Toronto: University of Toronto Press, 1997.

Williams, Michael. "Burwell, Adam Hood." *Dictionary of Canadian Biography*. Vol. 6. University of Toronto/Université Laval, 2003–. http://www.biographi.ca/en/bio/burwell_adam_hood_7E.html.

– "Editorial Emendations and Explanatory Notes." In Burwell, *Talbot Road*, 31–83.

Witham, John. "Building the Trent-Severn: A Summary." In Cole and Cole, *Kawartha Heritage*, 29–34.

Wood, J. David. *Making Ontario: Agricultural Colonization and Landscape Re-Creation before the Railway*. Montreal: McGill-Queen's University Press, 2000.

Wood, S.T. *Rambles of a Canadian Naturalist*. Toronto: Dent, 1916.

Wordsworth, William. "Lines Written a Few Miles above Tintern Abbey." In *Lyrical Ballads* by William Wordsworth and Samuel Taylor Coleridge, 111–17. 1798. Edited by W.J.B. Owen. 2nd ed. Oxford: Oxford University Press, 1996.

Zeller, Suzanne. *Inventing Canada: Early Victorian Science and the Idea of a Transcontinental Nation*. Toronto: University of Toronto Press, 1987.

Index

www.ingramcontent.com/pod-product-compliance
Lightning Source LLC
LaVergne TN
LVHW090155080826
844660LV00013B/820/J

* 9 7 8 1 4 4 2 6 5 0 1 2 1 *